IMAGES
of America

MERCHANTVILLE

To Mike, Andy, and Peter, with love.

IMAGES
of America

MERCHANTVILLE

Maureen A. McLoone

ARCADIA
PUBLISHING

ISBN 978-0-7385-0912-9

Published by Arcadia Publishing
Charleston, South Carolina

Printed in the United States of America

Library of Congress Catalog Card Number: 2001091058

For all general information contact Arcadia Publishing at:
Telephone 843-853-2070
Fax 843-853-0044
E-mail sales@arcadiapublishing.com
For customer service and orders:
Toll-Free 1-888-313-2665

Visit us on the Internet at www.arcadiapublishing.com

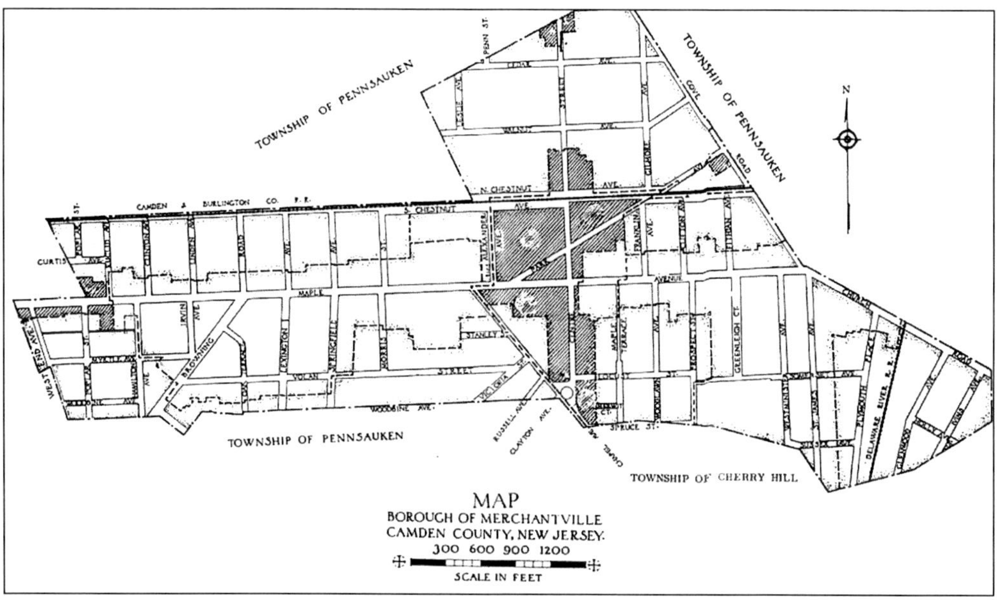

Shown is a map of Merchantville, Camden County, New Jersey. (Merchantville Historical Society.)

Contents

ACKNOWLEDGMENTS

Access to photographic materials was crucial to this book. Thanks to several enthusiastic, caring people, my sources were abundant. For their sharing of their treasured images and memories, I truly thank John Alloway; Jeff Brown; Cindy Clark; Helen and Vernon Collins; Andy Grant; Bob Hanna; Kay Hussong; Sr. Alice Ivanyo, M.P.F.; Rudy Klock; John A. Mead Jr.; Ruth Curran Neild; Joy Perry; Irene Powers; Tony Repice; Tina Schmidt; Hope Scott; Bobbi Stagliano; Sue Walker; and Karl Wirth.

Merci to Brooks and Randy Oakford, who went the extra mile for me and fueled my energy with chocolate-covered pretzels. Special kudos to Edith Silberstein of the Merchantville Historical Society, who gave me the "keys to the kingdom"—the archives. Thanks go to my "forever friend," June Wahl Fitzgerald, for mastering the drill of maneuvering through the proofs to judge the presentation. It pays to know the right people. Finally, Brad Walker commendably handled all my photographer requests.

Especially, a heartfelt thank-you to my son Peter, age 13, who took me by the hand and convinced me that the computer was my friend.

—Maureen A. McLoone

INTRODUCTION

Nearly 300 years ago, the area that became Merchantville was among the land holdings of a Samuel Cole. On the 13th day of the third month of 1682, he sold 500 acres of land to Samuel Spicer. Thus began the property transactions that eventually led to the founding fathers' arrival in the village of Merchantville.

While Merchantville was still developing as a community, it was part of Waterford Township. In 1848, a piece of Waterford was reorganized into Old Delaware Township. Then, in 1859, Stockton Township was formed from part of Waterford, and within it all of Merchantville. In 1850, the new, beautifully shaded Moorestown-Camden Turnpike was attracting the attention of certain Philadelphia merchants. Between 1852 and 1860, Patrick Cunningham, Samuel McFadden, John Loutey, Frederick Gerker, and Matthias Homer purchased extensive lands. At the beginning of this transition from a rural to a select suburban site, these pioneer merchants built substantial residences along the turnpike. All but Cunningham selected land on the north side of the turnpike near Cove Road, which was once a private road from Thomas Spicer Jr.'s home to Colestown.

Many people were dissatisfied being part of Stockton Township due to how little of their revenue was spent on improvements to their town. George Crump, an interested resident who served as England's vice consul to Philadelphia, drew up a proposed charter for self-rule. He and six other residents took this document to Trenton. Approval of the charter led to Merchantville's incorporation on May 18, 1874. When it came to naming the infant town of 400 residents, one of the merchants' wives, Rebecca Loutey, suggested calling it Merchantsville (soon changed to Merchantville) because of their common profession.

The completion of the Camden & Burlington Railroad in 1867 was the impetus for the growth of the community by providing good transportation. Residents of Philadelphia were attracted to the town, where they built permanent or summer homes.

In the 20th century, Merchantville's population continued to increase until it reached about 4,000. In the 1920s, the second largest boom in building took place, largely due to the completion of the Delaware River Bridge (now the Benjamin Franklin Bridge) in 1926.

The founding of this suburban village represents one of the first efforts made to relieve congestion in a great city, Philadelphia, and to give to busy workers something of this beautiful country as part of their home environment. Merchantville remains the residential community envisioned by its founders a century ago. This is the borough's charm. The same spirit that has enabled this small hometown to thrive for more than 125 years will be the driving force for its progress in the years to come.

BIBLIOGRAPHY

Benenson, Carol A. *Merchantville, New Jersey: The Development, Architecture, and Preservation of a Victorian Commuter Suburb*. 1984.

Cordery, M. Blanche. *Merchantville Past and Present*. Borough of Merchantville, 1964.

Eastlack, Francis F. *History of Merchantville, Camden County, NJ*. 1899.

Ladies of the Presbyterian Church. *Standard Recipes for Cooking*. Philadelphia: Press of A.H. Sickler & Company, 1891.

Lewis, Earl P., ed. *Centennial Yearbook*. Merchantville. 1974.

Directory of Merchantville, North Merchantville, and Pennsauken. Camden: Herbert F. Freeman & Company, 1911.

Merchantville 50th Anniversary Program Committee. *Merchantville, the Borough Beautiful, 50th Anniversary*. 1924.

Merchantville Historical Society brochures.

A Walking Tour of the Cattell Track. 1995.

A Walking Tour of the Oaks.

Merchantville Historical Society. *A Victorian Evening, April 15, 1989*. 1989.

Polk, Charles P. *The Annals of Merchantville*. The Community News, 1951.

Publicity and Historical Committee. *History of Camden County in the Great War*. Camden. 1919.

Wyckoff, Dr. J. Iredell. *History, Frederick W. Grigg Post No. 68, the American Legion*. Merchantville, New Jersey. 1940.

One

Borough Beginnings

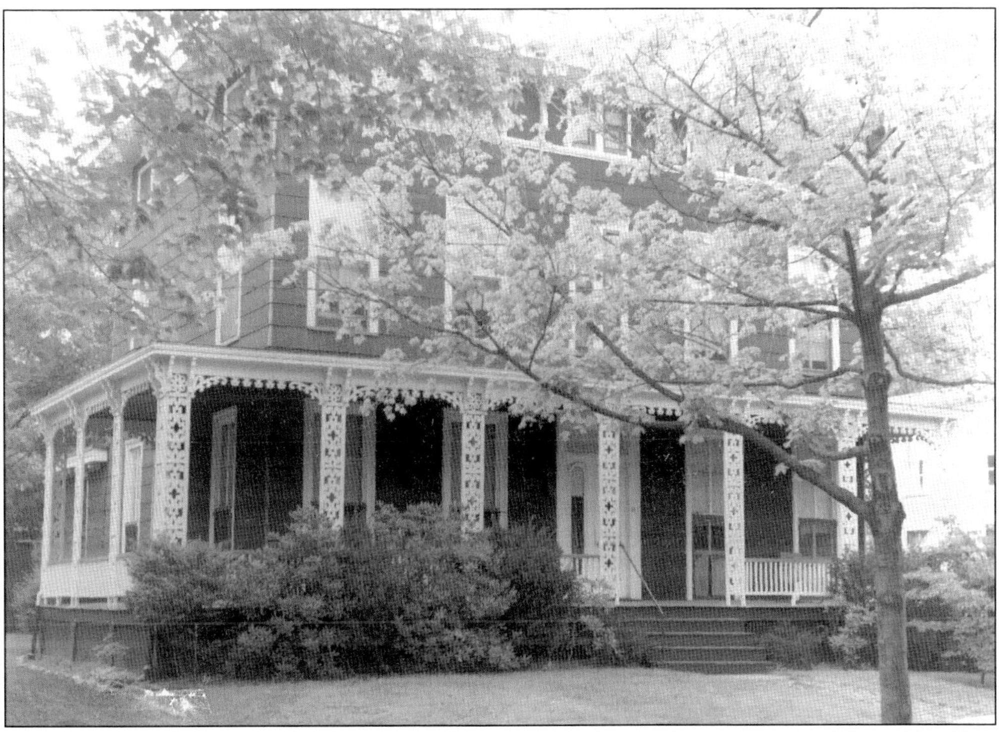

In 1857, at the home of Philadelphia merchant John Loutey, several citizens met to decide a name for their newly incorporated town. They had practically agreed on Martinsville in honor of Ben Martin, the genial and popular owner of the local pub, the Stockton House. Rebecca Loutey suggested that Merchantville would be an appropriate name, since the founding fathers were all merchants. (Merchantville Historical Society.)

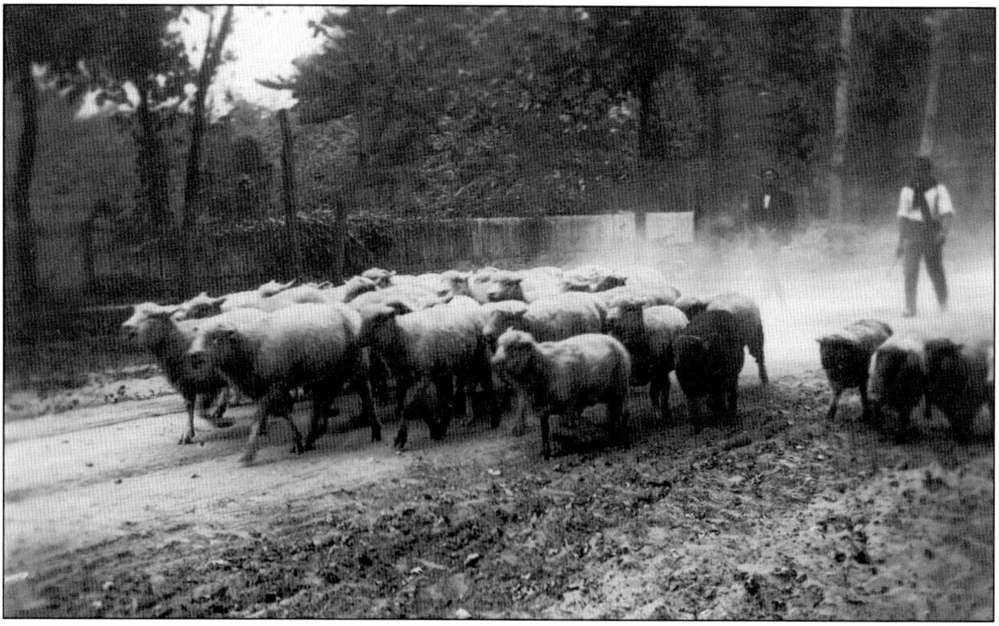

Two men take sheep to market along Wellwood Avenue at the Woodbine Avenue intersection. Wellwood Avenue later became Browning Road. Before the development of Merchantville, the area was a sparsely settled agricultural community. The primary interest was in leading prosperous agricultural lives, not in the founding of a suburb. (Merchantville Historical Society.)

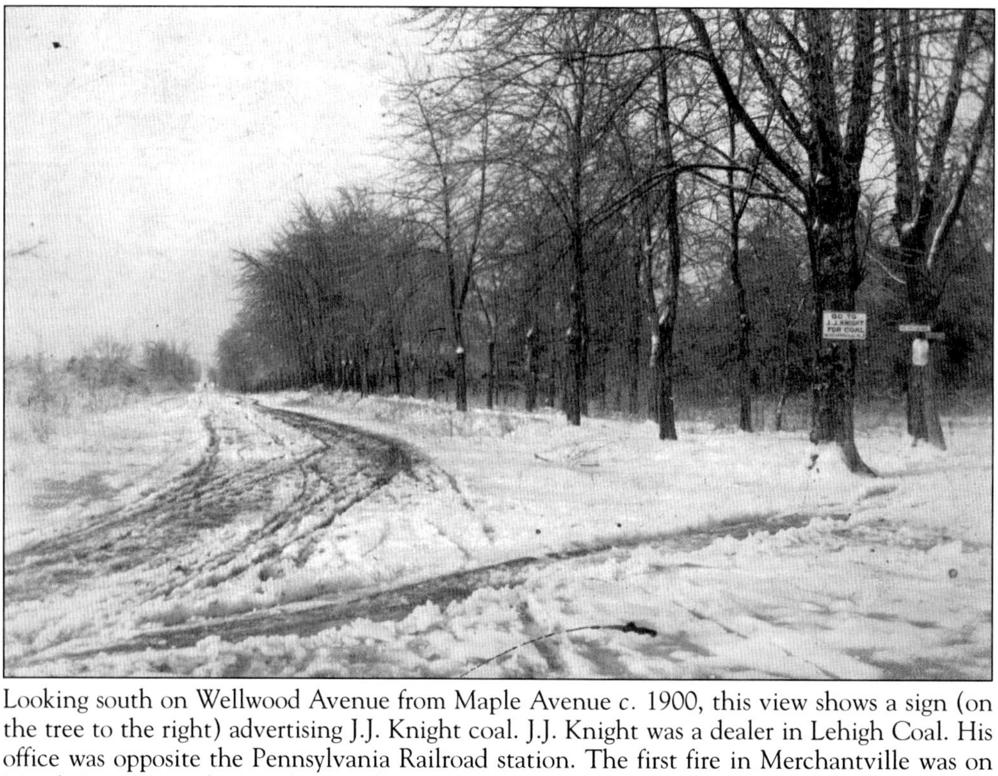

Looking south on Wellwood Avenue from Maple Avenue *c.* 1900, this view shows a sign (on the tree to the right) advertising J.J. Knight coal. J.J. Knight was a dealer in Lehigh Coal. His office was opposite the Pennsylvania Railroad station. The first fire in Merchantville was on March 3, 1889, in the woods of Wellwood. (Merchantville Historical Society.)

This view is looking down Hamilton Avenue from Wellwood Avenue (Browning Road). There was nothing but Native American trails passing through Merchantville until 1747, when the Ferry Road, which linked Camden and Mount Holly, was constructed. (Merchantville Historical Society.)

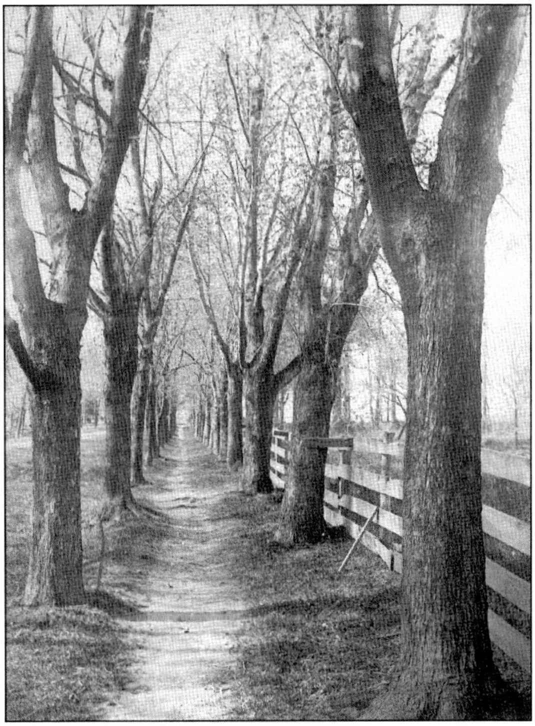

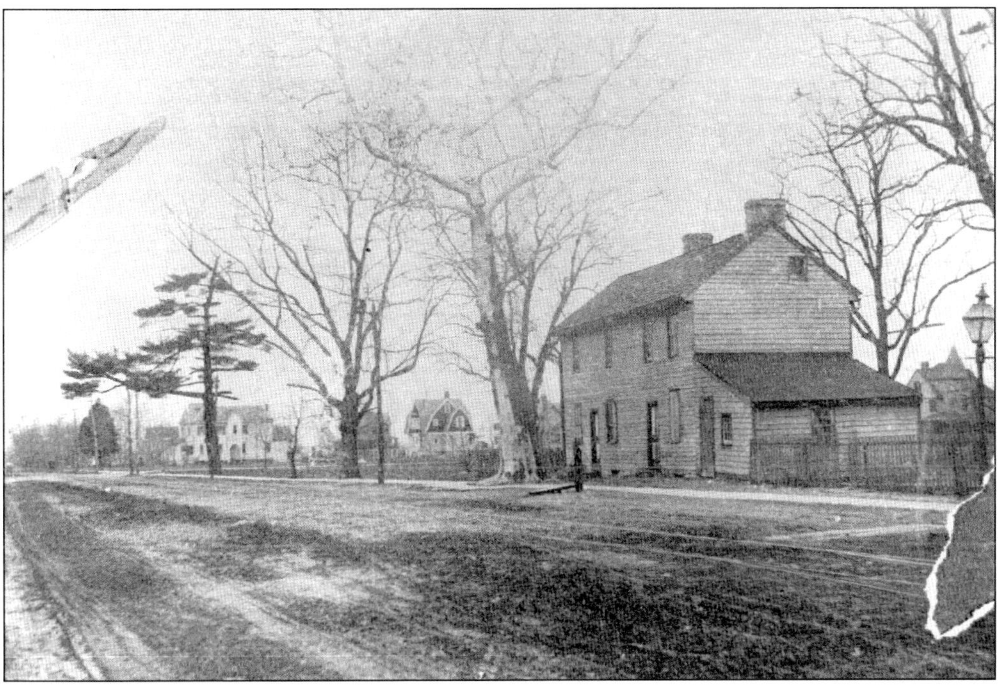

The Curtis Farm was situated on the northwest corner of Maple Avenue and Lexington Avenue. It was built in the 1790s by James Geghan. In 1823, it was sold to a member of the Curtis family. Many old maps show the extensive acreage of the Curtis estate in the so-called Wellwood section. It was razed in 1915. (Merchantville Historical Society.)

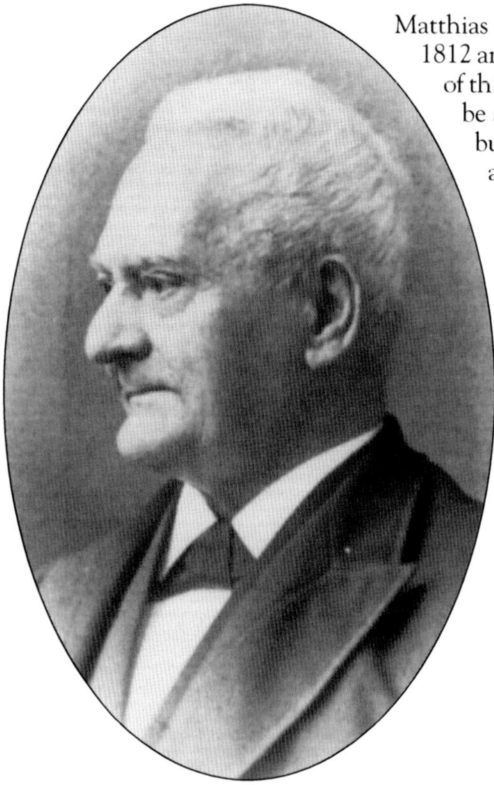

Matthias Homer was born in Birmingham, England, in 1812 and settled in Merchantville by 1860. The imprint of this man's prominence and active participation can be seen in borough matters, formation of churches, building associations, railroad or political matters, and more. He became Merchantville's first burgess. Homer died on December 16, 1893. (Merchantville Historical Society.)

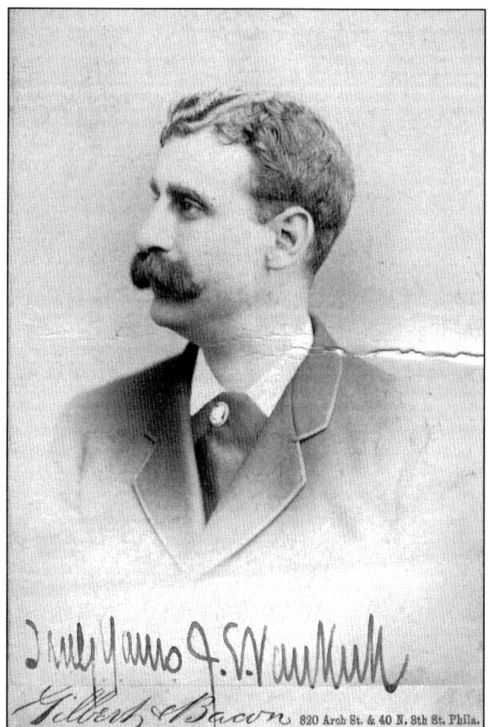

On May 18, 1896, Joseph E. Van Kirk became our seventh burgess. During his term, on May 24, 1897, the title of the borough executive was changed from burgess to mayor. Van Kirk served as mayor until March 18, 1898. He lived at 9 West Cedar Avenue with his wife, Bertha, who was the fourth president of the Merchantville Women's Club. (Merchantville Historical Society.)

Mayor Frank S. Walton (seen on the right in the rocker) served the community from March 19, 1900, to March 14, 1904. In 1890, resident and architect Arnold H. Moses designed Walton's residence at 16 Springfield Avenue. The home was an early example of Colonial Revival style architecture in Merchantville. (Merchantville Historical Society.)

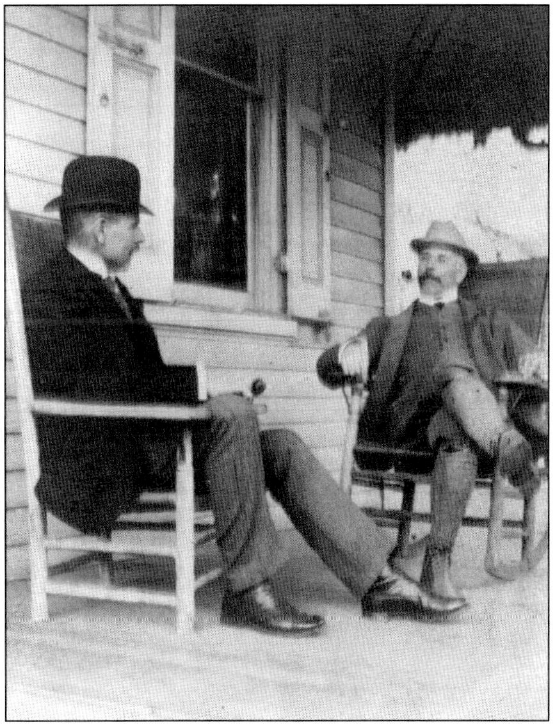

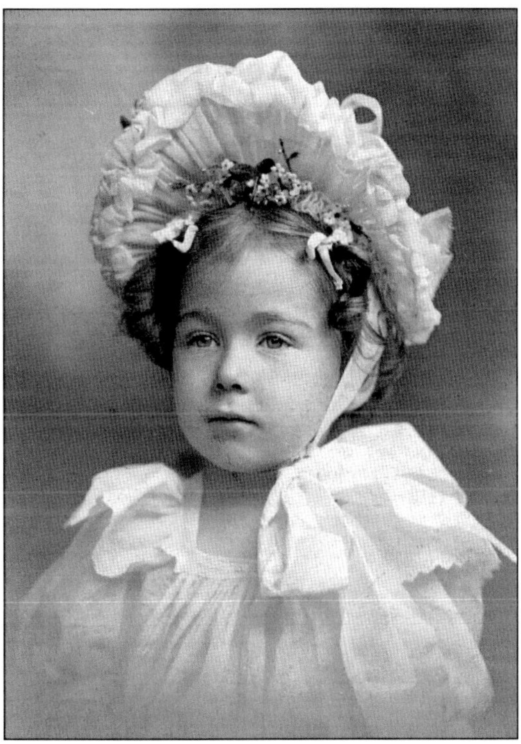

Thelma Fowler, age two, wears a ruffled hat and dress in this 1896 photograph. Francis F. Eastlack stated in his 1899 book, *History of Merchantville*, "But the women of Merchantville! God Bless them! Every one of them is an earth angel! Be she matron or maid, old or young, she is a physical beauty and a mental paragon!" (Merchantville Historical Society.)

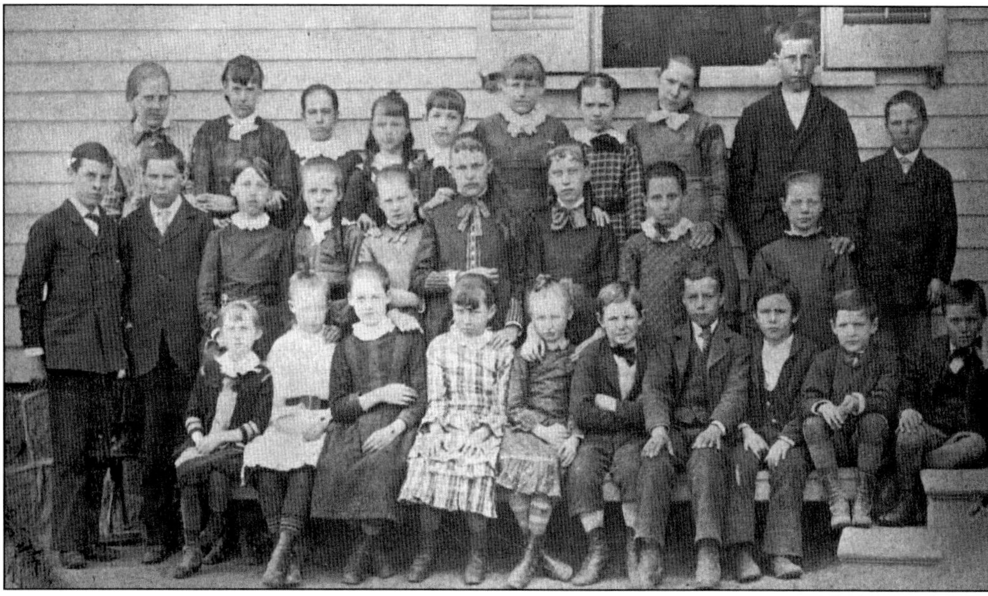

Posing at the Merchantville School *c.* 1880 are, from left to right, the following: (front row) Daisey Furber, four unidentified, Charley Laney, John Upham, Barney O'Donnell, Frank Homer, and James Laney; (middle row) Will Furber, Walter Eastlack, unidentified, Nellie Upham, unidentified, Nellie Penrose, May Bartine, Lizzie Eastlack, and unidentified; (back row) unidentified, Hattie Murray, Lottie Knight, Clara Knight, Katie Knight, unidentified, Annie Troute, Ida Eastlack, unidentified, and George Laney. (Merchantville Historical Society.)

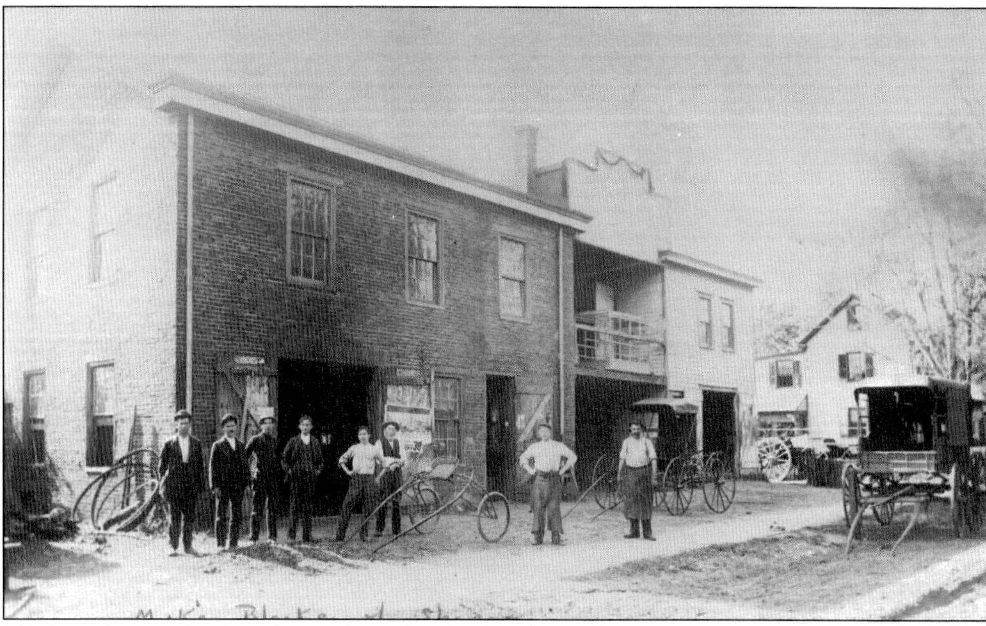

Blacksmithing, wheelwrighting, horseshoeing, and jobbing were the services offered at Jacob Mick's Blacksmith Shop at 62 Chapel Avenue, where Stanley Avenue is now cut through. The first Democratic mass meeting was held in the fall of 1884 over the shop (thereafter known as Mick's Hall). There were only six Democrats in the borough, but a large number of Republicans greeted them and applauded their audacity. (Merchantville Historical Society.)

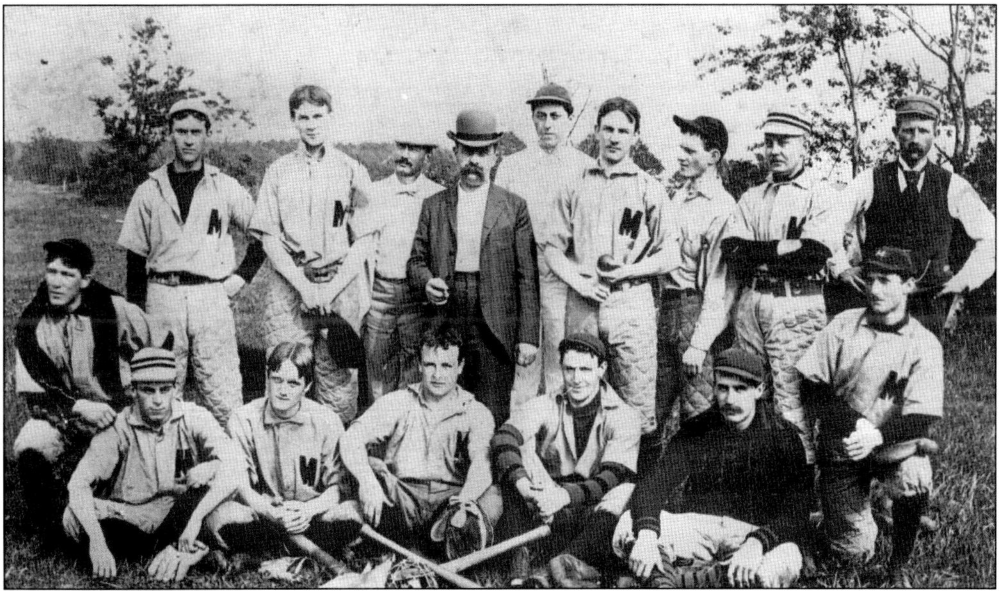

Athletics were but a casual part of outdoor life in the early days. Baseball games became more popular as the borough grew. In 1892, boys of Merchantville played baseball anywhere an open space and a field not roughened by the plow was available. Shown from left to right are the following: (front row) Otis Wallace, Coates Walton, Howard Street, and the rest unidentified; (back row) unidentified, Joseph Burroughs, Harry Homer, George Crump, and the rest unidentified. (Merchantville Historical Society.)

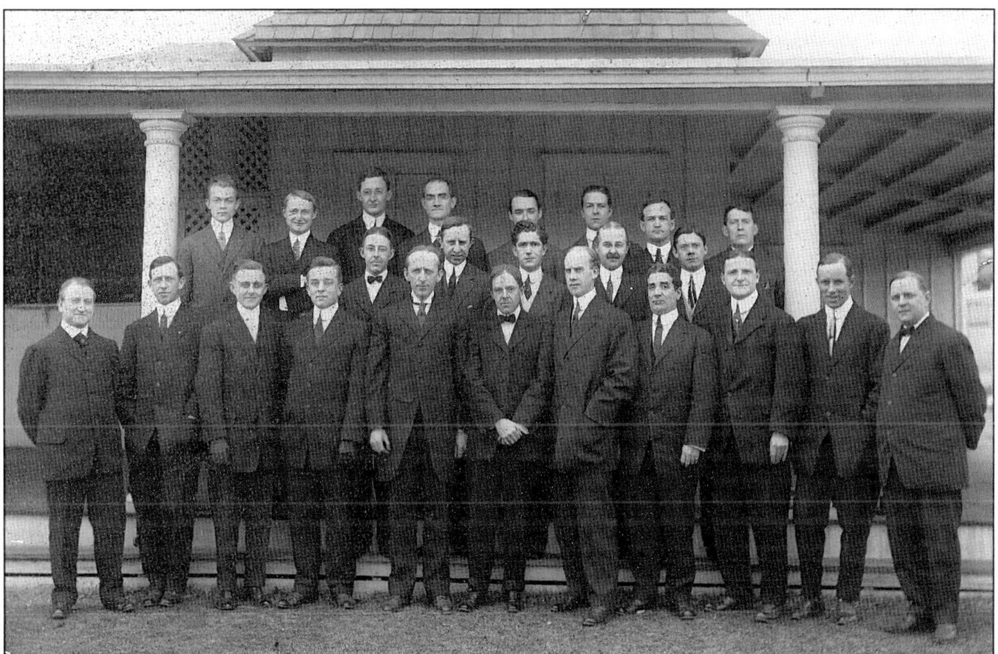

At a meeting held on the third floor of old Merchantville Hall, the Merchantville Field Club was named and its colors, red and white, were chosen. The first field, now the lawn in front of the present community center, held the original clubhouse. (Merchantville Historical Society.)

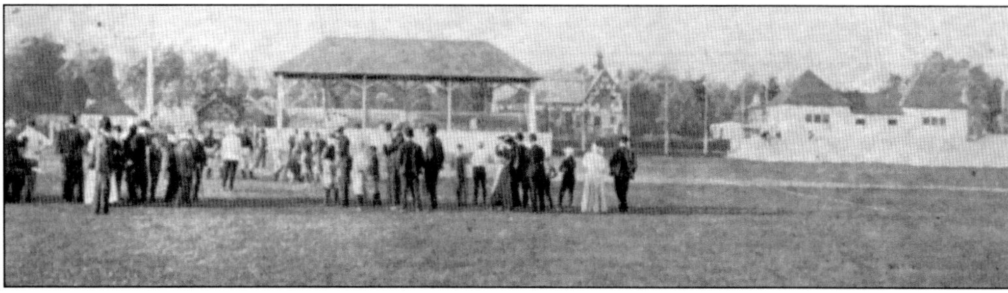

Spectators enjoy a game of football on the field grounds. The Cricket Club and the Athletic Club formed the nucleus of the handsomely equipped Merchantville Field Club, which was the favorite resort for lovers of outdoor sports, such as baseball, cricket, tennis, football, and golf. It controlled six acres of ground, with a membership of 200 in 1899. (Tina Schmidt.)

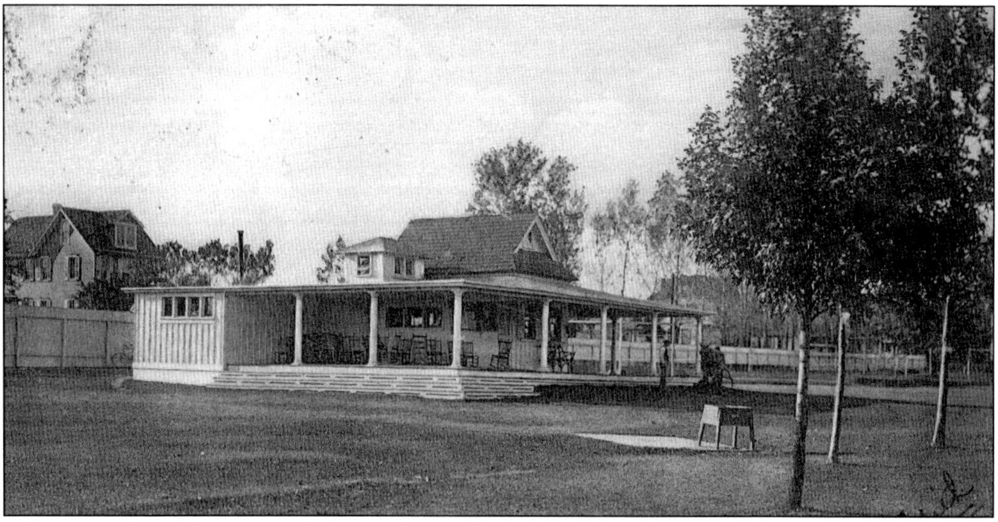

The original clubhouse for the Merchantville Field Club was vacated for the new, spacious brick house on September 10, 1921. The former clubhouse became the ladies' clubhouse. (Maureen McLoone.)

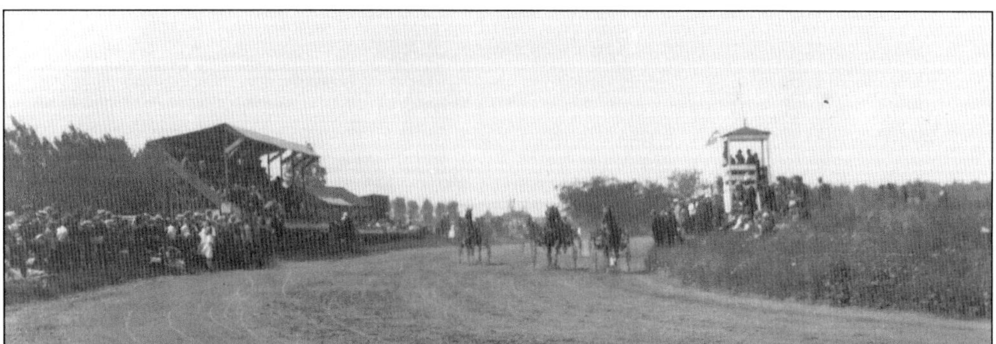

Harrison Robbins opened a racetrack, known as the Gentlemen's Driving Park, and ran it for some time. It was situated along the south side of East Maple Avenue, where Rice & Holman was located. The name was later changed to the West Jersey Country Club. (Merchantville Historical Society.)

Two

STATELY STREETSCAPES

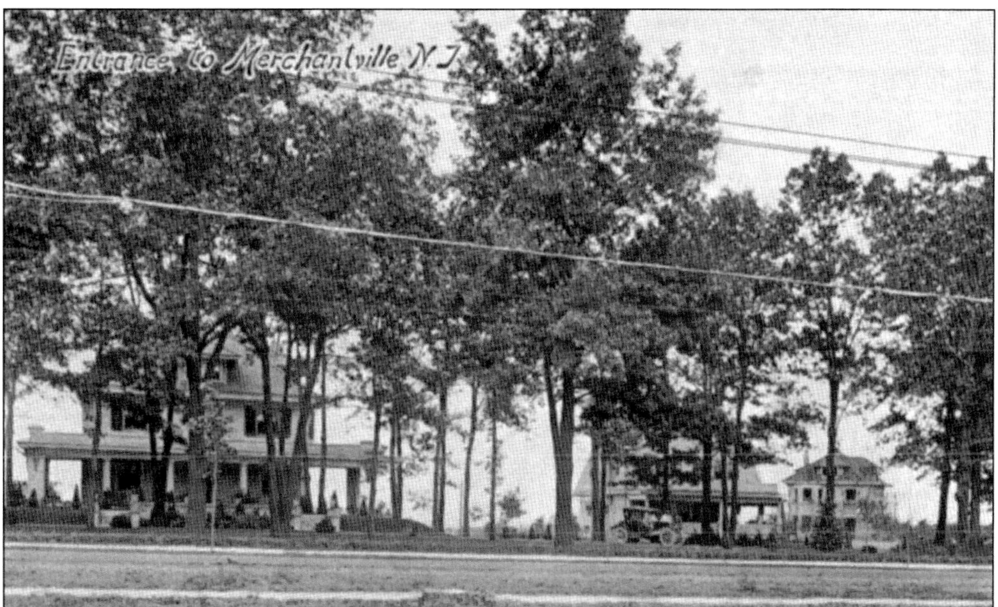

The Oaks, the "Entrance to Merchantville," is a planned neighborhood of upscale homes built in the early 20th century. It is a classic example of suburban development. The Oaks was a late arrival in Merchantville, where the first significant housing development came in the 1870s. In many ways, the Oaks was the jewel of automobile age development in the borough. It served as a gateway for vehicular traffic entering the borough along Wellwood Avenue. (Bobbi Stagliano.)

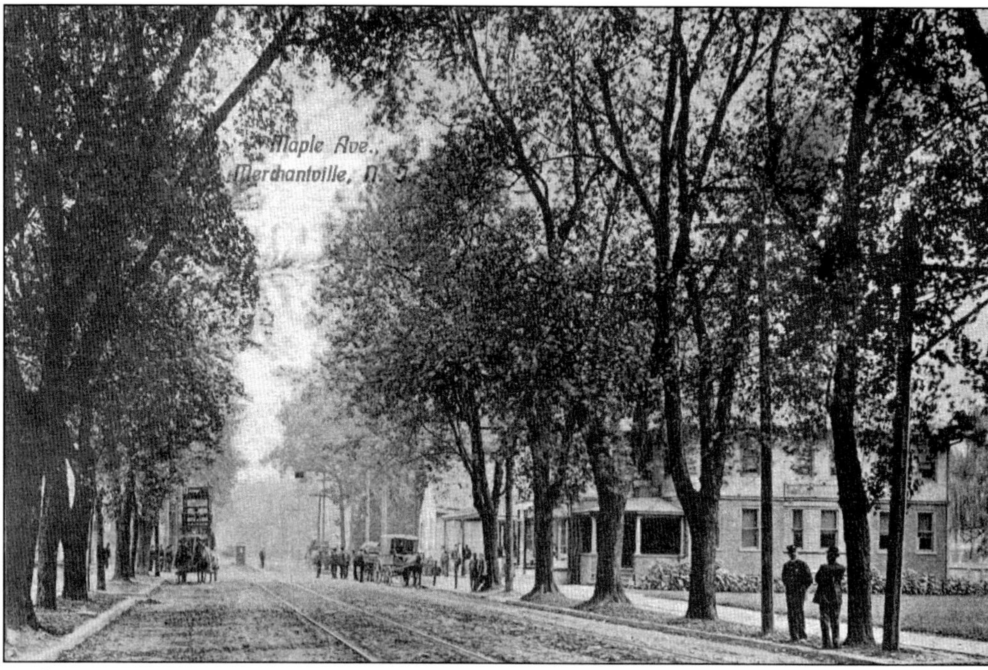

In this scene on Maple Avenue, in the heart of the borough, trolley tracks are clearly visible. The Camden Horse Car Company finished the line from Camden to Merchantville in September 1893. The fare each way was 10¢ for some time. The first monthly ticket was issued to A. Macray on October 24, 1893. The name of the company later changed to the Camden and Suburban Railroad Company. (Tina Schmidt.)

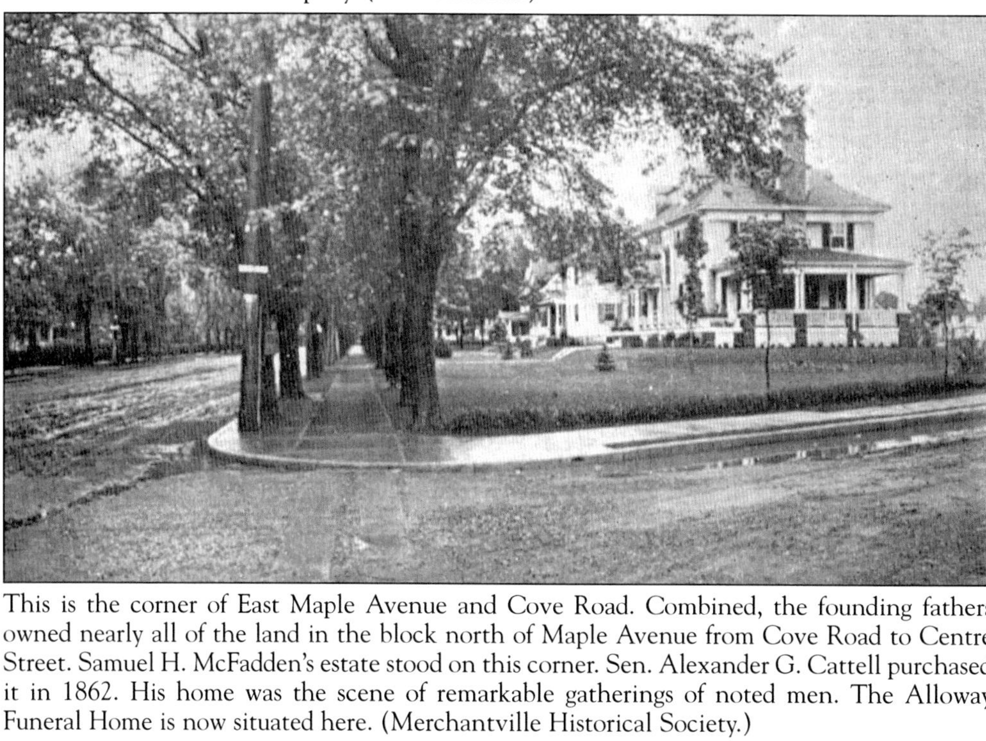

This is the corner of East Maple Avenue and Cove Road. Combined, the founding fathers owned nearly all of the land in the block north of Maple Avenue from Cove Road to Centre Street. Samuel H. McFadden's estate stood on this corner. Sen. Alexander G. Cattell purchased it in 1862. His home was the scene of remarkable gatherings of noted men. The Alloway Funeral Home is now situated here. (Merchantville Historical Society.)

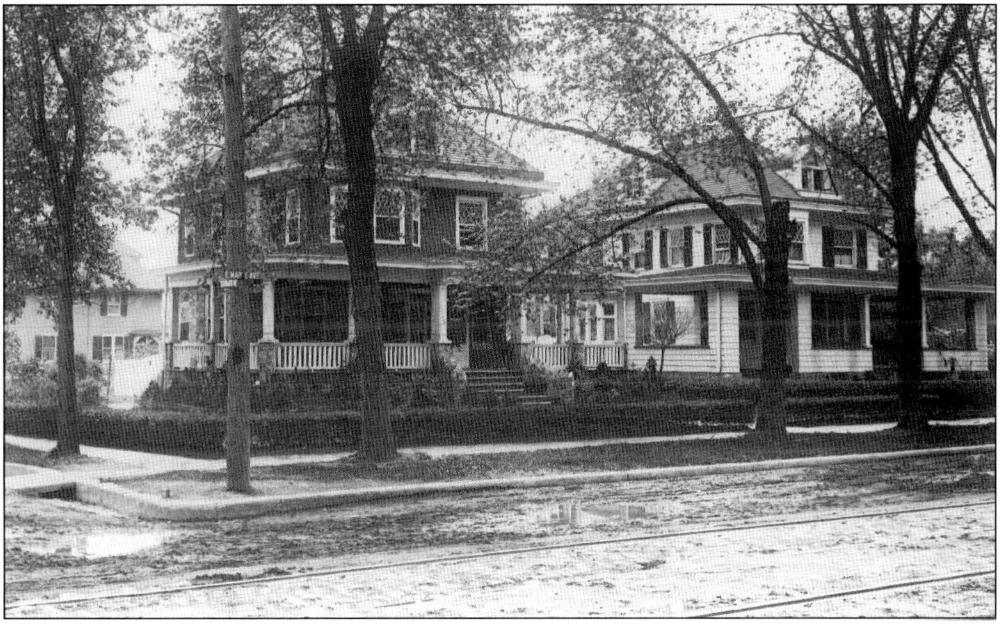

Maple Avenue mostly served as the early borough's boulevard for the upper middle class. Along this shady, tree-lined street, silverware manufacturer Harrison Robbins, dry goods merchant William Kempton, and architect Henry Alexander Macomb had their mansions built. Merchantville was "one of the most desirable locations for a suburban home," as reported c. 1900 in a realtor's circular. (Tina Schmidt.)

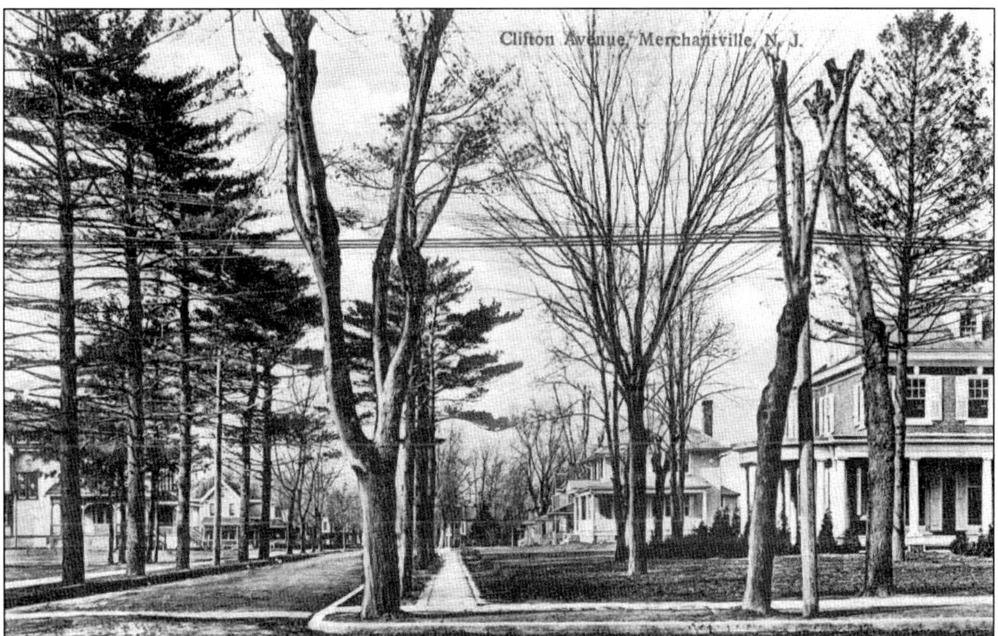

Clifton Avenue runs north of East Maple Avenue. James Ackeroyd, a wool merchant, and his wife, Anna, resided at 15 Clifton Avenue. Shown on the right is the onetime residence of George A. Crump and his mother, Elizabeth T. Crump, the widow of British vice consul George Crump. George A. Crump's sister Helen lived at 21 Clifton Avenue. (Tina Schmidt.)

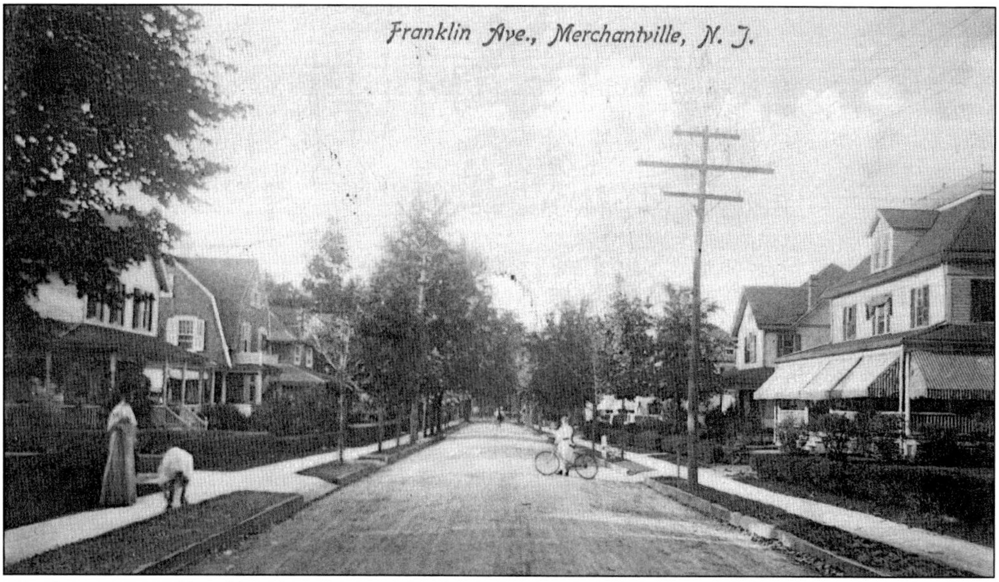

The house at 28 Franklin Avenue was built in 1896 for Arthur Dorrance, the originator of the Campbell Soup Company and president of the Joseph Campbell Company from 1894 to 1914. This dwelling was home to Dorrance and his wife, Charlotte, from 1896 until 1909. Nearly all the houses on Franklin Avenue were erected around the beginning of the 20th century. (Rudy Klock.)

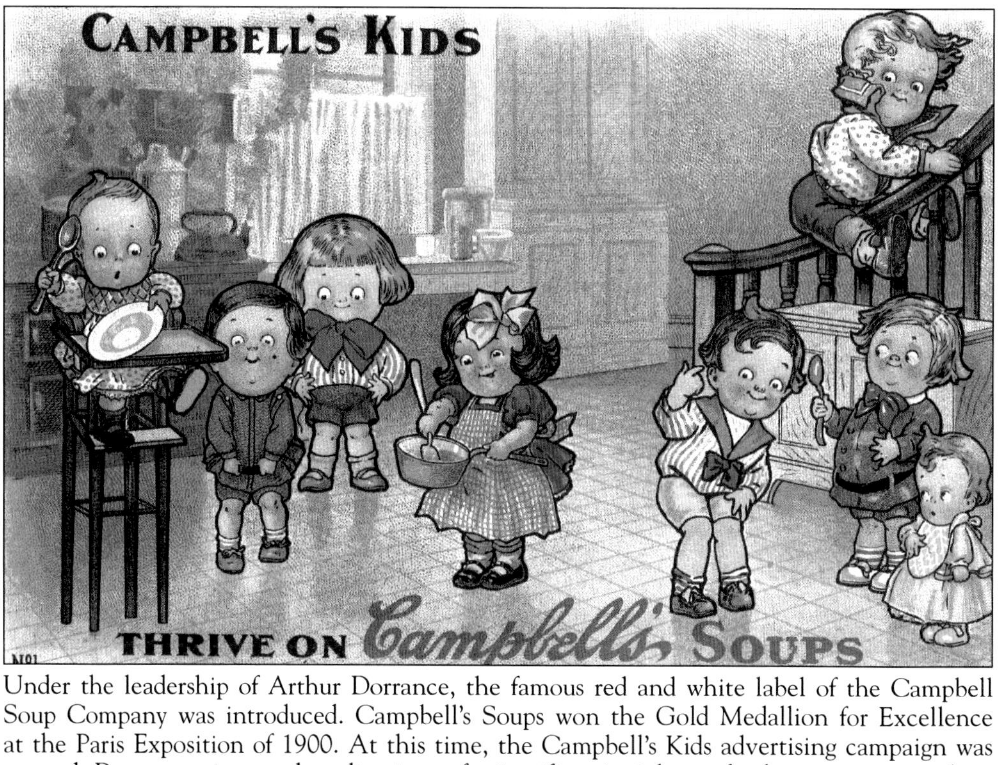

Under the leadership of Arthur Dorrance, the famous red and white label of the Campbell Soup Company was introduced. Campbell's Soups won the Gold Medallion for Excellence at the Paris Exposition of 1900. At this time, the Campbell's Kids advertising campaign was created. Dorrance pioneered applications of scientific principles to food preparation, such as the production of condensed soups. (Irene Powers.)

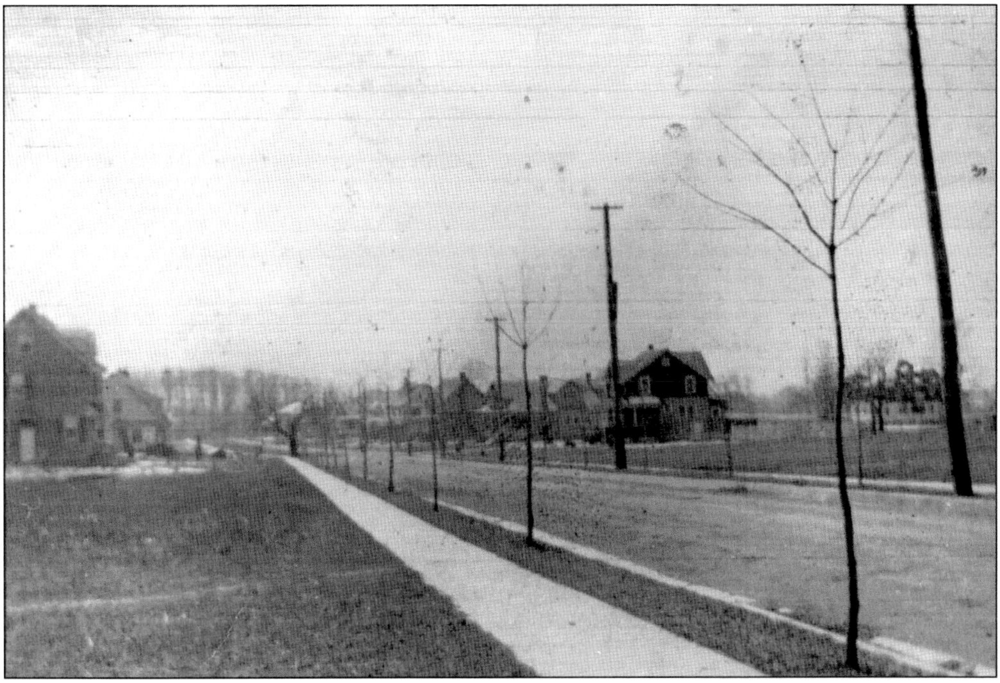

In 1914, Plymouth Place was barely developed. After World War I, lots were bought and development began anew in Merchantville. When the Delaware River Bridge opened in 1926, new streets on the southern side of Maple Avenue were cut through, individual homes built, and the borough's population gradually developed to near its present number. (Vernon Collins.)

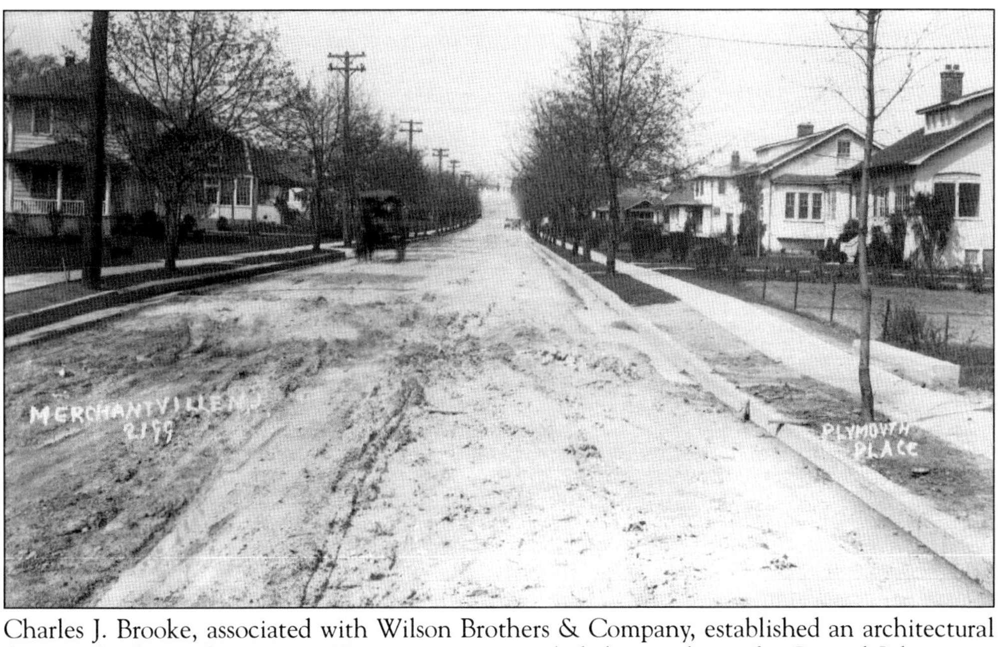

Charles J. Brooke, associated with Wilson Brothers & Company, established an architectural firm in the borough c. 1908. His commissions included a residence for Samuel Johnson at Plymouth Place near Church Road in 1910. (Merchantville Historical Society.)

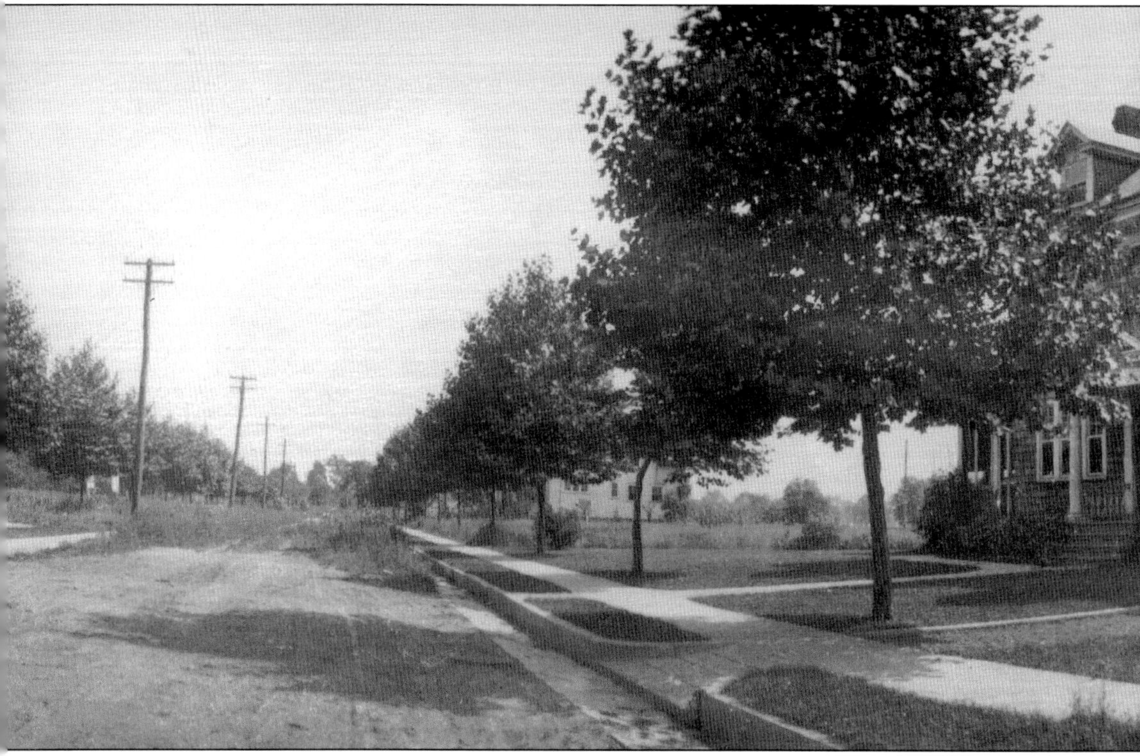

In 1918, St. James Avenue was impassable in rainy weather. The iceman, a Mr. Simon, would have to stop at the corner and carry the ice into the block. The street was paved about six years

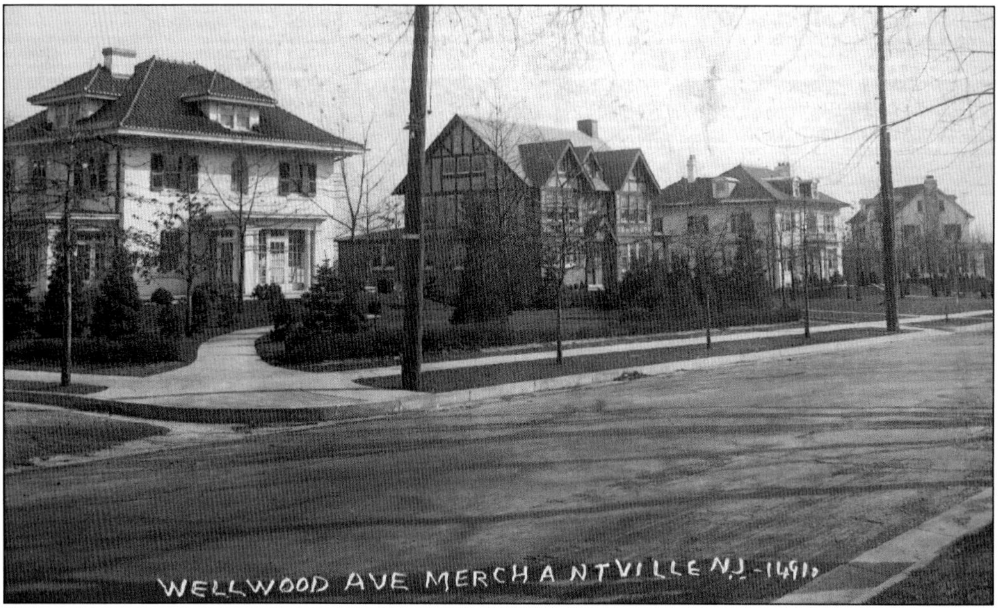

From 1760 until 1823, Wellwood Avenue was a private lane from a large farm of John Browning. The lane ran from the farm into Kaighn Avenue in Camden. Along this street could be found the grand homes of Emeline G. Bender, Harvey K. Partridge, Harry S. Bottomly, and Harry Humphreys. (Bobbi Stagliano.)

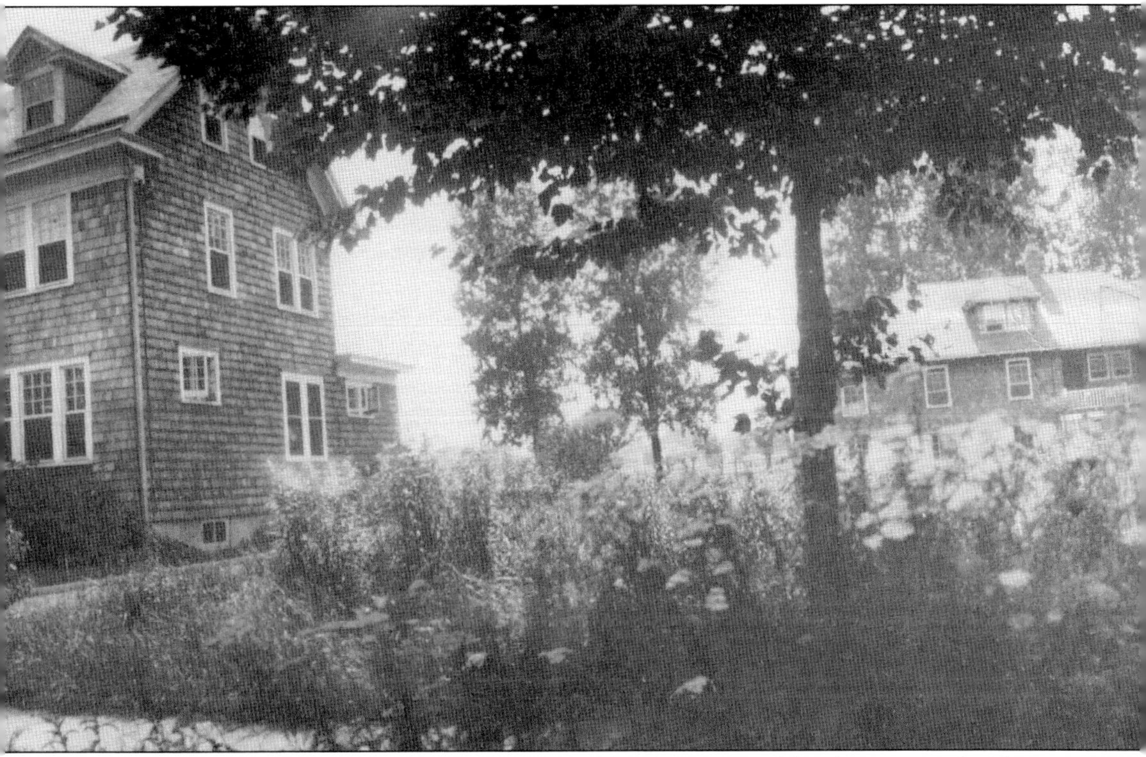

later. The house shown was built by a Mr. Mansfield and was owned by the Morgan family. It was purchased by John J. Brunson in May 1918. (Merchantville Historical Society.)

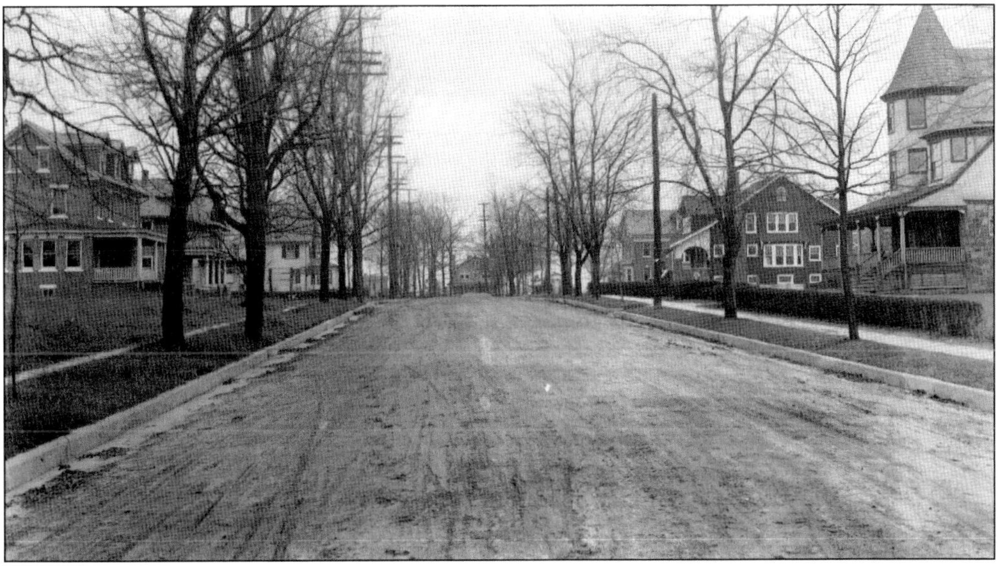

Patrick Cunningham selected "Wellwood" as the site for his "home in the country." There was a free-flowing spring of water in the midst of this beautiful tract of pine woodland that Cunningham formed into a square well. Thus the name was derived from this well in the woods. (Bobbi Stagliano.)

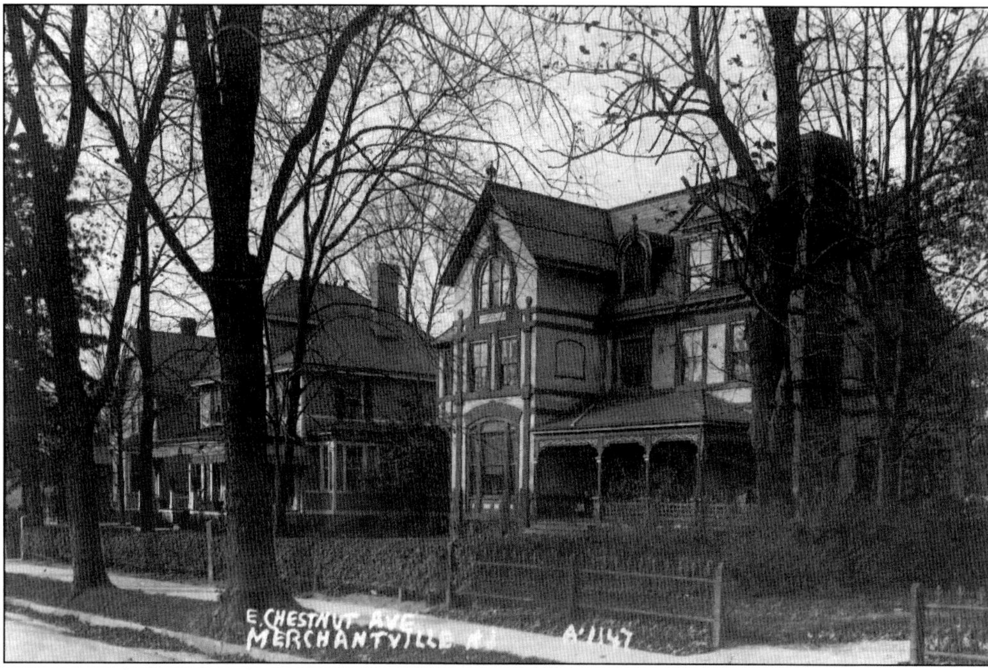

In 1877, John Crump began construction of single and double cottages along the north side of Chestnut Avenue. Crump built at least eight structures. The Ingersoll House, at 1 East Chestnut Avenue, was built in the Queen Anne style. Dr. Joseph D. Lawrence and his wife, Clara, lived here for many years. (Merchantville Historical Society.)

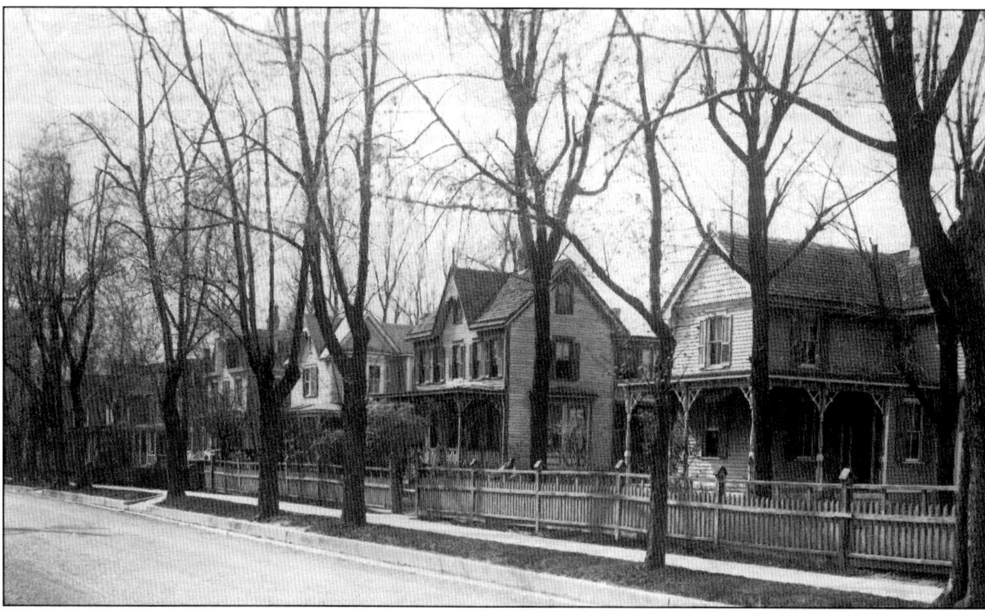

In 1883, Chestnut Avenue was continued westward to Morris Street. Samuel Carson acquired three lots belonging to Alexander Cattell on West Chestnut Avenue in the late 1800s. Chestnut Avenue was the location of the railroad line and had smaller dwellings that primarily housed members of the working class, like stonemasons, gardeners, and carpenters. (Merchantville Historical Society.)

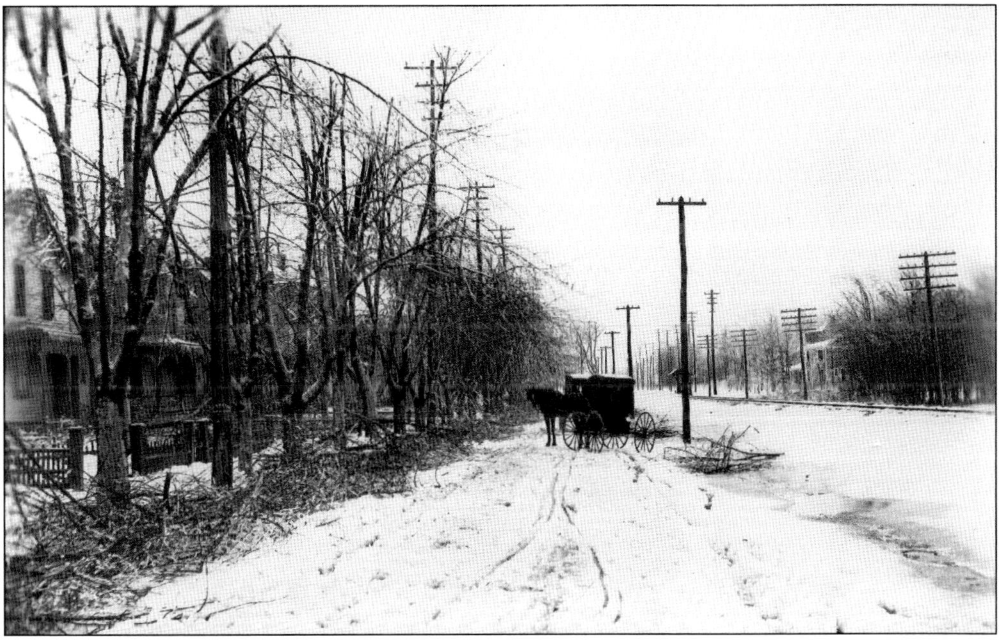

According to 1883 building announcements in the *West Jersey Press*, James Brown constructed at least seven cottages along the south side of West Chestnut Avenue: "These houses under the supervision of James Brown were occupied as rapidly as completed, and presented a neat appearance." (Merchantville Historical Society.)

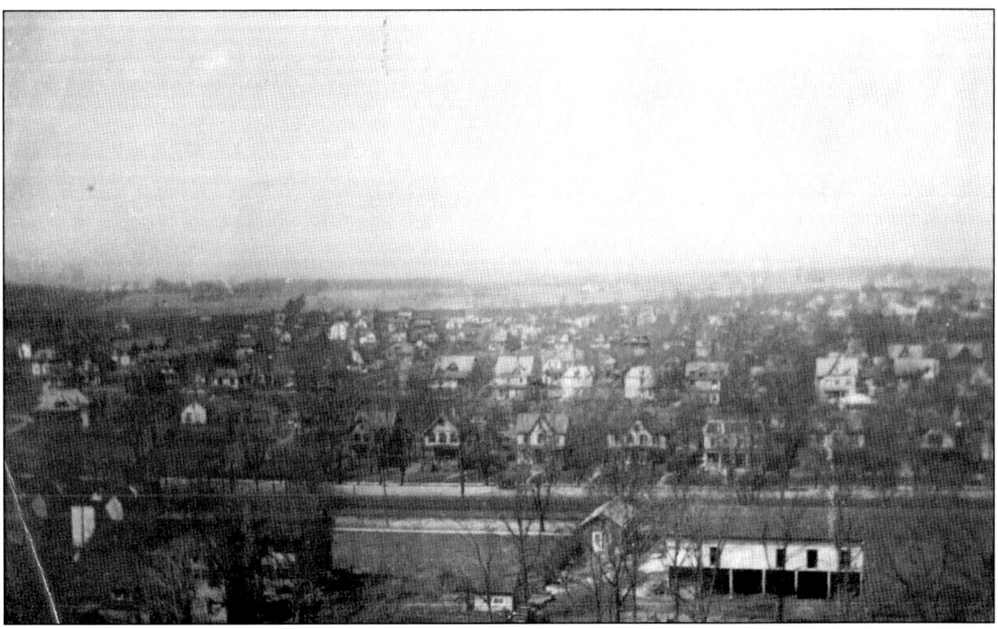

A price for a lot on West Chestnut Avenue in the mid-1880s cost between $350 and $500. Shown here is the Collins Lumber Yard, which began operation c. 1887 and provided materials for a land development undertaking known as the Cattell Development. (Merchantville Historical Society.)

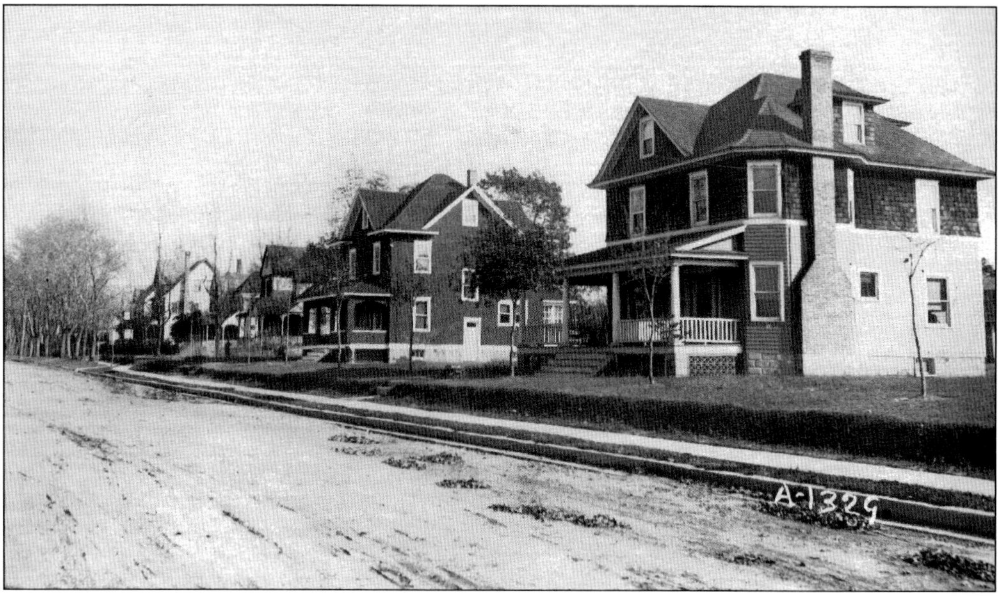

From 1868 to the mid-1870s, Alexander Cattell sold several 60-by-250-foot lots on East Chestnut, Park, and East Walnut Avenues for between $400 and $500. A few lots with speculative frame dwellings sold for $4,500. The first home, the Furber House at 25 East Walnut Avenue, was built in 1869. (Merchantville Historical Society.)

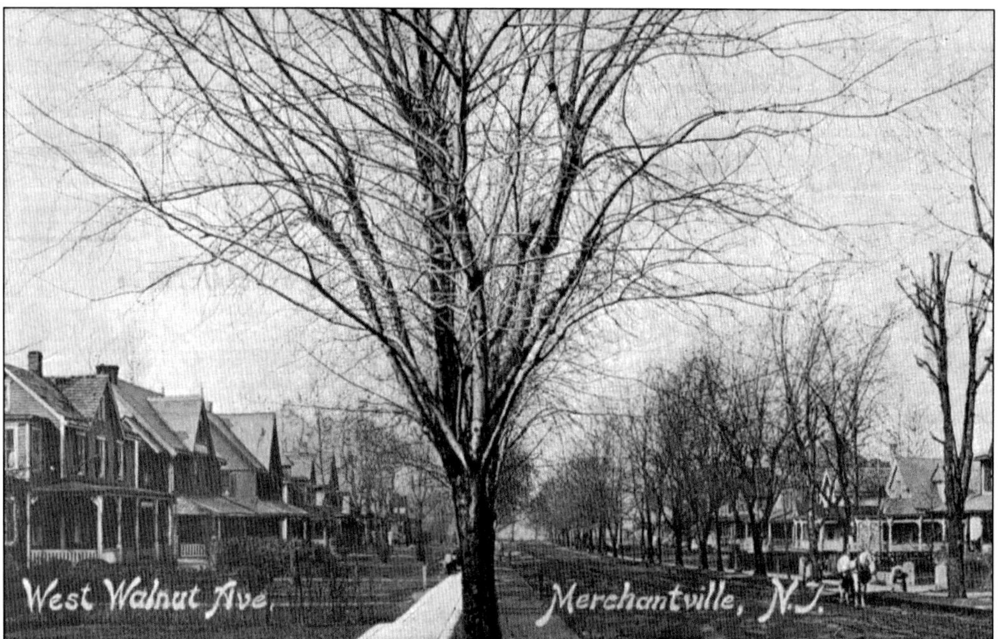

During the late 1880s, Arnold H. Moses and his partner, Guy King, were designing frame cottages in the Cattell Development for $5,000. These builders dominated construction along Chestnut, Walnut, and Cedar Avenues. The summer cottages at 23–27 West Walnut Avenue were originally used as summer retreats from the heat of the city. (Tina Schmidt.)

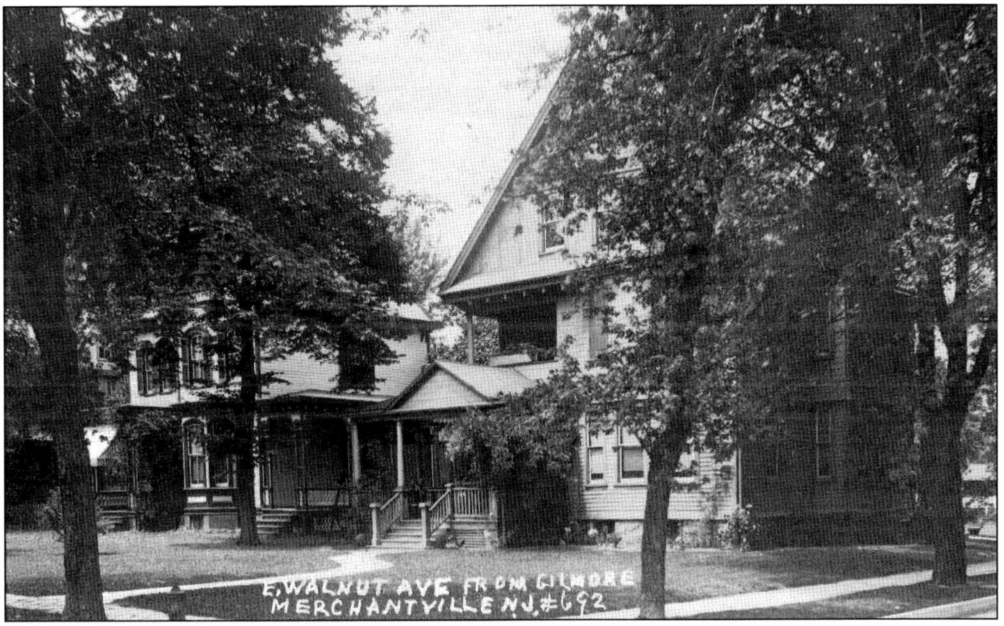

The Sarah Jesson House, at 30 East Walnut Avenue, was built in the Second Empire style. It has been altered over the years but has been returned to its former elegance. Walnut Avenue, located in the heart of the Cattell Development, was home to manufacturers of frames, envelopes, dental instruments, and hosiery. This general clustering of industry by street existed throughout the borough. (Tina Schmidt.)

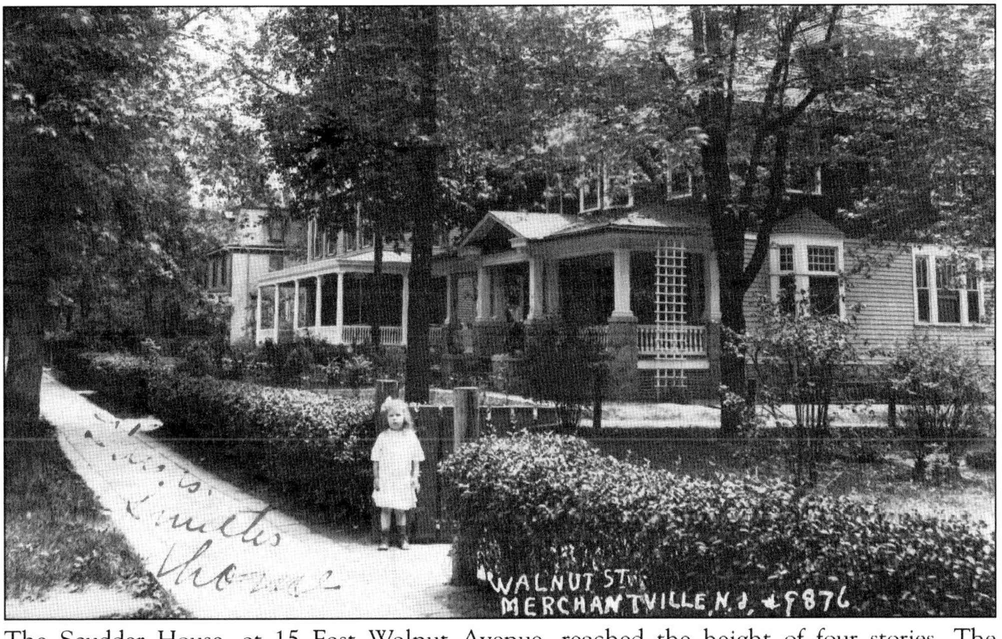

The Scudder House, at 15 East Walnut Avenue, reached the height of four stories. The skyline of Philadelphia was visible from the top windows. It was built in the Queen Anne style and retains its original splendor. Christian E. Spangler moved to 6 East Walnut Avenue in 1872. He was an envelope manufacturer and a board member of the Pennsylvania Railroad. (Maureen McLoone.)

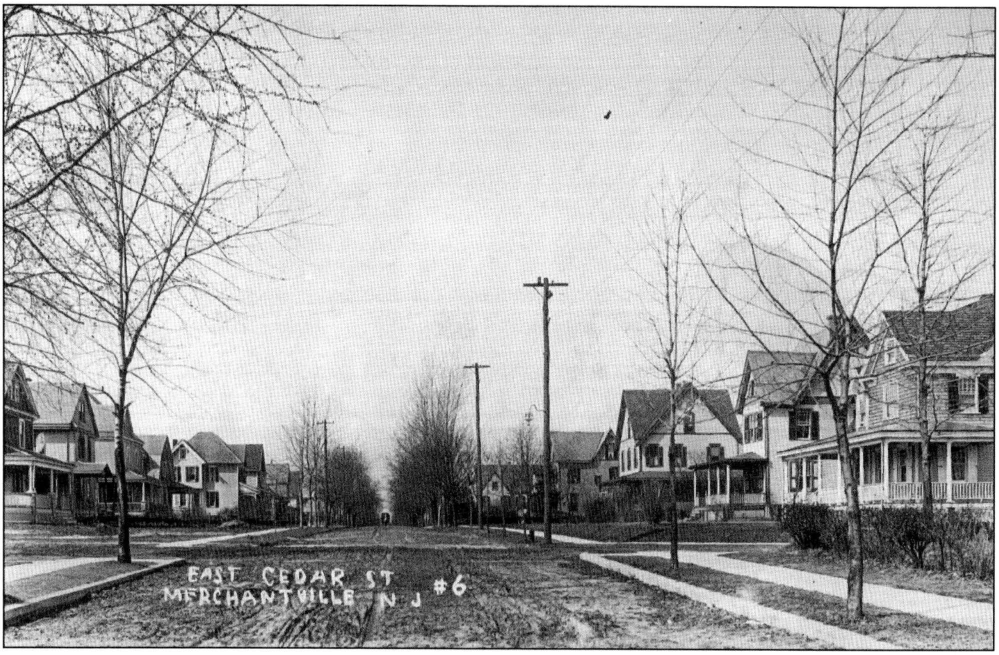

Deed searches of Cattell's 143 lots indicate multiple purchases by builders and developers during the 1880s and 1890s. George W. Gilbert acquired five lots on East Cedar Avenue. D. Leonard Moore, who built numerous dwellings in surrounding Pennsauken, secured a lot on East Cedar as well. (Merchantville Historical Society.)

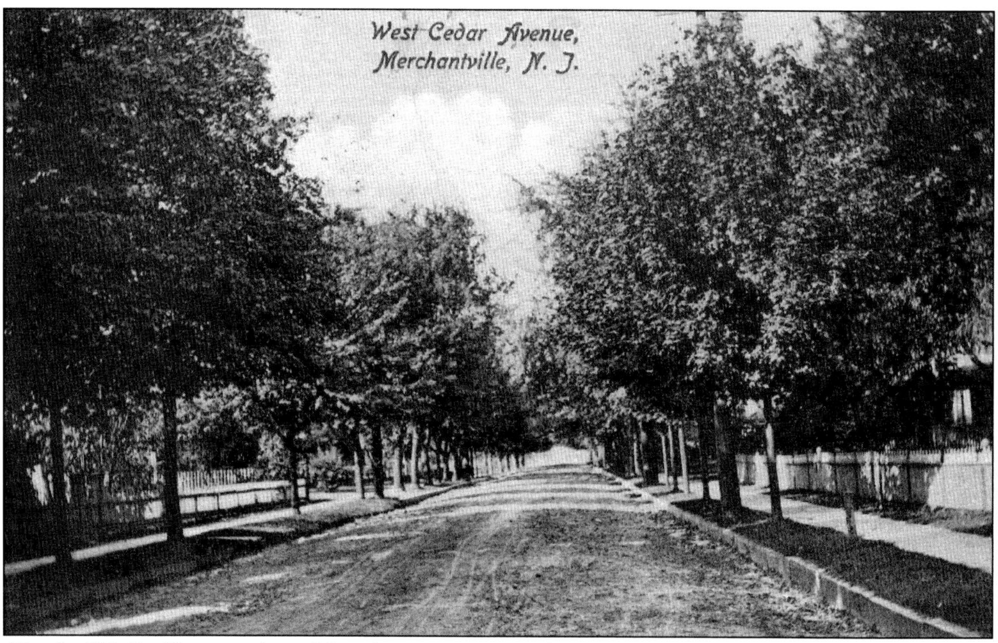

Charles W. Godfrey purchased five lots on West Cedar Avenue from the Cattell Development. George C. Tilton likely constructed at least nine residences on West Cedar Avenue. Tilton, along with his partner David Howell, appeared to have been the most popular builders. (Tina Schmidt.)

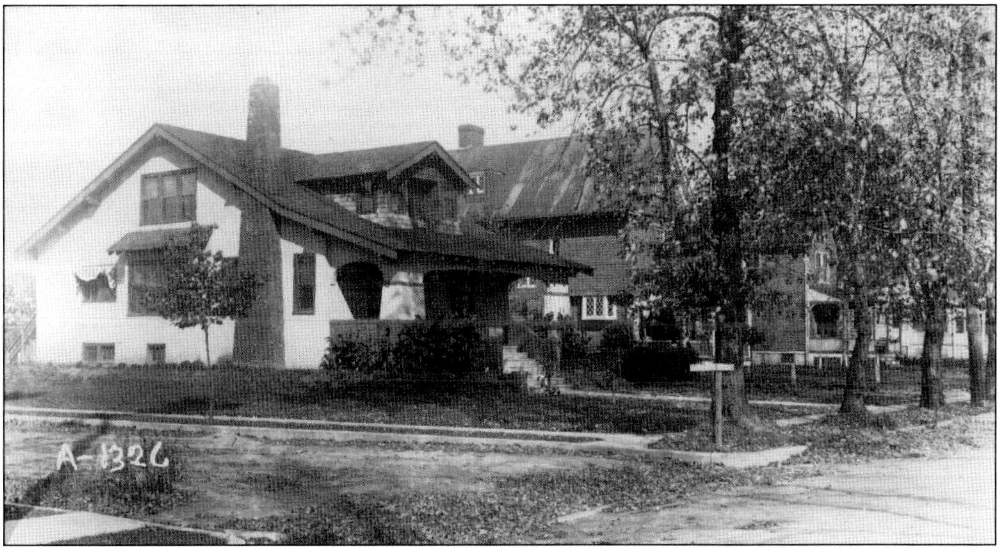

The bungalows along Leslie Avenue were examples of the smaller houses built in the second decade of the 20th century. The homes were built along the newly cut street and are examples of the Craftsman style. (Bobbi Stagliano.)

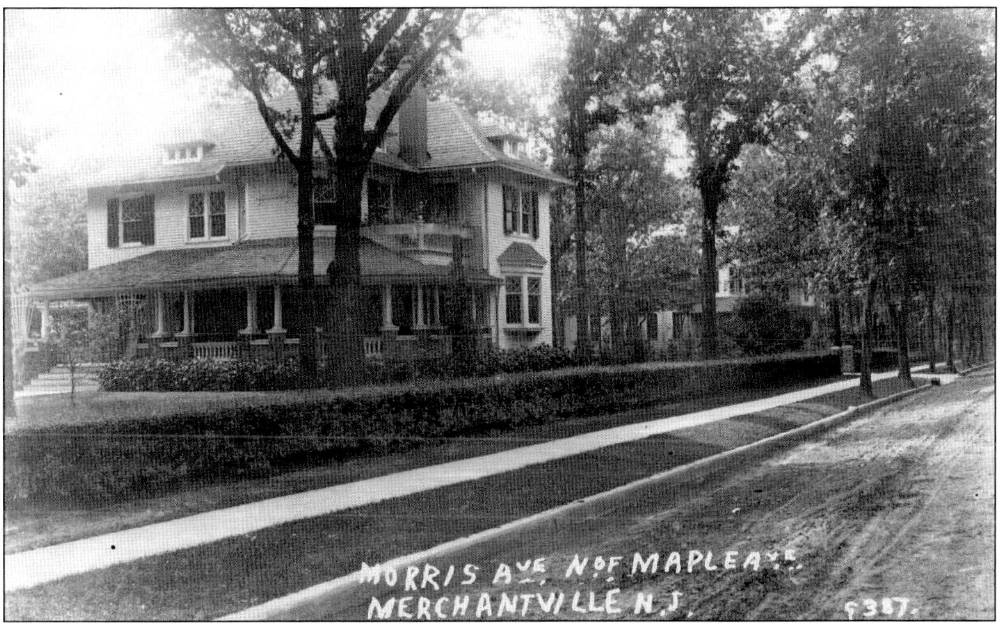

In 1887, scattered buildings appeared on Maple Terrace and South Centre, Volan, and Morris Streets. Edward S. Hall, a Philadelphia banker, built his home in Merchantville in 1869. It is still standing at the northeast corner of West Maple Avenue and Morris Street. In this home, the first meeting for the founding of the Grace Episcopal Church was held. Six men and women attended. (Bobbi Stagliano.)

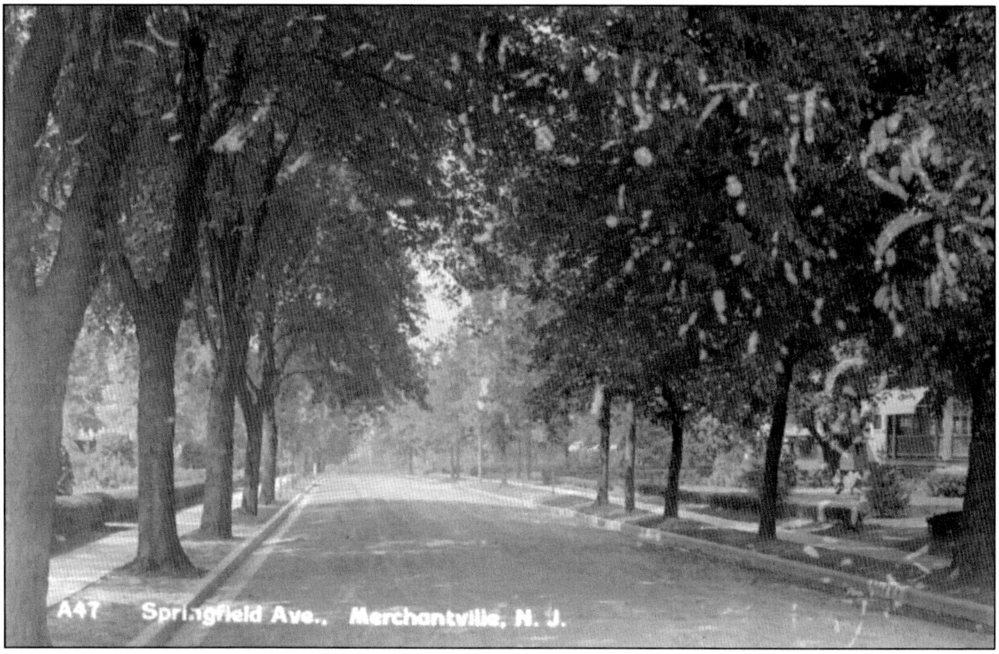

Frank S. Walton, the ninth mayor of the borough, lived at 16 Springfield Avenue. This was an early example of Colonial Revival architecture. The individual responsible for introducing this middle-class interpretation is Arnold H. Moses. This house is significant because it marks one of Moses's early architectural projects in Merchantville. (Bobbi Stagliano.)

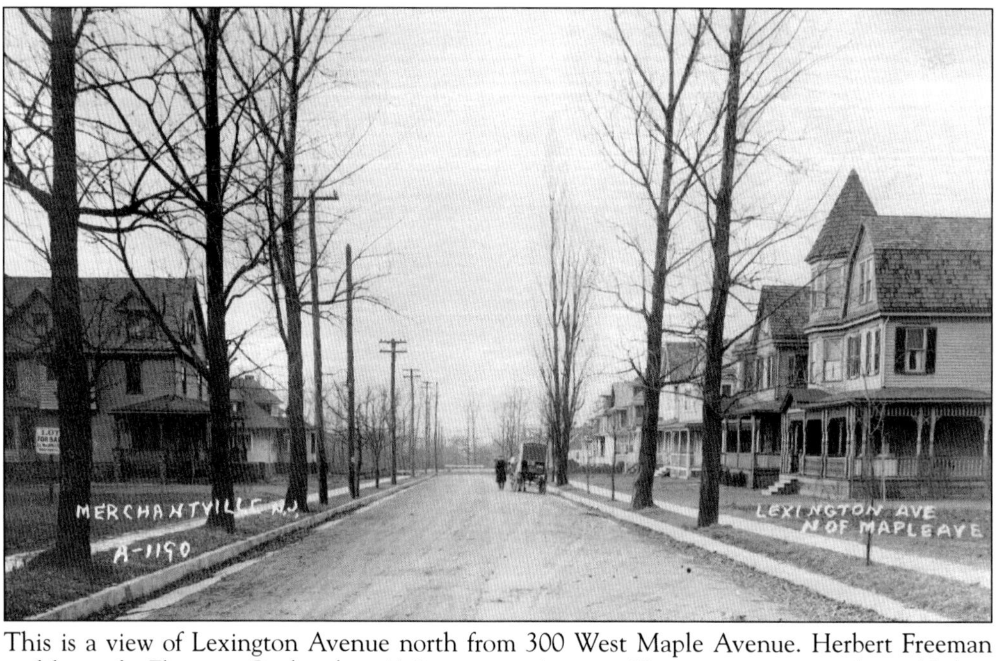

This is a view of Lexington Avenue north from 300 West Maple Avenue. Herbert Freeman and his wife, Florence G., lived at 11 Lexington Avenue. He was a printer and a publisher. The 1911 *Directory of Merchantville, North Merchantville, and Pennsauken* was compiled and published by Herbert F. Freeman & Company. (Merchantville Historical Society.)

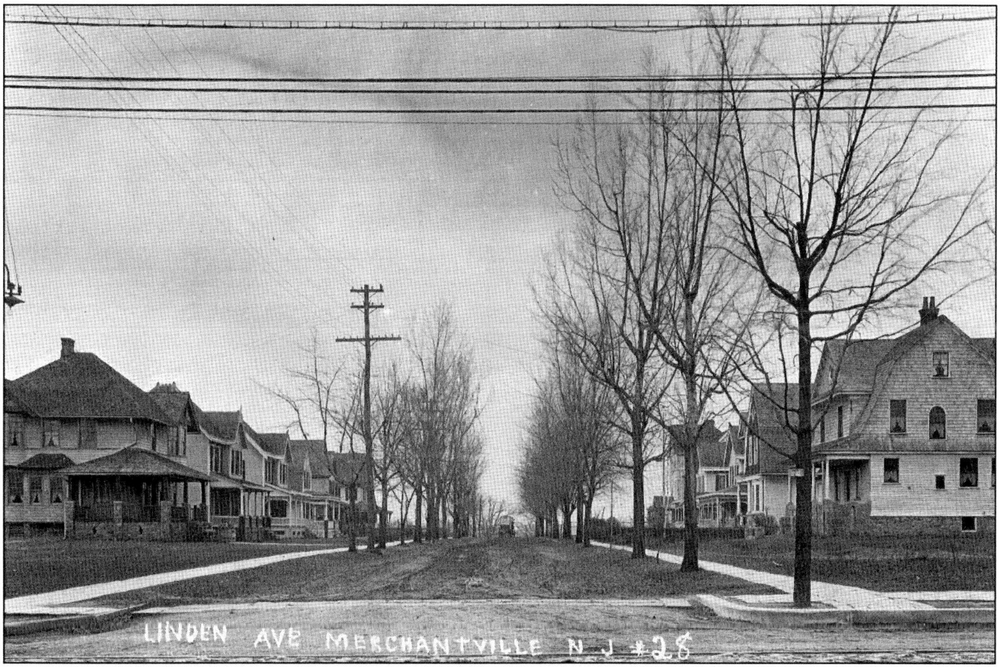

The Thomas Stephen residence, at 23 Linden Avenue, was designed and inhabited by its namesake. Stephen, who maintained an architectural office in Camden, was among the most prolific architects in that city and throughout South Jersey. He lived in Merchantville for 61 years. (Bobbi Stagliano.)

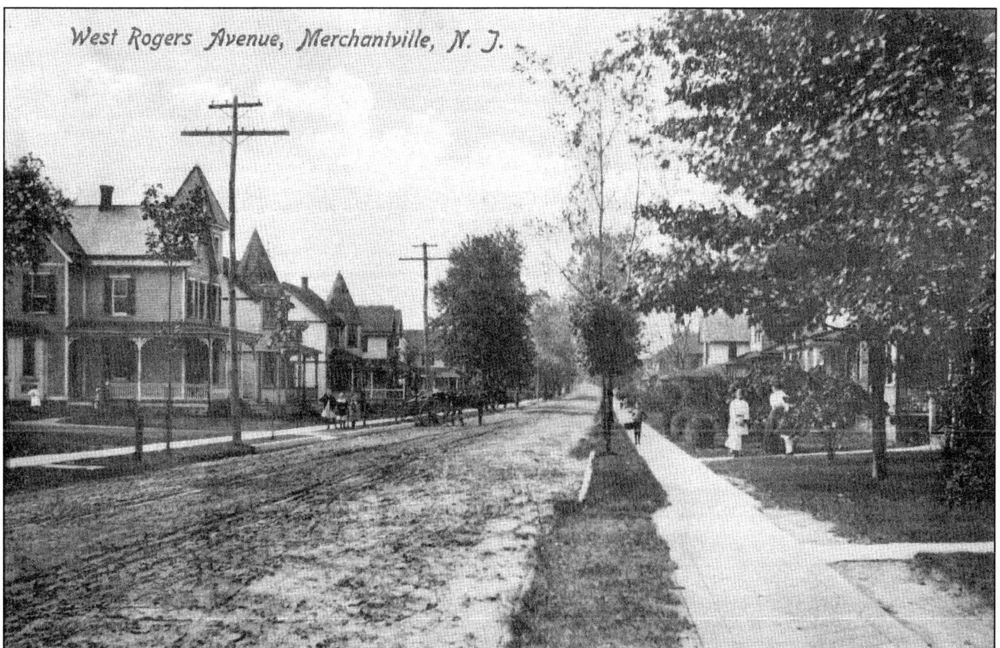

West Rogers Avenue runs west beginning at 300 North Centre Street. Charles Dobson lived with his wife, Rose, at 28 West Rogers Avenue. His occupation was listed as a trunk maker in the 1911 directory, which also indicated that this residence was outside the borough limits. (Tina Schmidt.)

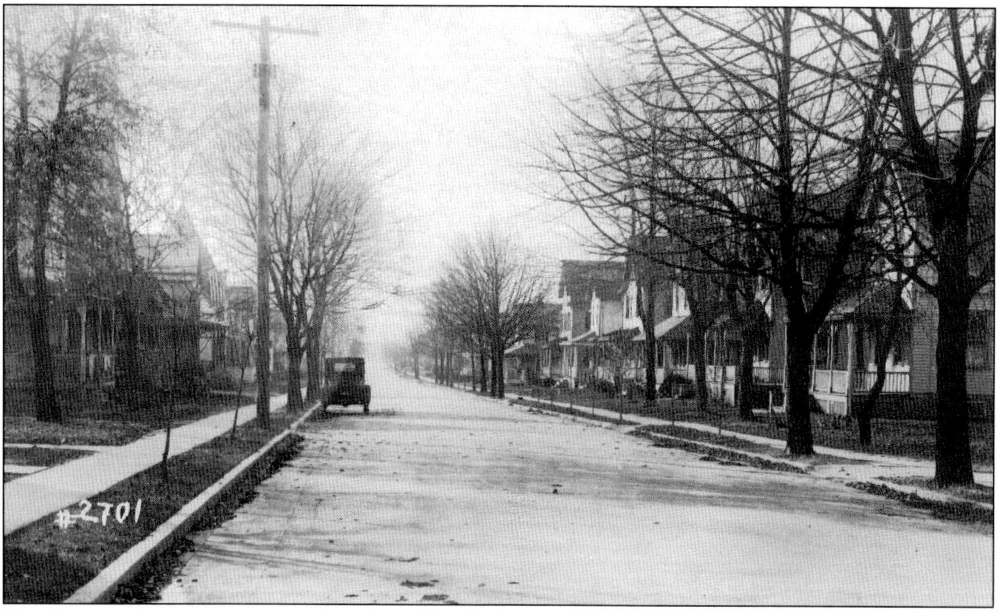

East Rogers Avenue runs east from 300 North Centre Street. Josiah B. Borton and his wife ran a grocery store at the southeast corner of Centre Street and Rogers Avenue. Henry Matthews, painter, and his wife, Jennie, lived at northeast corner of Centre Street and East Rogers Avenue, as listed in the 1911 directory. (Tina Schmidt.)

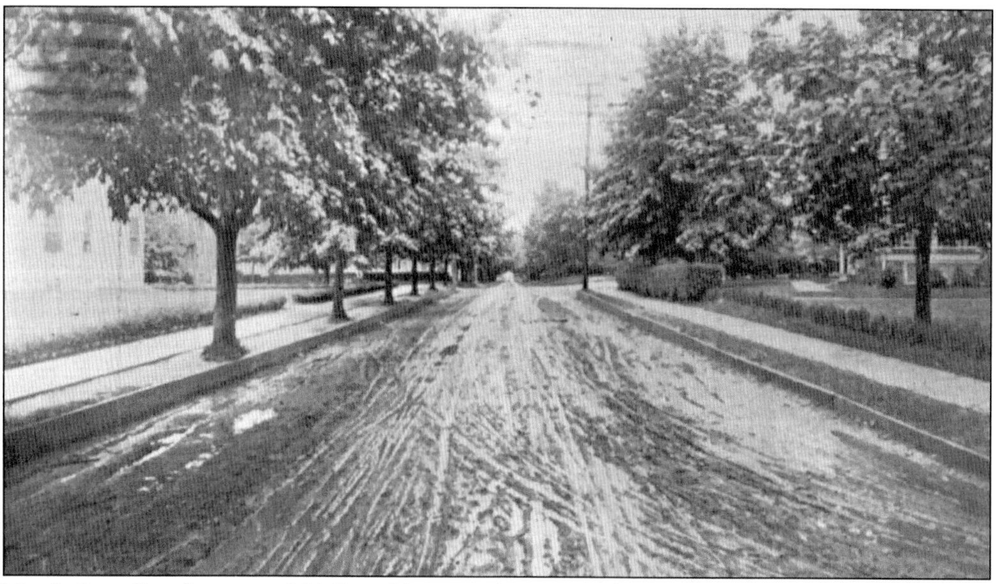

North Cove Road starts at 200 East Chestnut Avenue and runs north. In the early 1900s, the Cooper brothers sold groceries at the northeast corner of Cove Road and Park Avenue. Richard J. Watson and his wife, Ella, lived at 37 North Cove Road. A picture of his residence appears in chapter 5. (Bobbi Stagliano.)

Three

FOREVER FAITHFUL

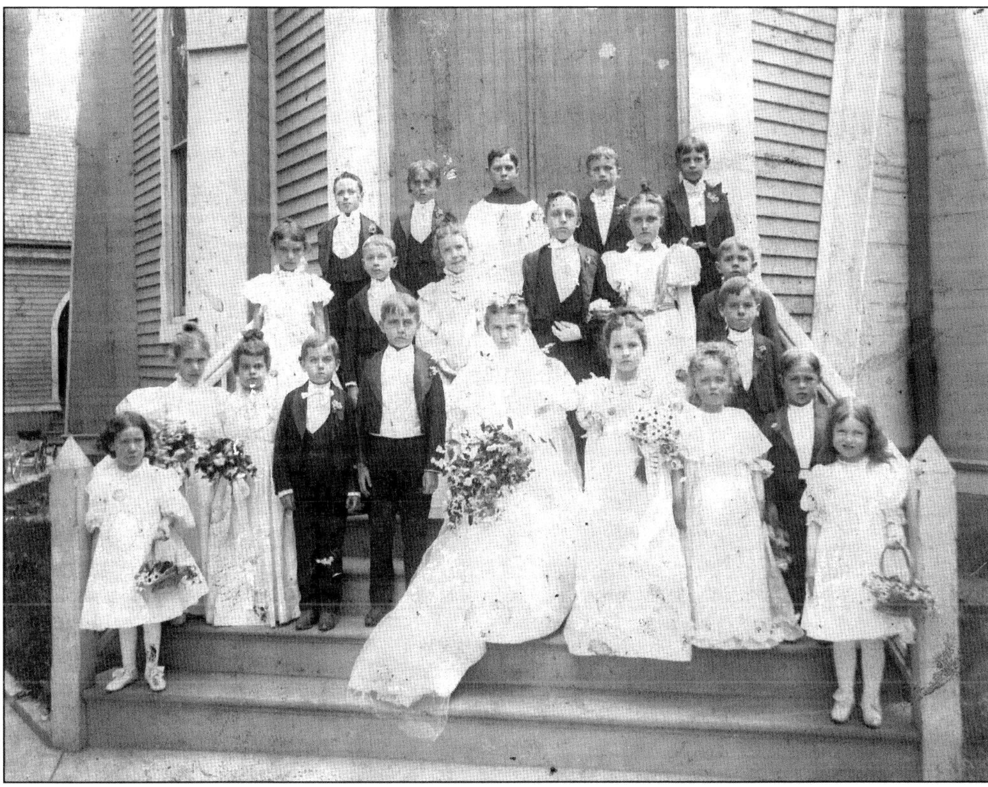

In 1905, the Merchantville First Presbyterian Church presented a Tom Thumb wedding. The participants were many of the children of the church community. Harry Knox Oakford and his twin brother, Charles Brooks Oakford, were in the production. Charles is the first on the right in the third row. Harry is in the second row, third from the left. Harry was the borough collector and Charles founded Aunt Charlotte's Candies. (Aunt Charlotte's.)

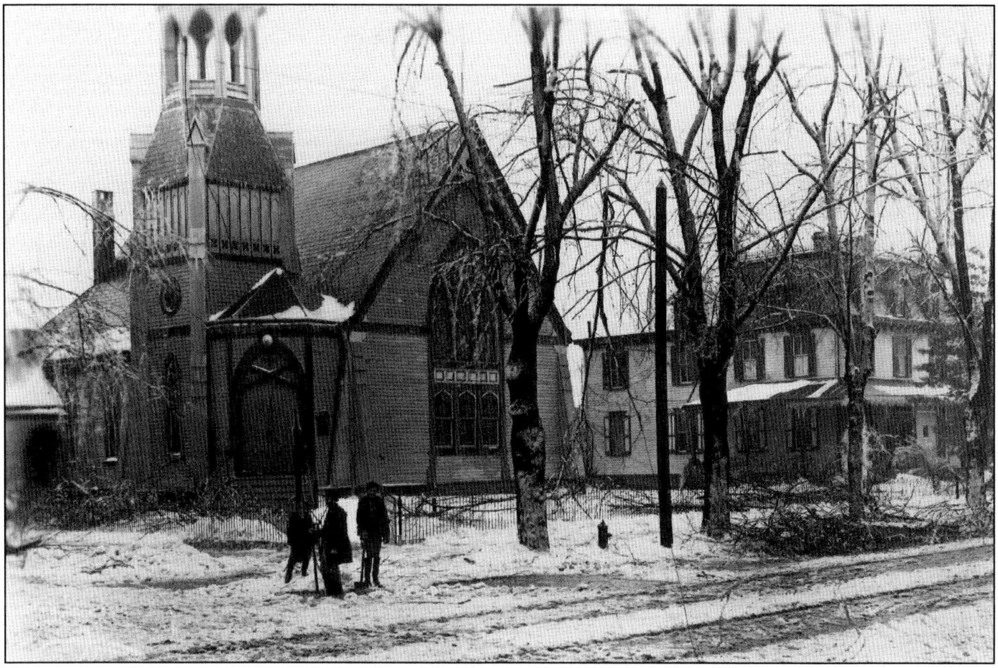

The work of erecting a church building for the First Presbyterian Church was decided upon at the third congregational meeting, held on March 11, 1875. Construction began that October, the final cost of which was $5,624.09. The membership at this time was 48. The new chapel was built and dedicated in December 1893. The First Presbyterian Church is situated on the southwest corner of West Maple Avenue and South Centre Street. (Merchantville Historical Society.)

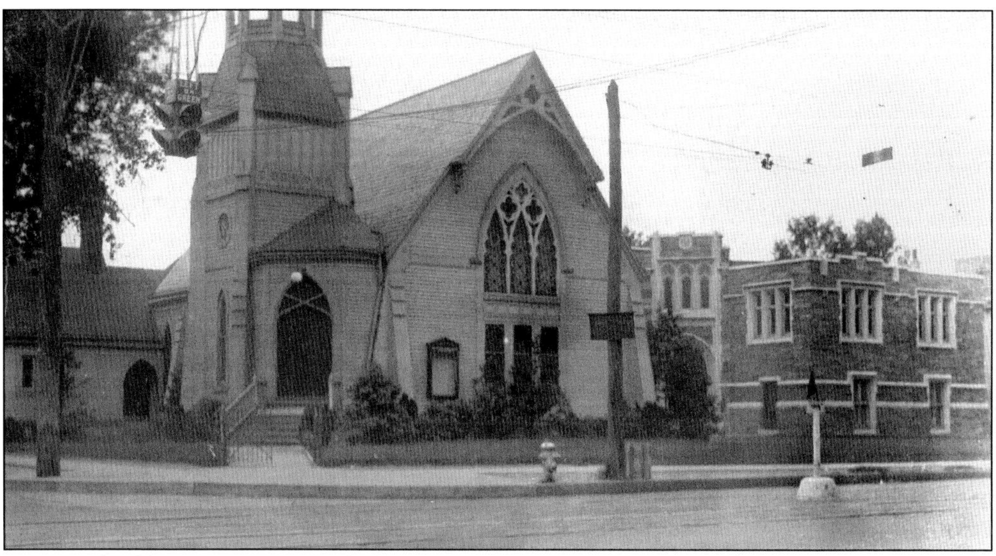

A major building expansion took place in 1924–1925, when the church-school building was erected. This addition contained a modern Sunday school room, social rooms, a kitchen, and a gymnasium. Its estimated cost was $60,000. Following World War II, the church shared in the rapid growth of the community. The congregation reported a communicant membership of 1,072 as of December 31, 1962. (Merchantville Historical Society.)

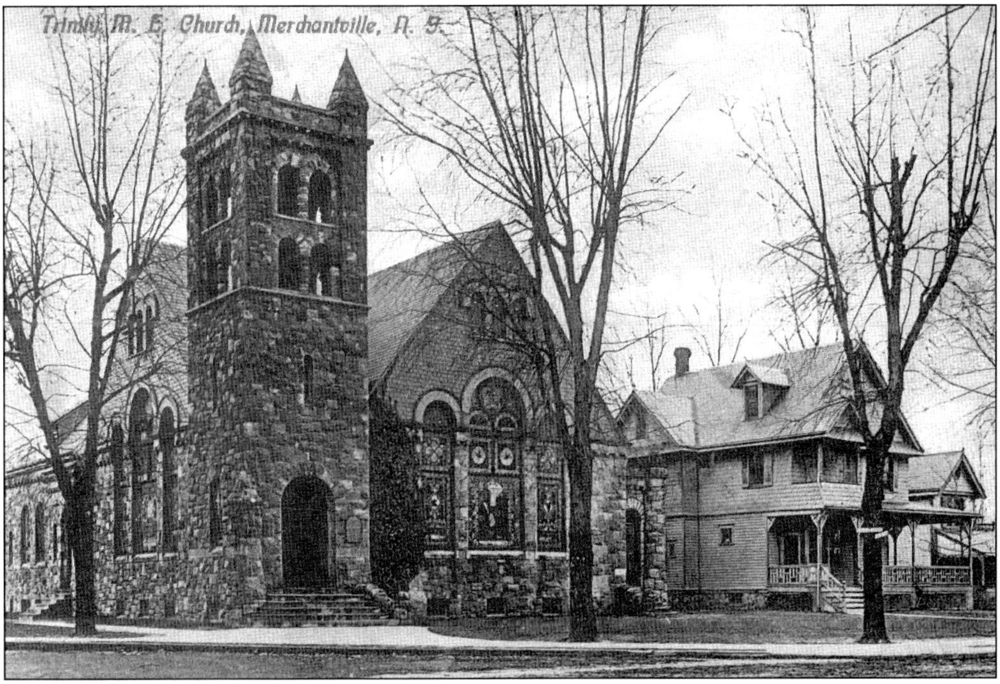

The Trinity Methodist Episcopal Chapel was the only public place of worship for miles around in the 1860s. The church was incorporated on March 11, 1865. It was a quaint and cozy wooden structure set back from the road, through an avenue of sturdy oaks and surmounted by a modest belfry. The granite edifice was finished and dedicated on May 9, 1894. The church is located at the corner of West Maple and Chapel Avenues. (Bobbi Stagliano.)

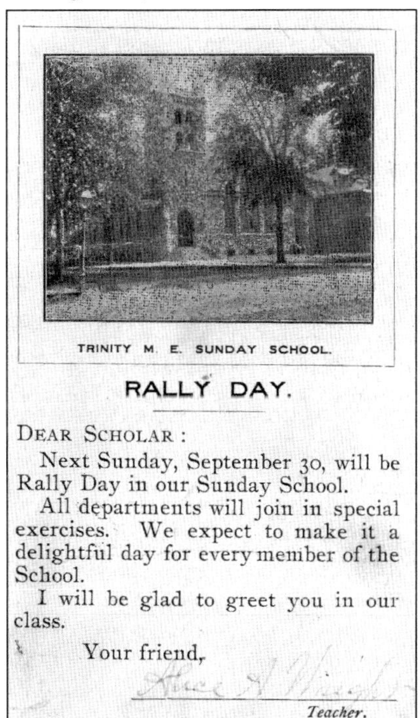
TRINITY M. E. SUNDAY SCHOOL.

RALLY DAY.

DEAR SCHOLAR:

Next Sunday, September 30, will be Rally Day in our Sunday School.

All departments will join in special exercises. We expect to make it a delightful day for every member of the School.

I will be glad to greet you in our class.

Your friend,

Teacher.

In the spring of 1863, David S. Stetson, an active member of Bethel Methodist Church in Camden, started a Sunday school in his home on East Maple Avenue. Rapid growth of this school led to the organization of a Methodist Episcopal church by the name of Trinity Chapel. In the 1890s, Samuel C. Gilmore was the superintendent of the church's Sabbath school, supported by 18 teachers and officers, with 178 scholars on the roll. (Bobbi Stagliano.)

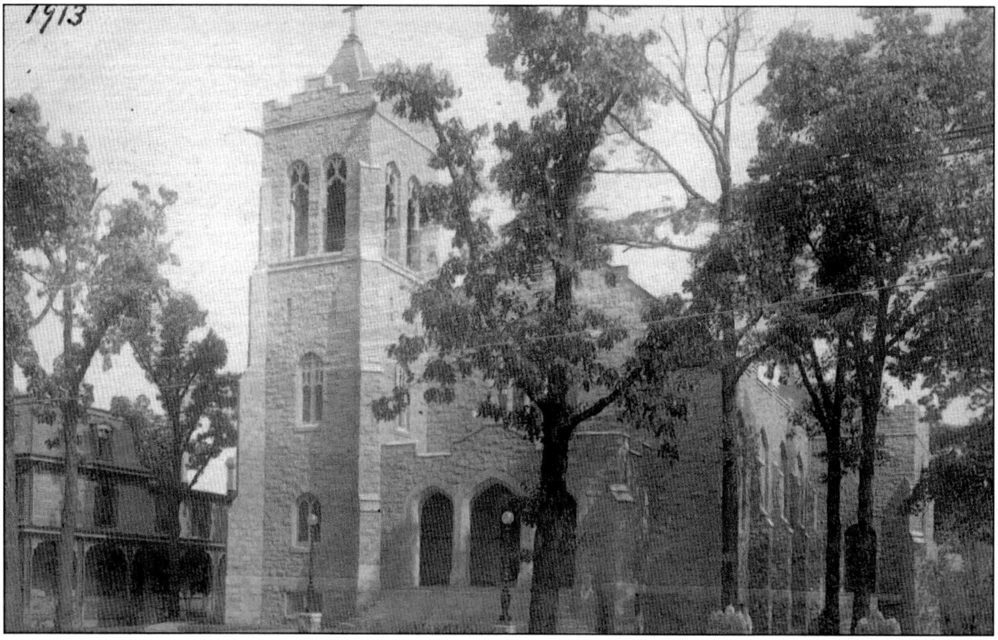

On November 3, 1906, the cornerstone was laid for a stone edifice on West Maple Avenue. The parish of St. Peter's Roman Catholic Church included Merchantville, Pennsauken, and Delair. On January 6, 1924, a disastrous fire completely destroyed the interior; only the foundation and the walls remained intact. Rebuilding was immediately started, during which worship services took place in the Park Movie Theatre. (Vernon Collins.)

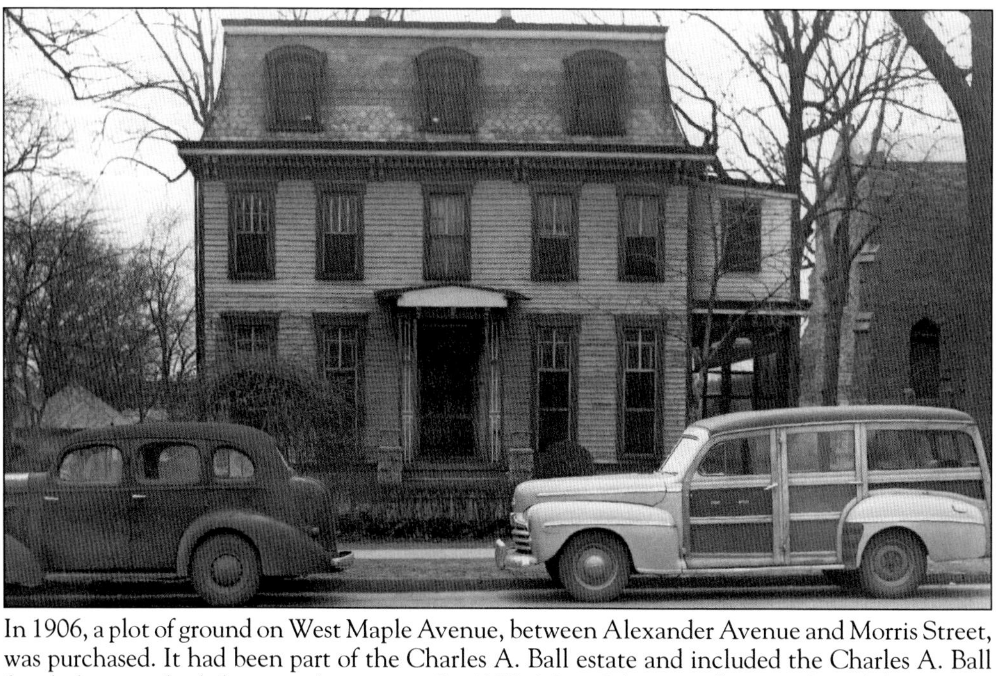

In 1906, a plot of ground on West Maple Avenue, between Alexander Avenue and Morris Street, was purchased. It had been part of the Charles A. Ball estate and included the Charles A. Ball family home, which became the rectory. In 1950, Msgr. John P. Fallon purchased the Martin property adjacent to the church on West Maple Avenue. This became the new and present rectory. (St. Peter's.)

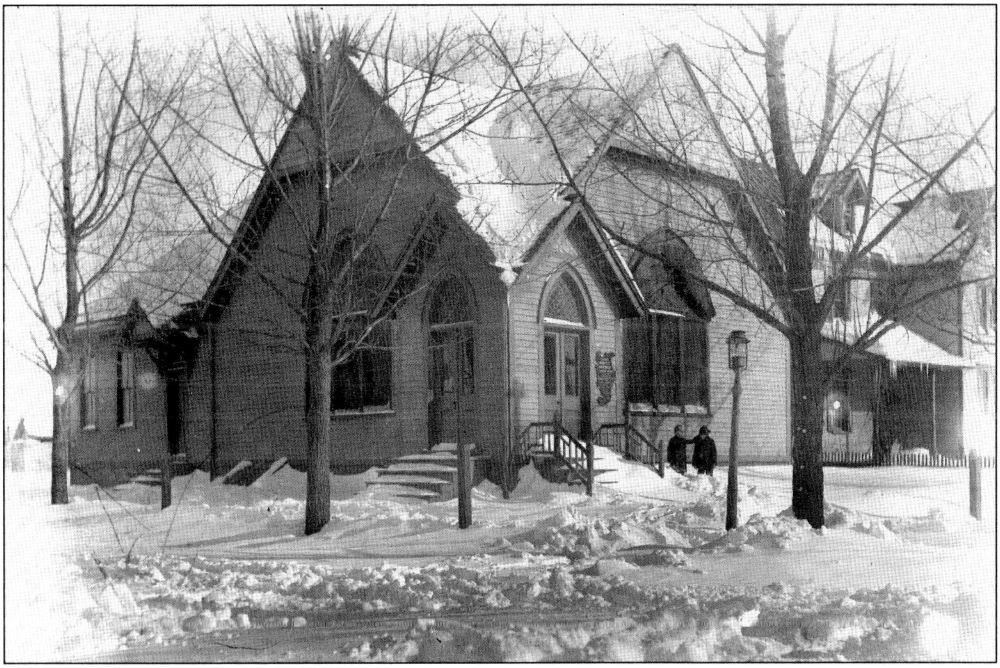

The First Baptist congregation was formally organized in 1889. In 1890, their first church, a neat and artistic wooden structure, was erected at the corner of North Centre Street and East Rogers Avenue. On May 18, 1890, the first service was conducted there. It was dedicated on June 22, 1890. After the church was relocated, John K. Jones opened a store at the site. (Merchantville Historical Society.)

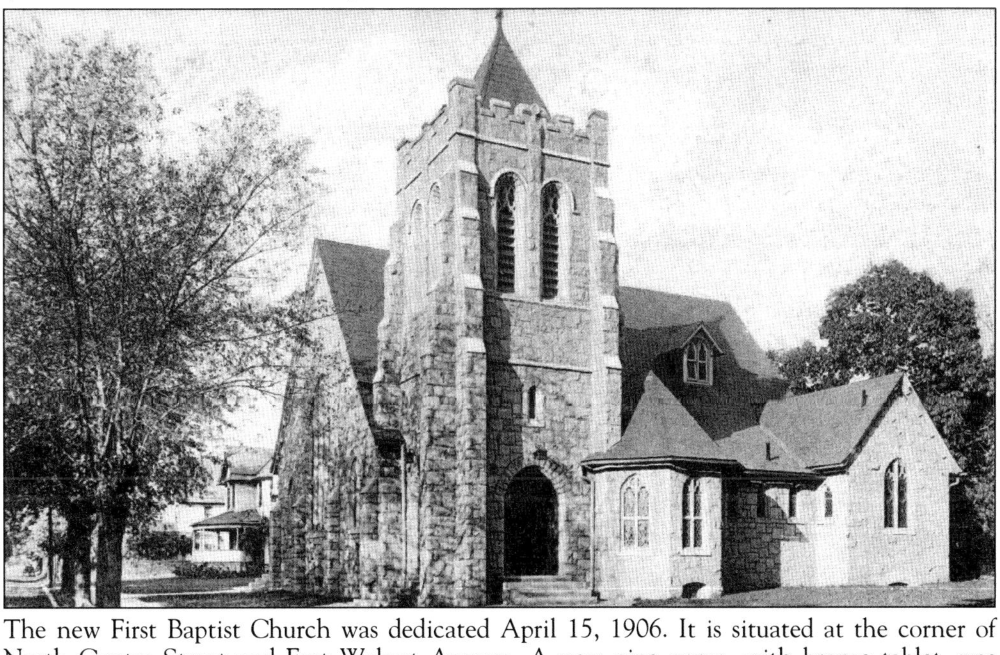

The new First Baptist Church was dedicated April 15, 1906. It is situated at the corner of North Centre Street and East Walnut Avenue. A new pipe organ, with bronze tablet, was dedicated on October 13, 1920, to Frederick W. Grigg, the only one of the 32 members of the congregation to give his life in World War I. (Merchantville Historical Society.)

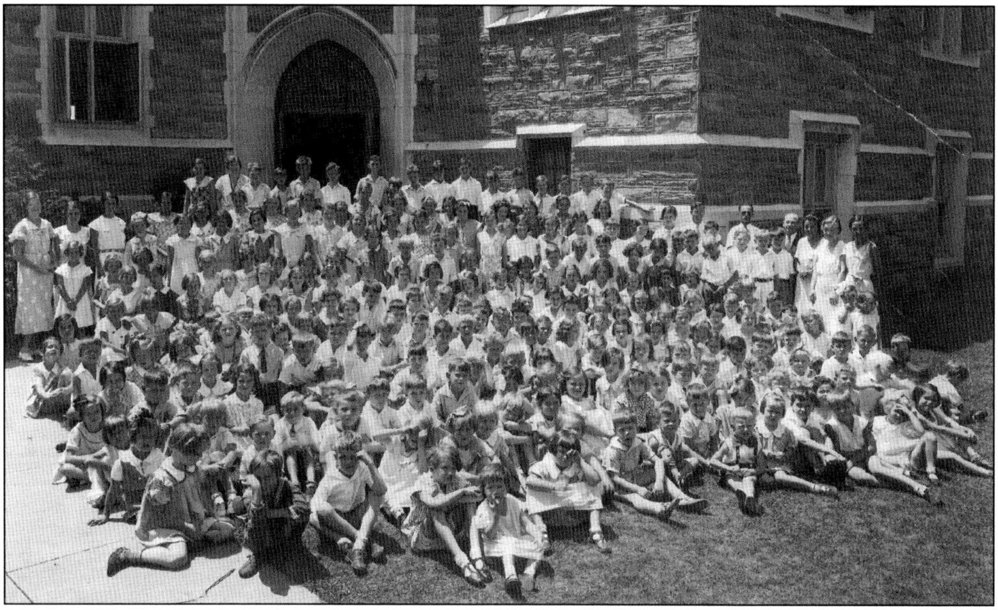

This is a 1934 vacation Bible school photograph. Joseph Wiltshire was the first superintendent of the First Baptist Church Sunday school, which is still in operation. He was assisted by 20 teachers and officers, with about 200 scholars on the roll. The Easter party invitation is just an example of the programs undertaken by the staff. (First Presbyterian Church; Irene Powers.)

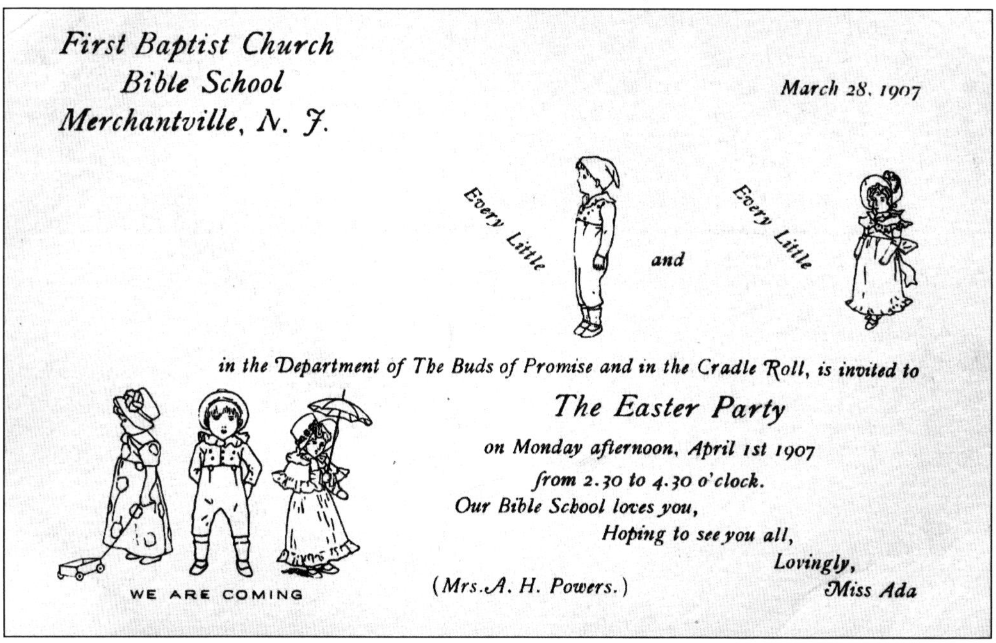

First Baptist Church
Bible School
Merchantville, N. J.

March 28, 1907

Every Little *and* *Every Little*

in the Department of The Buds of Promise and in the Cradle Roll, is invited to

The Easter Party

on Monday afternoon, April 1st 1907
from 2.30 to 4.30 o'clock.
Our Bible School loves you,
Hoping to see you all,
Lovingly,
Miss Ada
(Mrs. A. H. Powers.)

WE ARE COMING

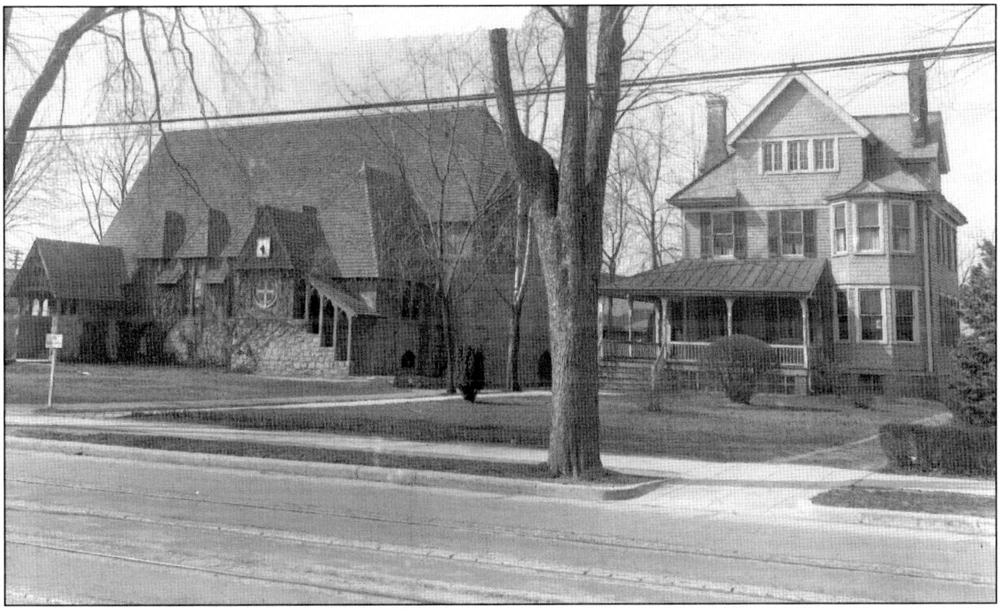

A neat wooden chapel was erected in 1878 at the corner of South Centre Street and West Park Avenue and became the Grace Episcopal Church. The chapel was then moved to the ground of the proposed new church in July 1890. The present imposing edifice was built during 1893 and 1894, and on September 30, 1894, the first divine service was solemnized. The first Sunday school superintendent was Henry A. Macomb. (Merchantville Historical Society.)

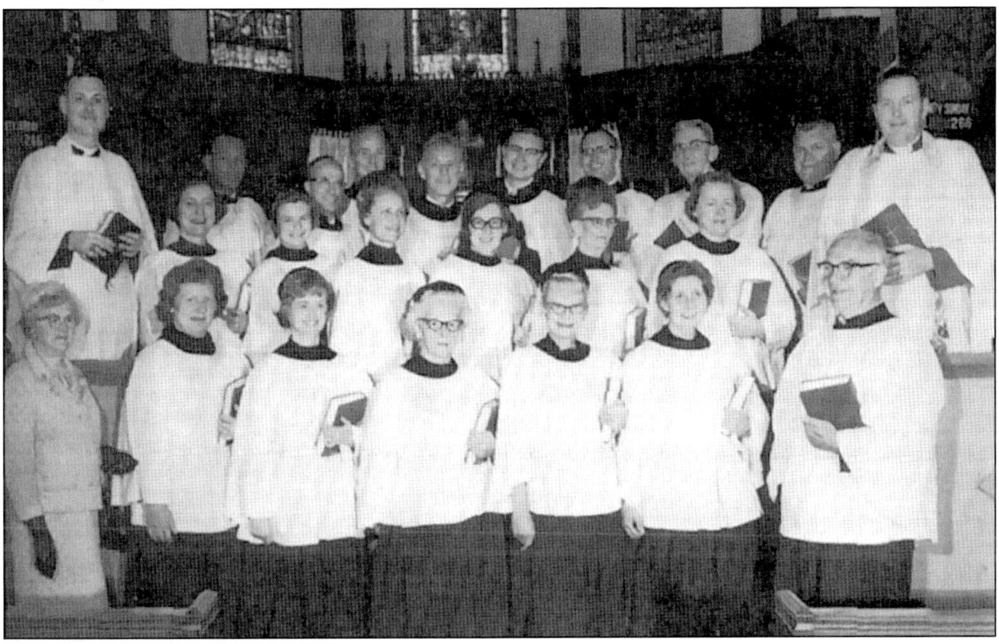

In 1894, the choir of the church consisted of nine members. Macomb was the leader and William Early played the organ. The choir stalls were erected in June 1896, and the vested choir sang its first service on the fourth Sunday after Trinity, in early summer. Shown in this c. 1960s photograph is the senior choir with canon James E. Purdy, curate Walter Krieger, and choirmaster Fred K. Homes. (Grace Episcopal Church.)

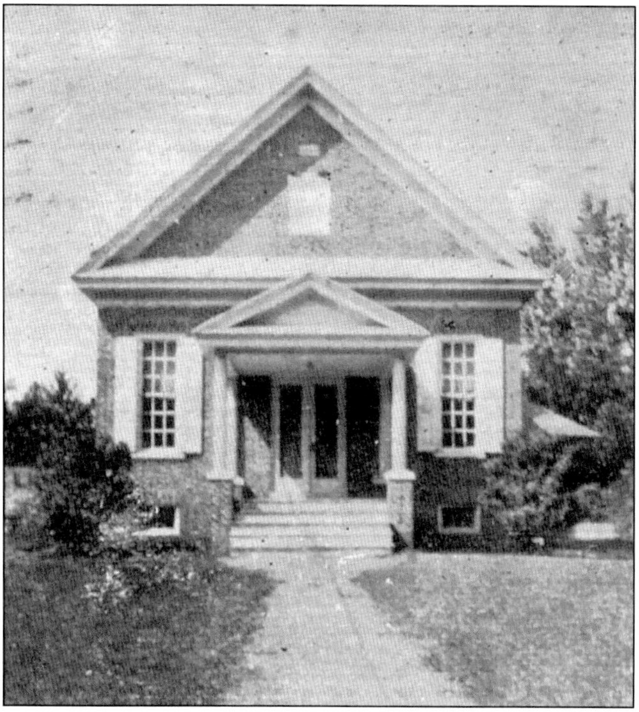

A number of Friends had for some time been holding meetings in Davenport Hall on East Park Avenue. Edwin L. Pierce, a Moorestown Friend, was deeply interested in finding an organization of Merchantville Friends, and was instrumental in building the meetinghouse on East Maple Avenue. This building, erected in 1901, was the site of the meetings until April 1922. In January 1923, it was sold to the Bell Telephone Company. (Maureen McLoone.)

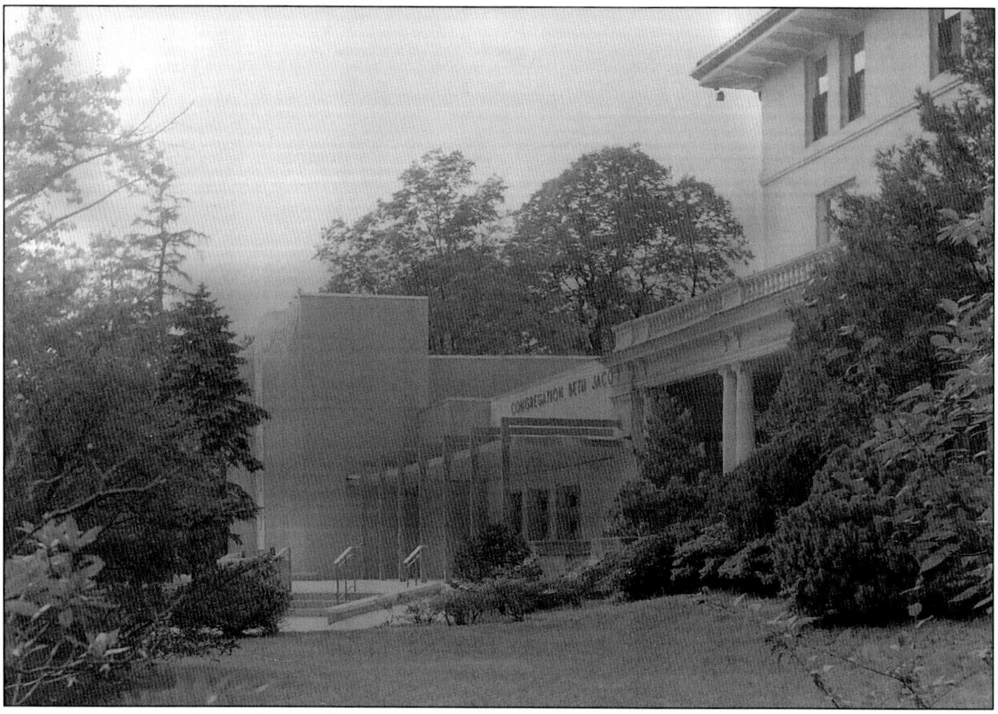

Congregation Beth Jacob purchased the former Atkinson estate at 109 East Maple Avenue in 1961. The old residence was completely reconstructed to provide classrooms, a chapel, a library, and other rooms. In 1987, Congregation Beth Jacob moved to another location, and the property at 109 East Maple was sold. (Merchantville Historical Society.)

Four

School Spirit

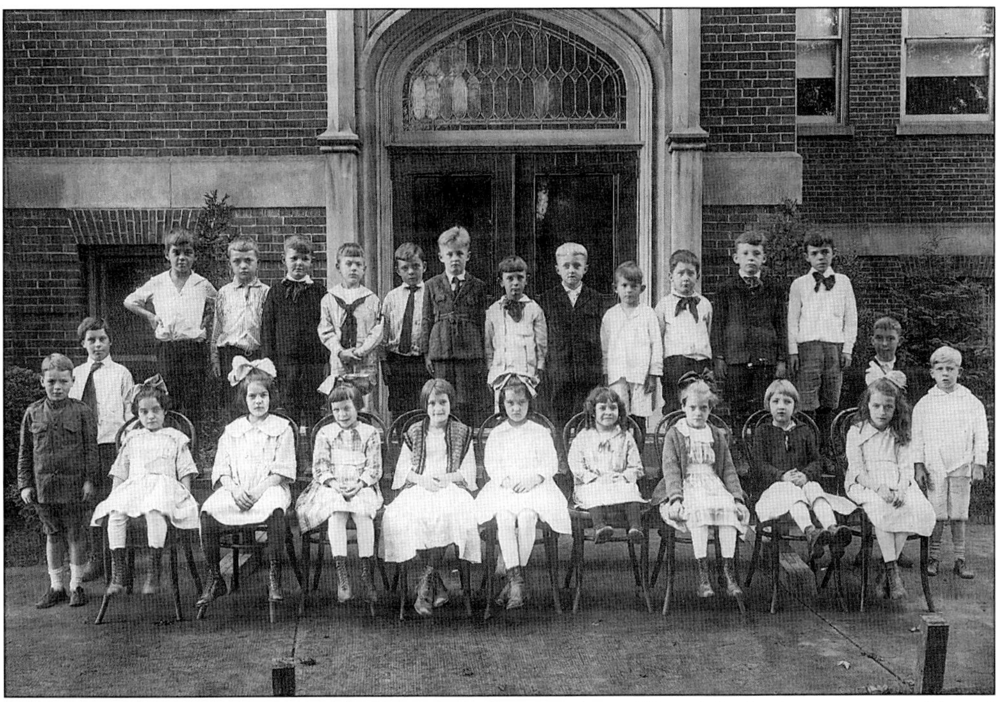

The first school in Merchantville was erected in 1863 on West Maple Avenue near Chapel Avenue. A public school district was formed and was later known as School No. 5. On the first Monday of September 1869, D.T. Gage, E.S. Hall, and T.L. DeBow were elected trustees and, on March 6, 1870, were authorized to build a schoolhouse. More land was purchased over time, and the school was enlarged. (Merchantville Historical Society.)

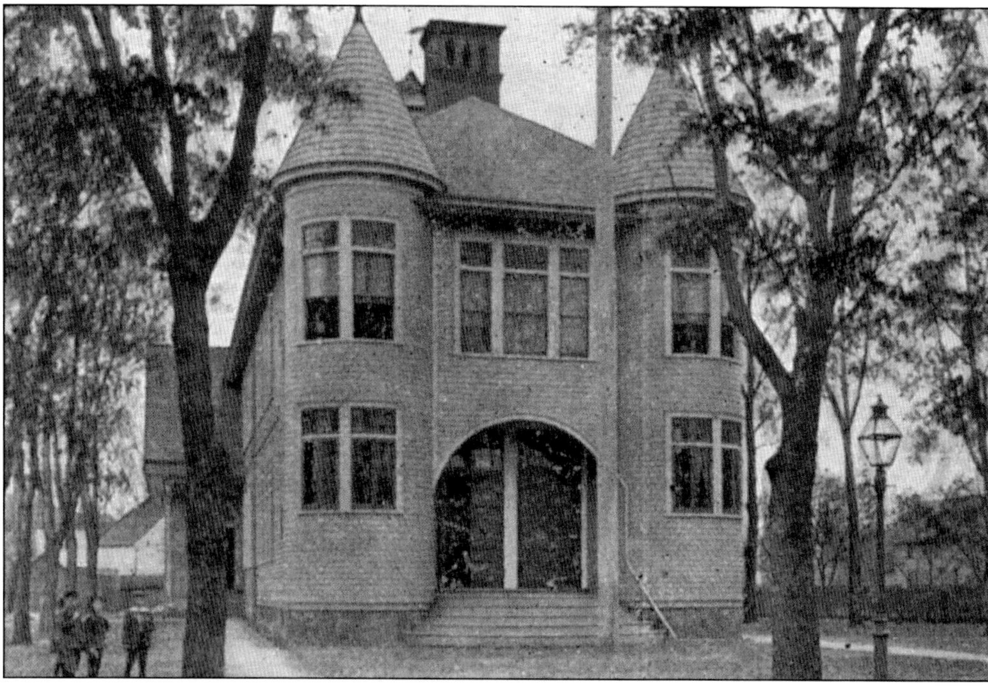

The purchase of a lot on Finn Avenue (now Centre Street) was confirmed on April 12, 1871, and a one-story, two-room building was constructed for use as a school. The first principal, appointed in September 1871, proved unsatisfactory; E.F. Way was appointed principal on November 13, 1871. About 90 pupils were registered at School No. 5. (Irene Powers.)

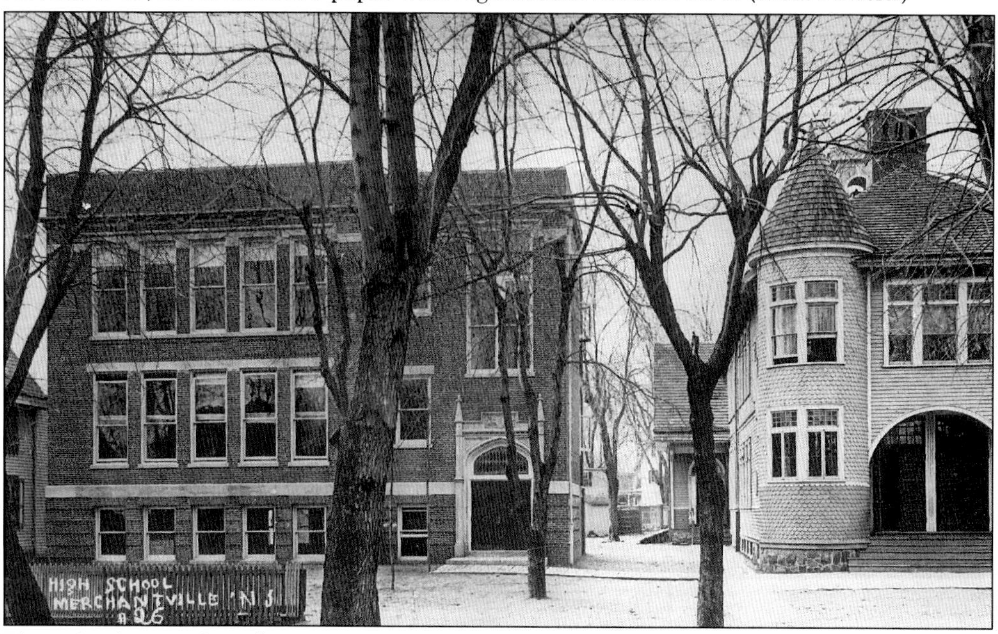

This school was enlarged over time as well. After it became outdated, a modern brick building was completed in 1915. In the early 1920s, the school was graded and included two years of high school. There were recreation grounds in the rear of the school and on Locust Street at Maple Terrace. (Merchantville Historical Society.)

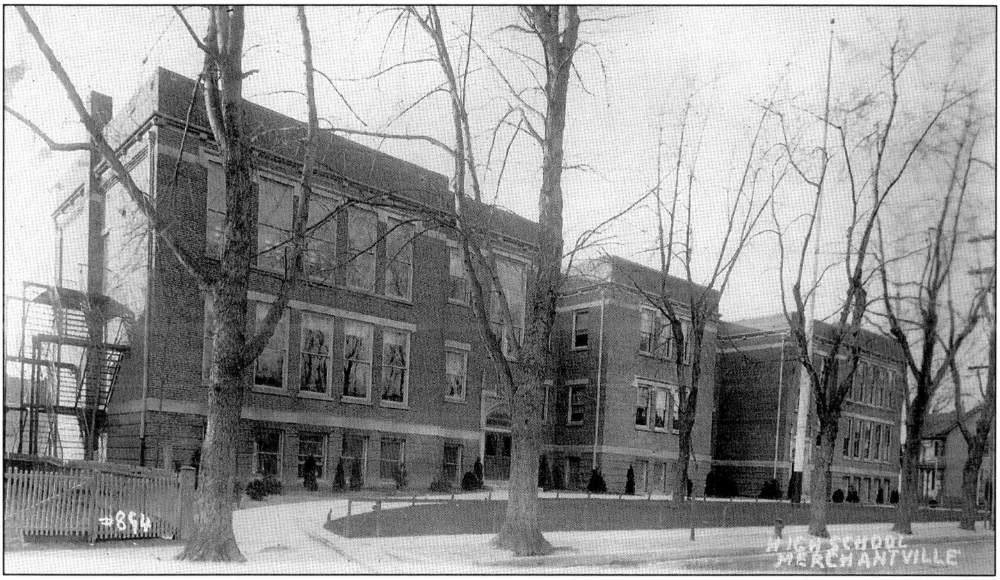

Early in the 1920s, the Pennsauken and Merchantville Board of Education visualized the increasing demand for high school facilities and, by agreement with Pennsauken, a large percentage of its students were sent to Merchantville. On June 13, 1929, the first senior class, 19 pupils, graduated from Merchantville High School. (Merchantville Historical Society.)

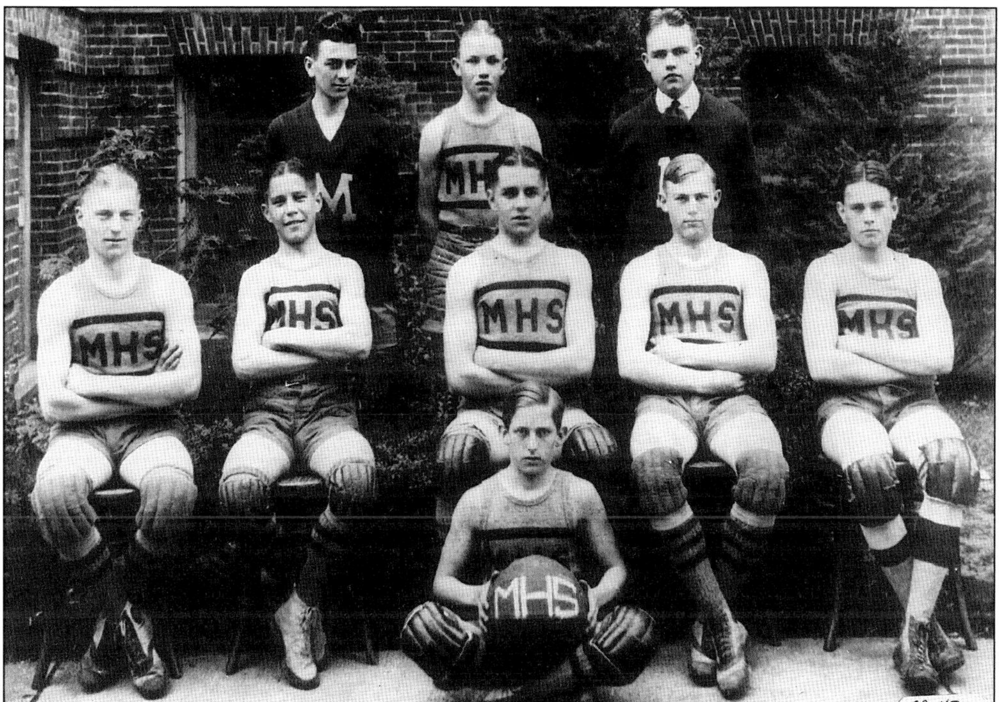

This is the 1922 Merchantville basketball team. By 1936, the need for a new physical education program resulted in the building of one of the finest gymnasiums in South Jersey. In 1941, the last external growth of the Merchantville Public School took place with the addition of the library. (Merchantville Historical Society.)

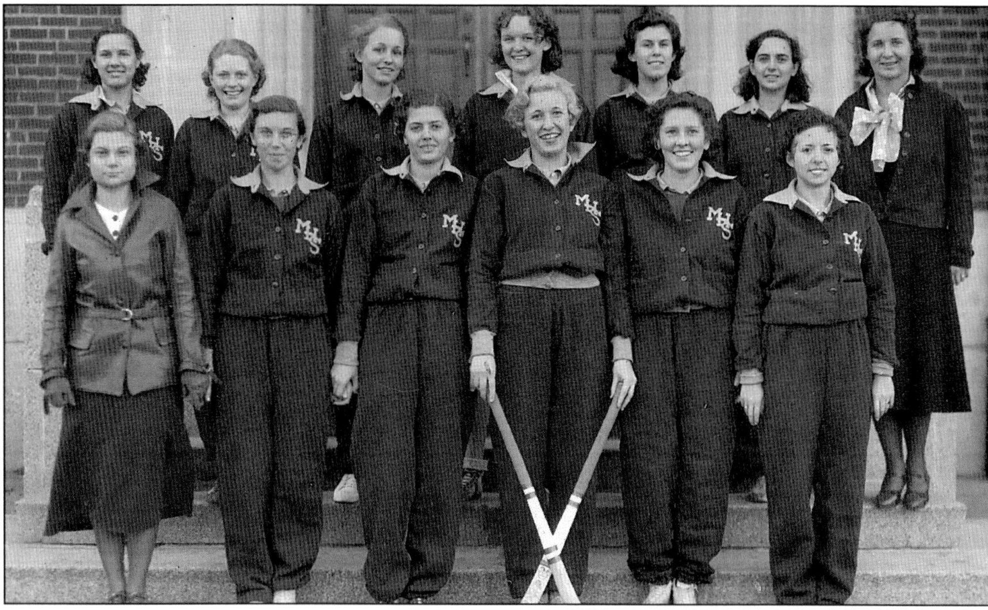

In front of Merchantville High School, the 1930–1931 girls' hockey team poses for the camera. From left to right are the following: (front row) Isabel Brickley, Georgetta Marlor-Rothgerber, Edith Barnard, and unidentified; (back row) Betty Evens, unidentified, Betty Young, unidentified, Pat Seaton, and Myrtle Walkdon (coach). (Aunt Charlotte's.)

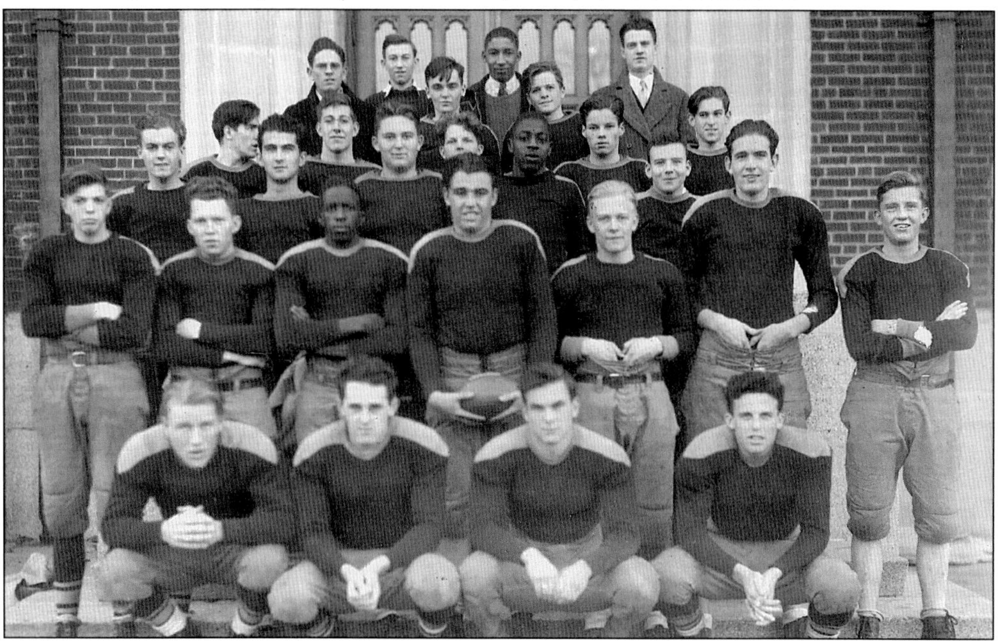

Pictured here is the 1934 Merchantville High School championship football team. From left to right are the following: (first row) Jim "Horse" Flowers, "Cap" Grear, Sam Warren, and Mike Lennon; (second row) Charles Sutton, unidentified, Joe Druce, Pearce Edwards, unidentified, and Howard Pfieffer; (third row) Newton Mac Nichol, Charles Campbell, Winfield Fink, Joe Sikorski, unidentified, and Burt Mac Nichol; (fourth row) Bob Elder (coach), E.D. Myres, three unidentified players, and J. Broomal (assistant coach). (Aunt Charlotte's.)

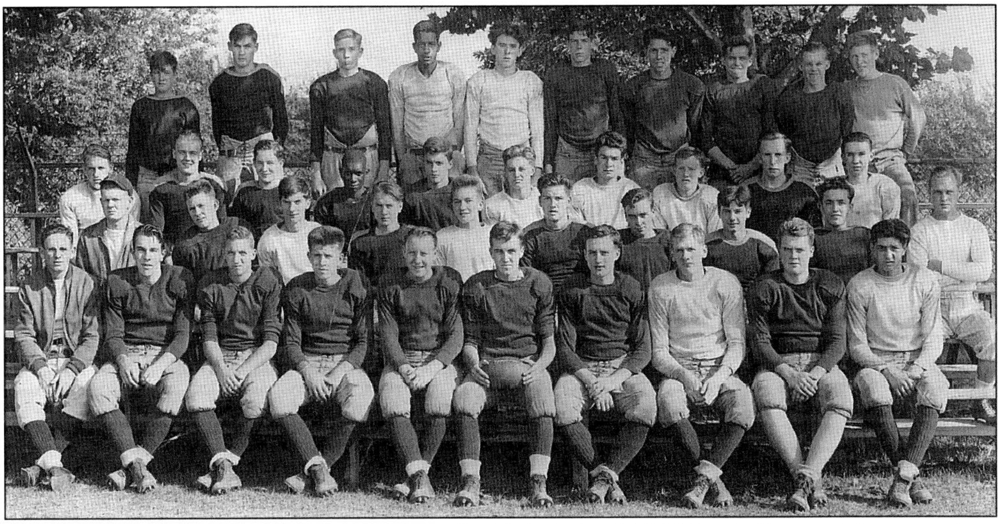

Shown are the members of the Merchantville High School 1937 football team. They are, from left to right, as follows: (first row) Bob Elder, Bill Federman, Dick Casper, unidentified, Frank Bailey, Bob Loughery, Bill Paradee, Bill Markley, Frank Seward, and Frank Coucci; (second row) George Berry, Joe Hanners, unidentified, Elmer Baxdale, Dick Stevenson, unidentified, Vernon Collins, two unidentified players, and Ron Long; (third row) John Murdock, two unidentified players, James Gaymon, three unidentified players, Bill Ferris, Paul Minnich, and Verton Rockafello; (fourth row) four unidentified players, Frank Dreyer, unidentified, Pat Coucci, Bobby Emerson, unidentified, and Pete Crane. (Vernon Collins.)

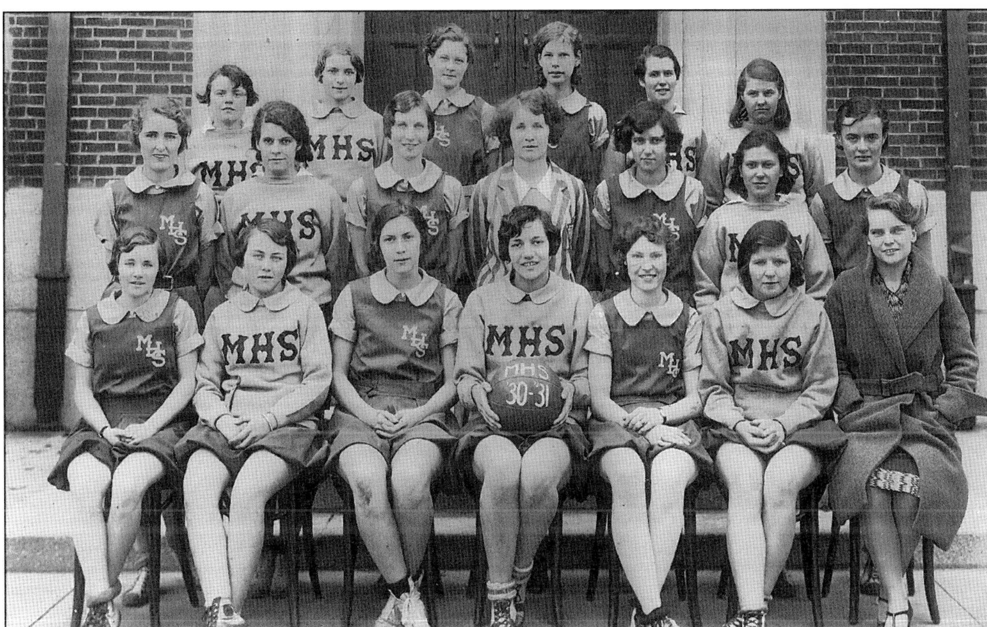

The members of the 1930–1931 girls' basketball team are, from left to right, as follows: (front row) two unidentified players, Winnifred Armstrong, Georgetta Marlor-Rothgerber, Marian Clements, and T. Troth; (middle row) Ruth McCaulley, Florence Mac Nichol, unidentified, and Myrtle Walkdon; (back row) five unidentified players and Elvinia Ebling. (Aunt Charlotte's.)

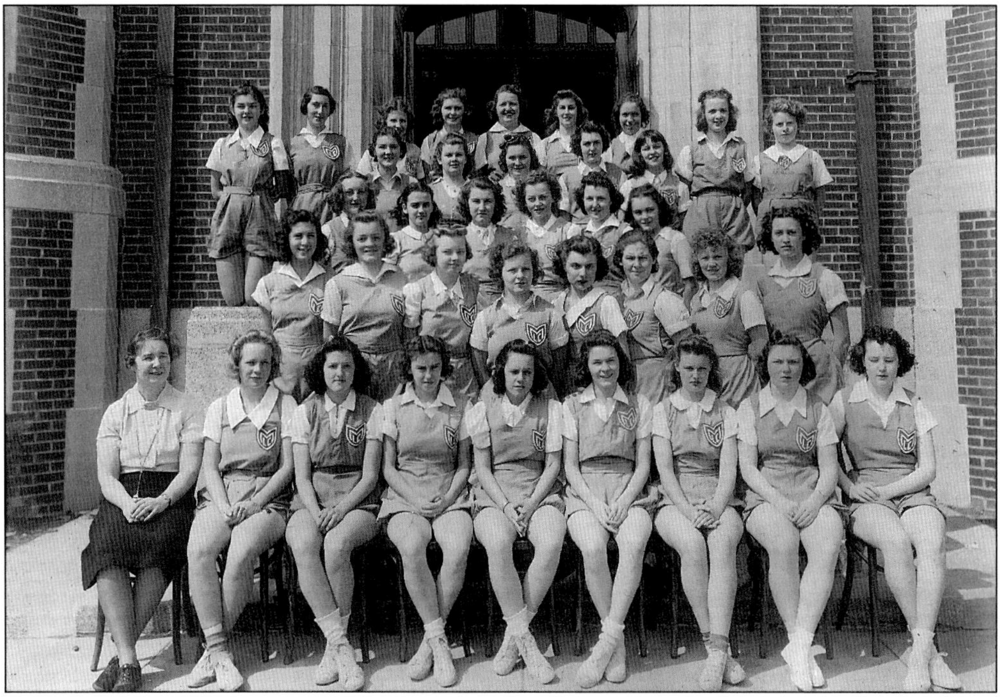

Helen Oakford Collins is sitting in the front row, fifth from the left, in this image of the 1938 Leaders Club of Merchantville High School. (Helen Collins.)

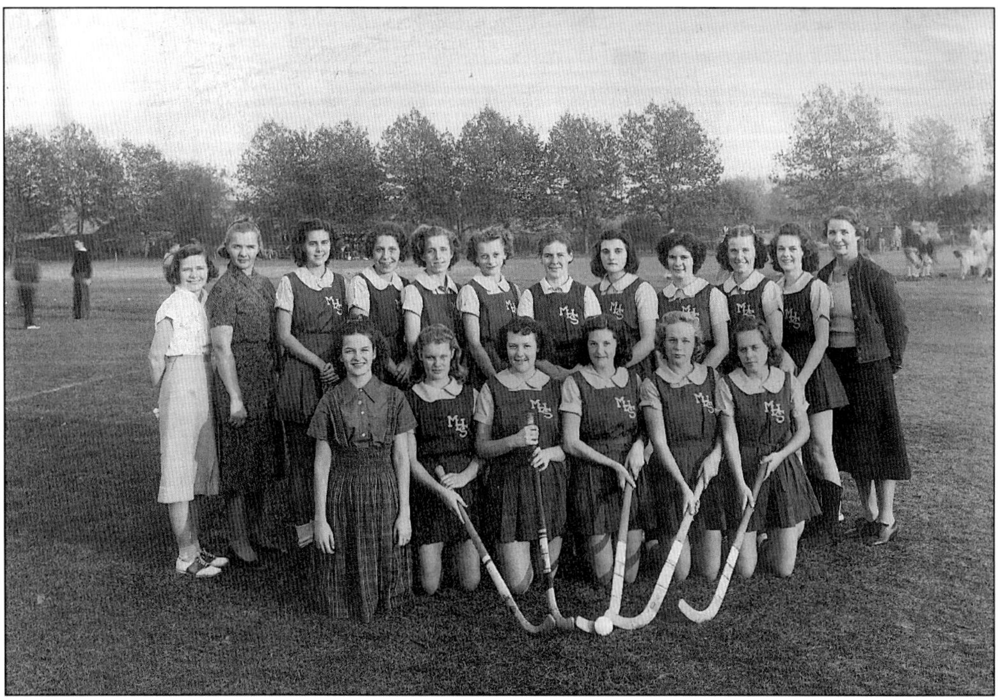

The 1939 Merchantville High School girls' hockey team takes a time-out to have their photograph taken. Hallahan Girls High School traveled from Philadelphia to play the girls from Merchantville. (Helen Collins.)

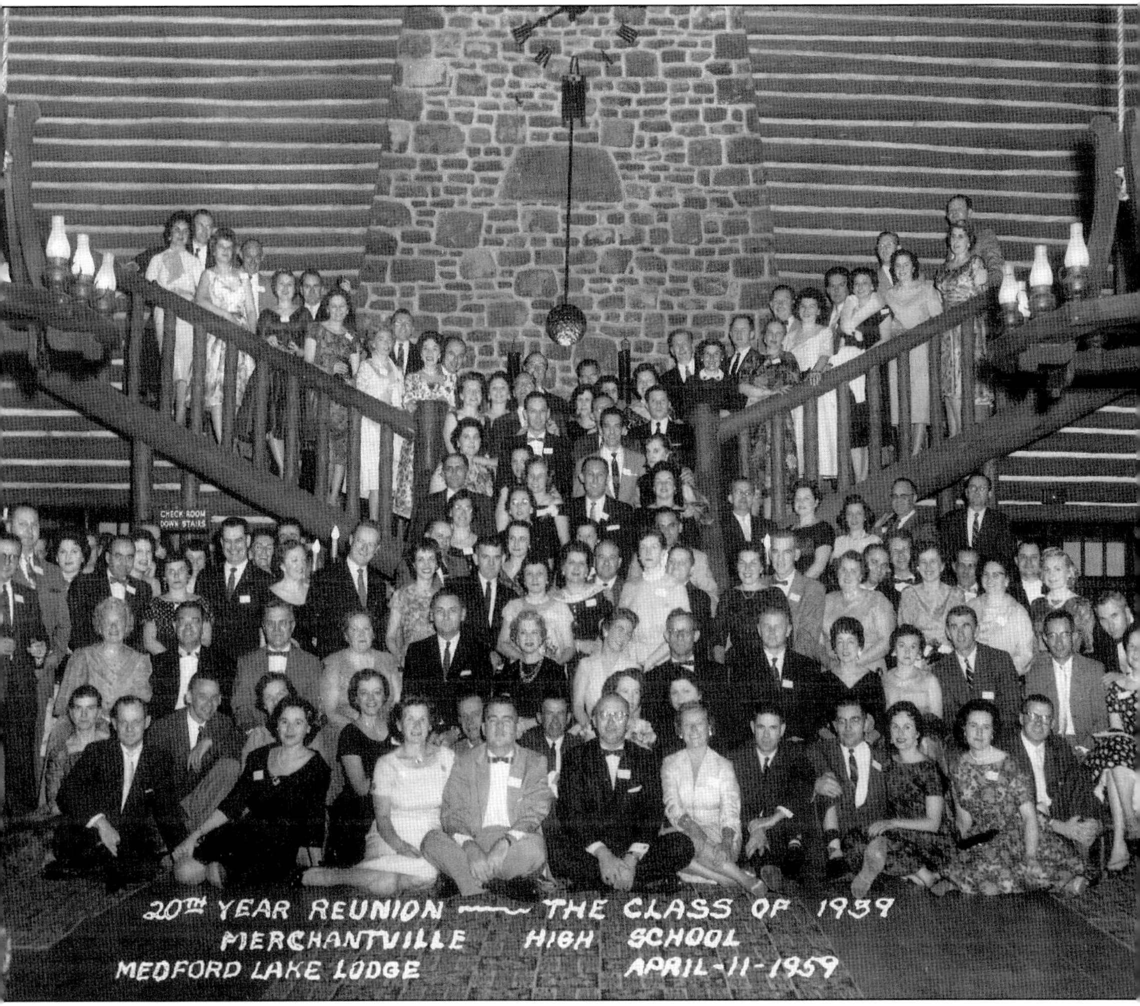

The Merchantville High School Class of 1939 held their 20th high school reunion on April 11, 1959, at the Medford Lake Lodge. (Vernon and Helen Collins.)

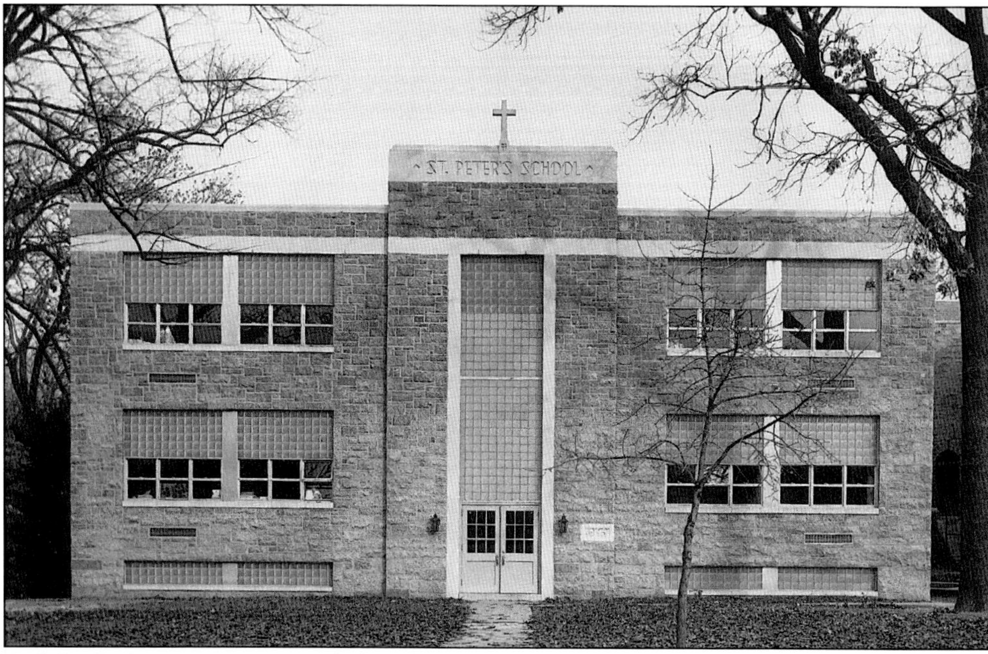

Fr. John B. Conway inaugurated plans for the erection of a parochial school in 1926. A school building was constructed in the rear of the rectory. Msgr. John P. Fallon came to St. Peter's in 1950 and immediately commenced plans to build a new school. Work started on the new school in January 1951. The school faces West Maple Avenue. (St. Peter's.)

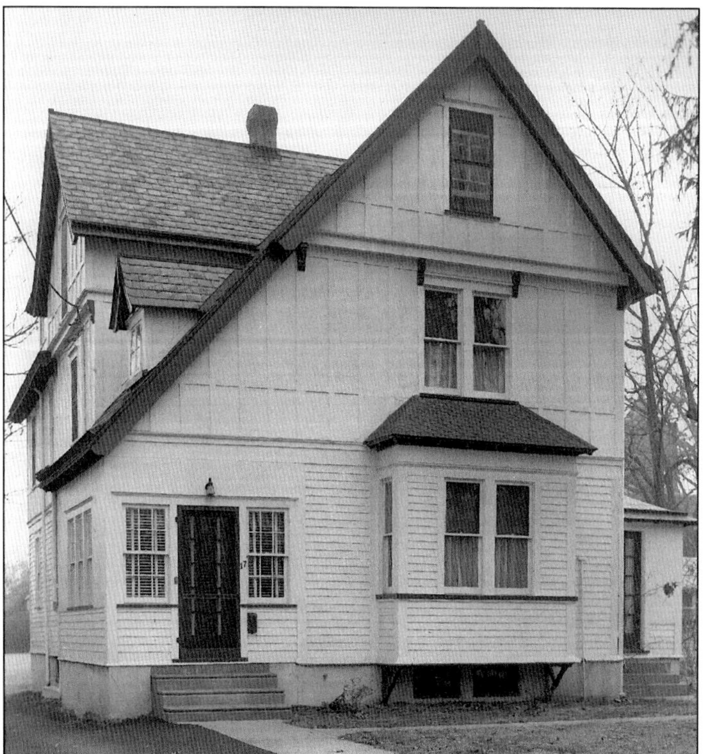

In September 1928, the Sisters of St. Francis from Allegheny, New York, arrived to teach at St. Peter's School. Their convent was at 17 Morris Street. In the 1960s, the Religious Teachers Filippini were assigned to St. Peter's to teach the nearly 1,000 students. (St. Peter's.)

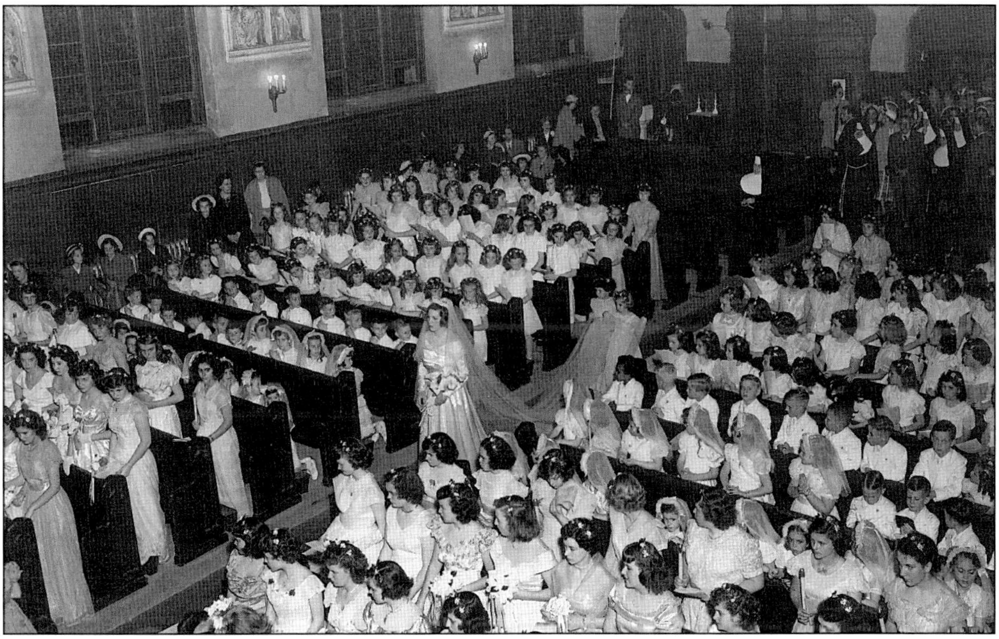

In May each year, St. Peter's held its May Crowning. In 1951, Mary Jeanne Robertson placed the crown of flowers on the statue of Mary, the Blessed Mother. All the schoolchildren participated, and some of the activity took place outside the church in a procession. (St. Peter's.)

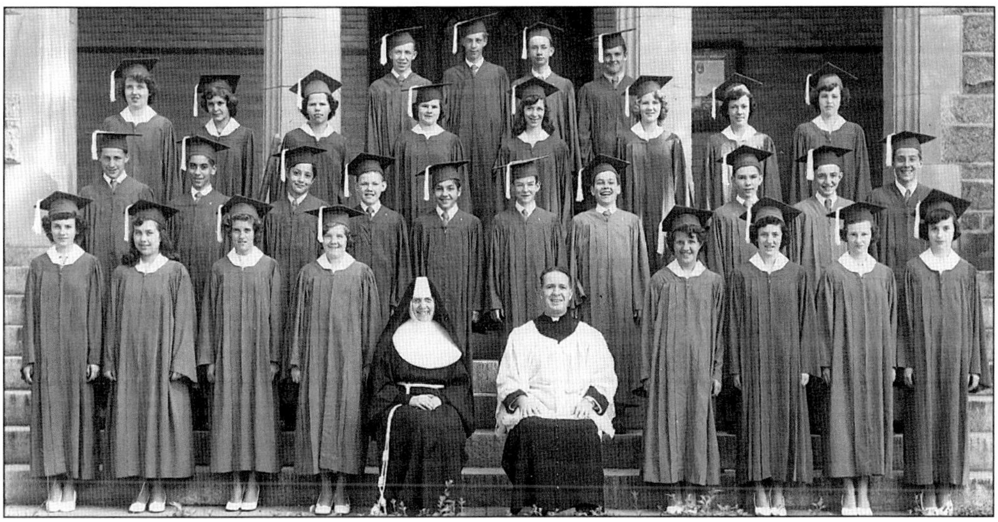

The 1952 graduating class of St. Peter's School stands on the steps of the church. Note that the doors in the front of the church have not yet been added. On the back of the photograph the graduates are listed, in alphabetical order, as follows: (boys) Joseph E. Alloway, Joseph C. Bonafiglia, Thomas R. Daley, James P. Deeny, Eugene P. DeLuca, Anthony F. Gargani, Thomas F. Hoover, Peter John Lavezzoli, James Lerro, Daniel E. McGranaghan, James P. McGranaghan, Joseph M. Mertsock, Bartholomew D. Myles, and John Sebastian Smith; (girls) Patricia Anne Barrett, Mary Edna Burke, Arlene Marie Burn, Irene Jane Cataldi, Dolores S. DiEttore, Judith Teresa Dunleavy, Carol Ann Faber, Margaret E. Grady, Marie P. Hines, Patricia Ann Messina, Patricia Anne Mullan, Madelon Marie O'Connor, Diane Theresa Panciera, and Ann P. Ricords. (St. Peter's.)

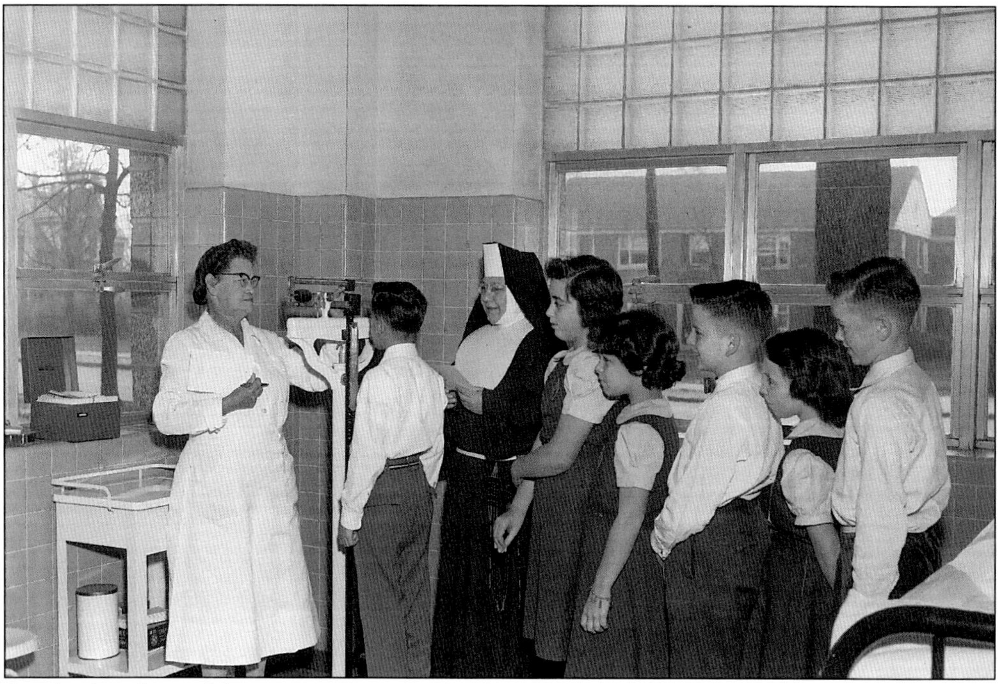

On the first floor of the new St. Peter's School were five classrooms, a principal's office, offices for a doctor and nurse, and lavatories. In this photograph, some students have their height and weight checked by the school nurse. (St. Peter's.)

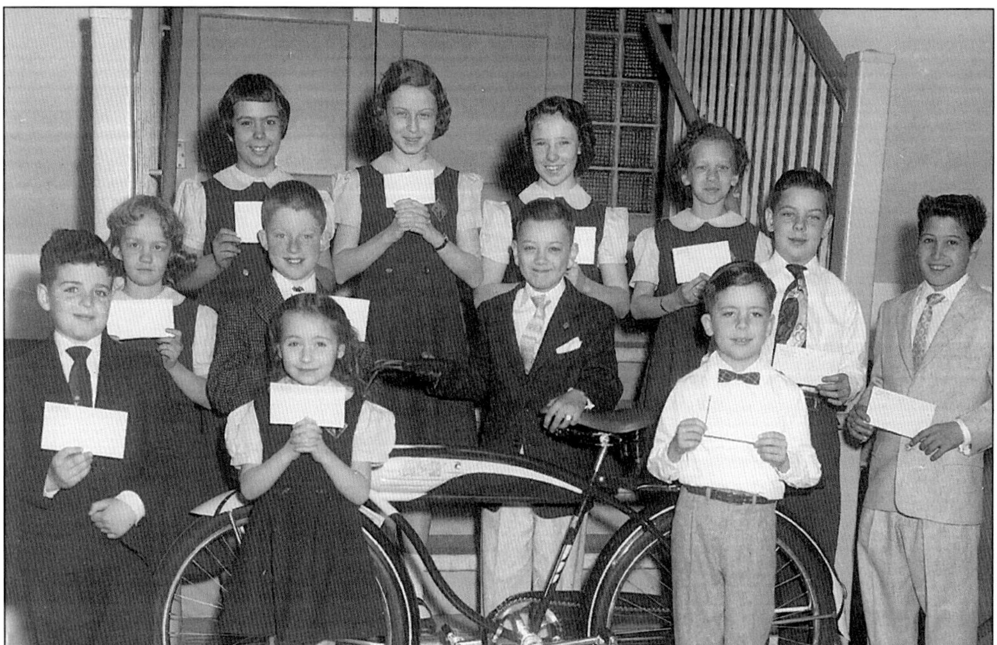

These children pose for a picture inside St. Peter's School. They were the finalists in one of the contests (such as essay or poster contests) that students would enter from time to time. Tom Kenney is standing in the first row to the extreme left. (St. Peter's.)

Five

DECORATIVE DWELLINGS

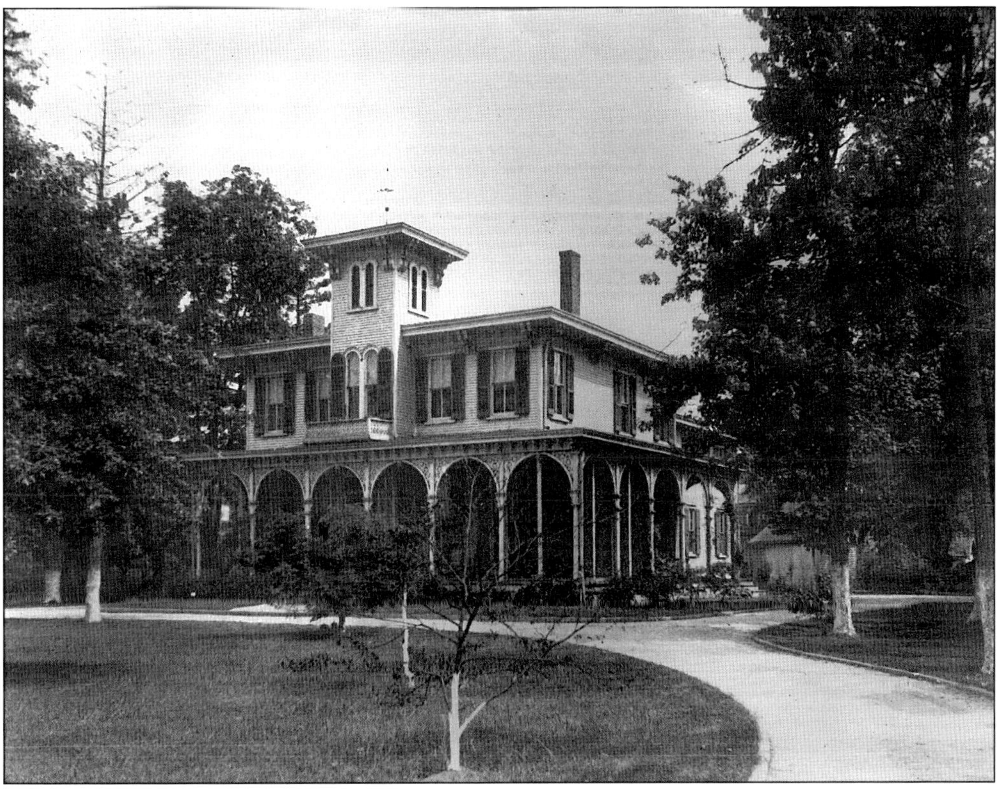

Thomas C. Knight was a prominent Philadelphia stockbroker and onetime president of the Philadelphia Stock Exchange. He served for three years on the first borough council. His home and grounds were located on East Maple Avenue where the Merchantville Mewes now stand. Knight passed away in June 1896. W. Tingle Dickerson bought the estate from Thomas Knight. (Merchantville Historical Society.)

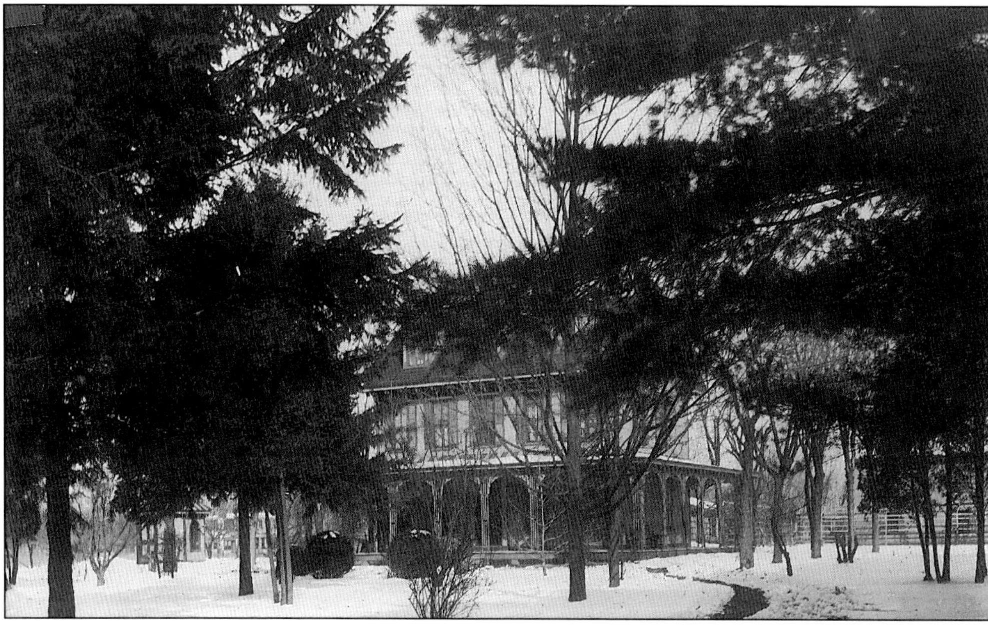

In 1888, John Rowbotham was sworn in as a councilman. His stately residence was located at the northeast corner of East Maple and Clifton Avenues. At the age of 35, in 1906, George Arthur Crump, a bachelor, bought the property at 203 East Maple Avenue. The house dated from 1885 and was the property of Elijah Cattell. Crump replaced the frame house with a larger brick home. (Merchantville Historical Society.)

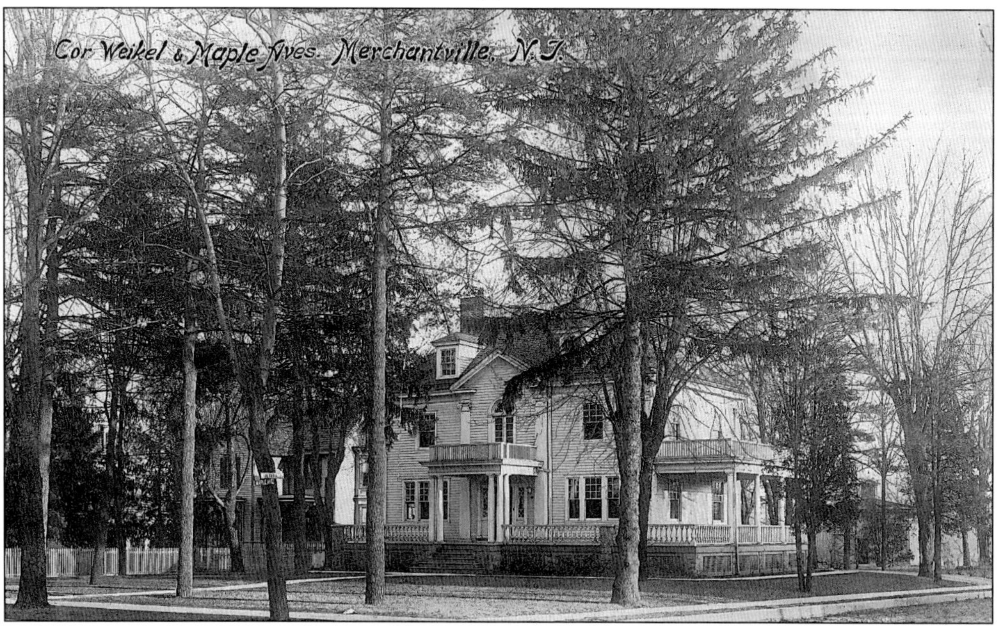

William D. and Nellie F. Weikel lived at 116 East Maple Avenue. Weikel was a spice merchant who also dealt in wholesale tea and coffee in Philadelphia. Weikel was active in the Merchantville-Pennsauken Water Company. He served on the borough council from 1904 to 1909. The home to the left in the picture is that of J. Frank Haig and his wife, Florence. Haig worked for the Pennsylvania Railroad. (Merchantville Historical Society.)

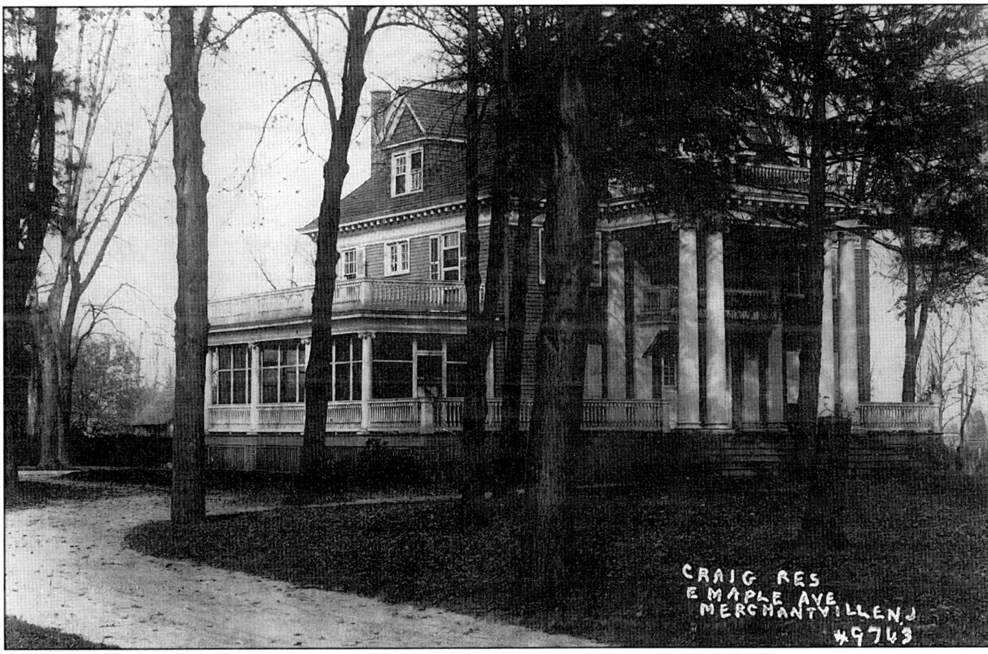

The Colonial home of William J. Craig, with large pillars reaching two stories high, was on the northeast corner of East Maple and Fithian Avenues. It next became the home of the Honorable Francis F. Patterson Jr., a congressman. Craig was a sugar broker who lived with his wife, Margaretta, in this house, which no longer exists. (Bobbi Stagliano.)

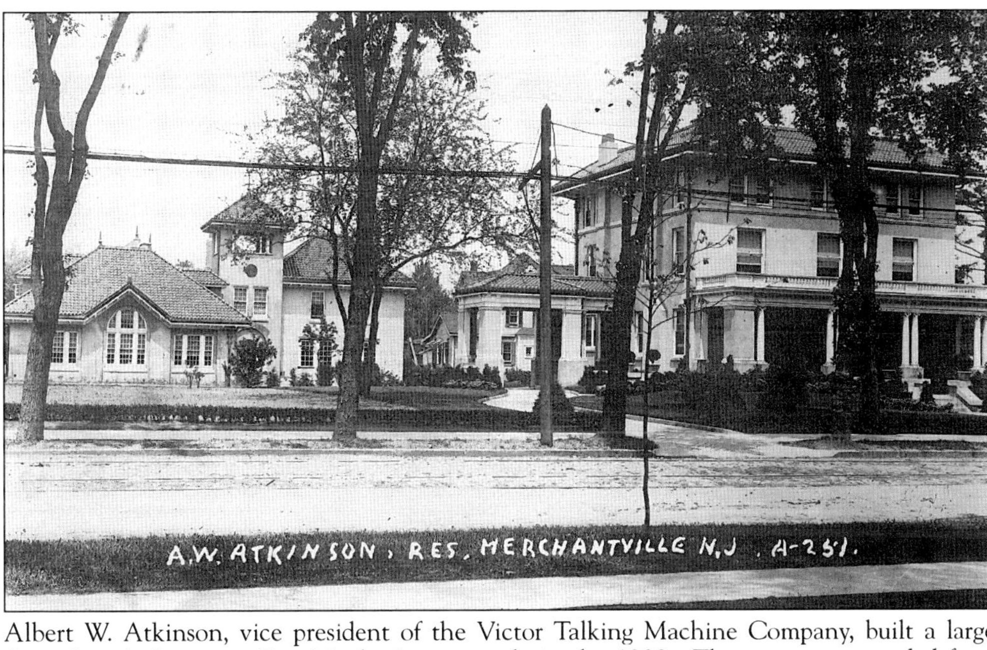

Albert W. Atkinson, vice president of the Victor Talking Machine Company, built a large Spanish-style home on East Maple Avenue early in the 1900s. The property extended from Franklin Avenue to Clifton Avenue and had space in the rear for a coachman's house and a paddock for horses. Trolley cars ran up and down East and West Maple Avenue and made a stop right in front of the Atkinson residence. (Merchantville Historical Society.)

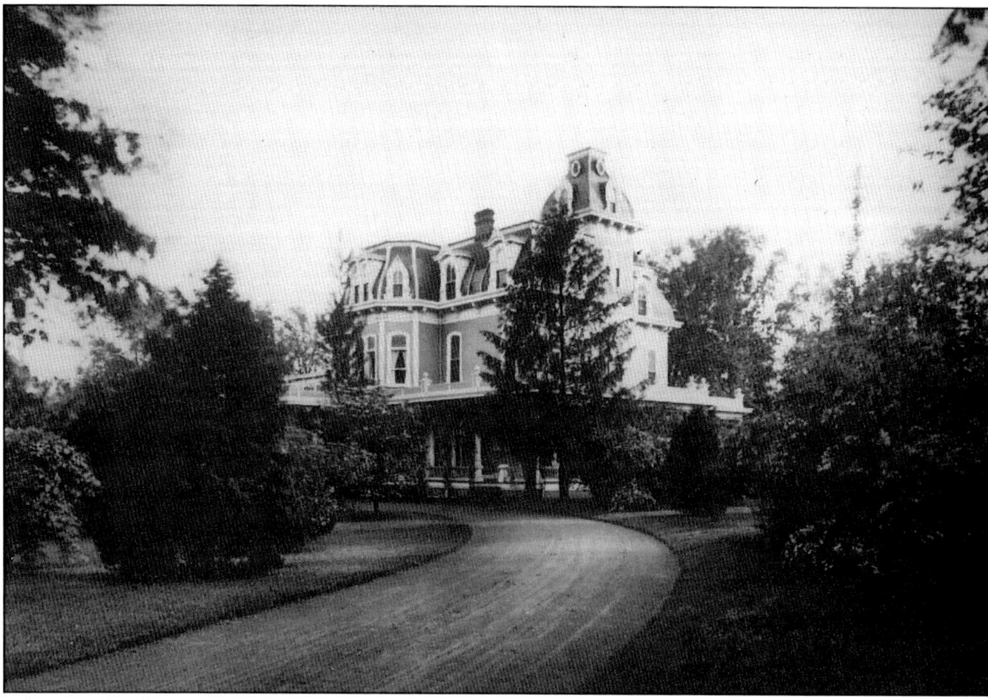

John Burleigh, vice president of Public Service Corporation of New Jersey, purchased a large Victorian home that had been built by Harrison Robbins in 1870. Greenleigh Court Apartments occupied the site after the demolition of the house. This location is on the south side of East Maple Avenue. Burleigh was also head of the Merchantville Water Company. (Merchantville Historical Society.)

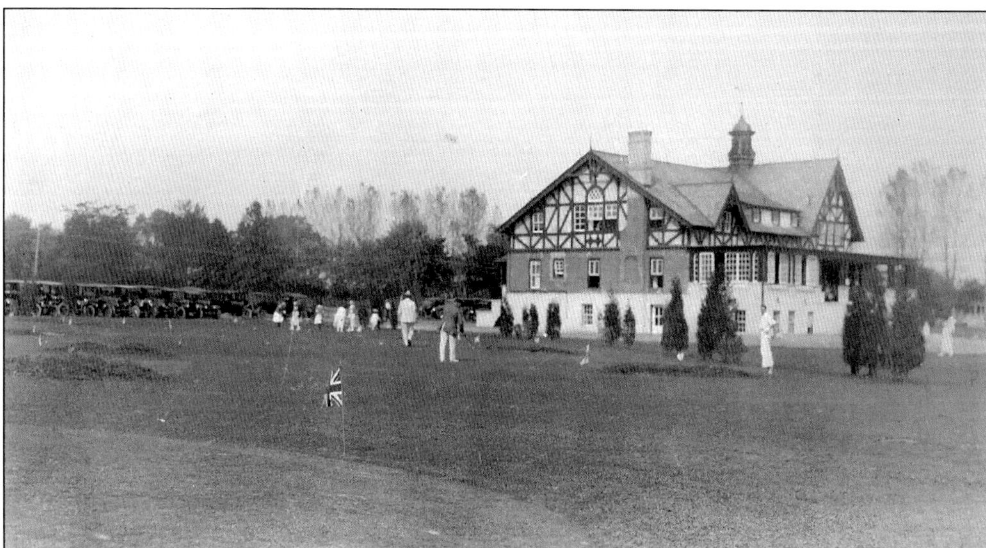

The brick, Robbins-Burleigh carriage house was moved to Somerset Street in 1921 after the demolition of the home on the estate. On September 10, 1921, the former carriage house opened as the Merchantville Country Club at 212 Somerset Street. A.W. Atkinson was the club's president. (Merchantville Historical Society.)

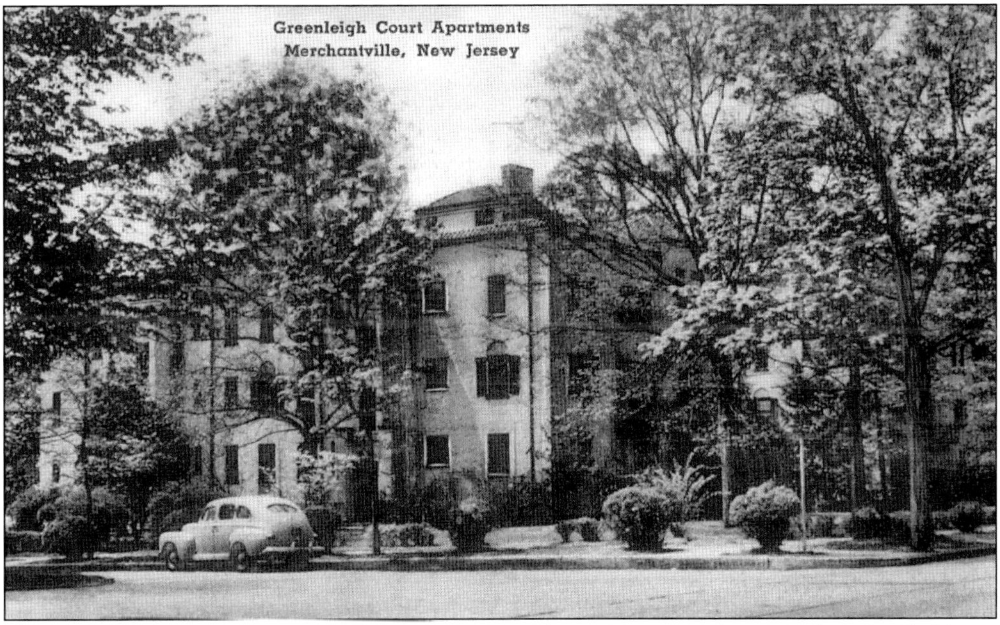

Greenleigh Court was cut through from East Maple to Somerset Avenue after the Robbins-Burleigh estate had been removed, and Greenleigh Court Apartments were built. The apartments were built in the Spanish style. Much later the apartments were converted to condominiums. (Maureen McLoone.)

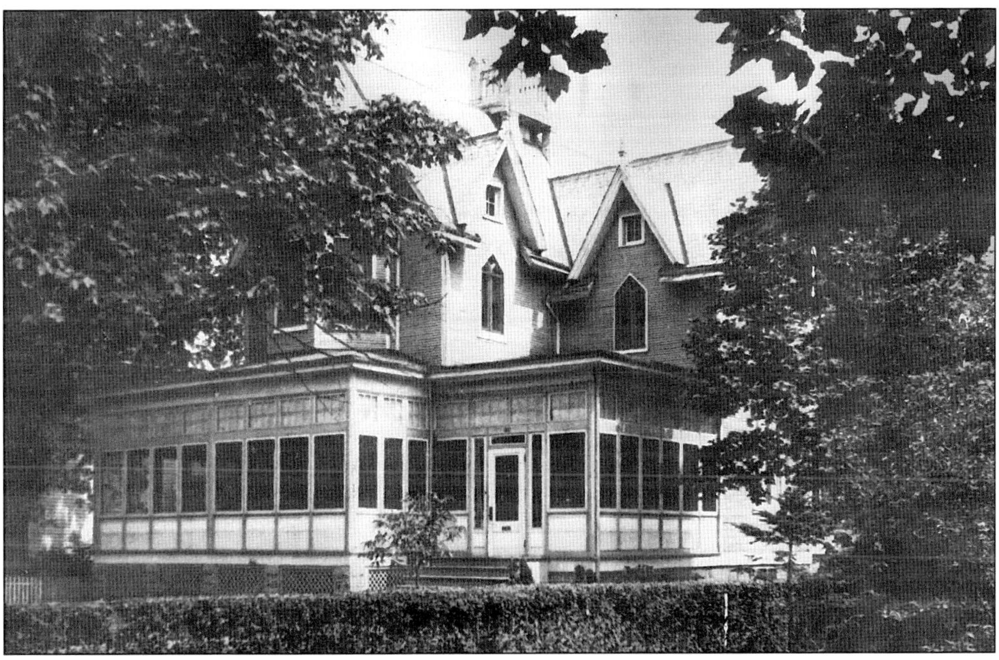

George Crump, Philadelphia's vice consul from England, had many business interests in town. He was largely responsible for drawing up the charter for Merchantville's incorporation as a borough. His home was on the south side of East Maple Avenue between Maple Terrace and Woodlawn Avenue at 102 East Maple and was demolished many years ago. (Merchantville Historical Society.)

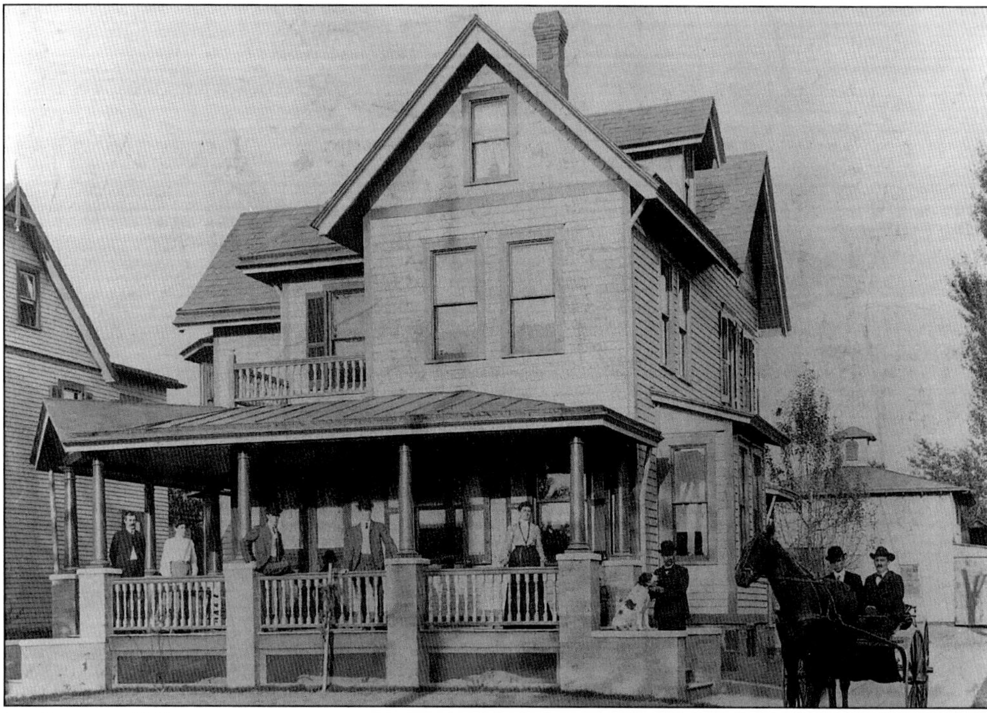

I. Clarence Wilson, assistant postmaster, lived at 213 North Centre Street according to the 1911 directory. John K. and Cornelia B. Wilson also resided at that address at another time. For Merchantville, extensive housing construction activity between 1850 and 1910 transformed the town into a commuter suburb. By 1880, North Centre Street supported businesses close to the railroad line. (Merchantville Historical Society.)

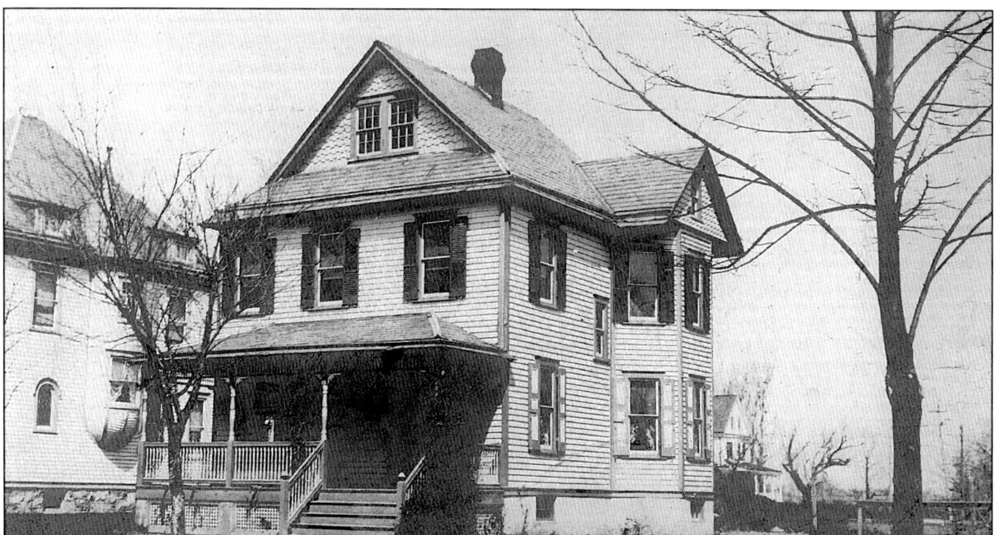

In the early 1900s, attorney Edward I. Berry and his wife, Anna, resided at 33 East Rogers Avenue. On January 2, 1911, Berry was appointed borough solicitor, succeeding William Early. In 1952, reference is made to the fact that Berry still held that position. (Vernon Collins.)

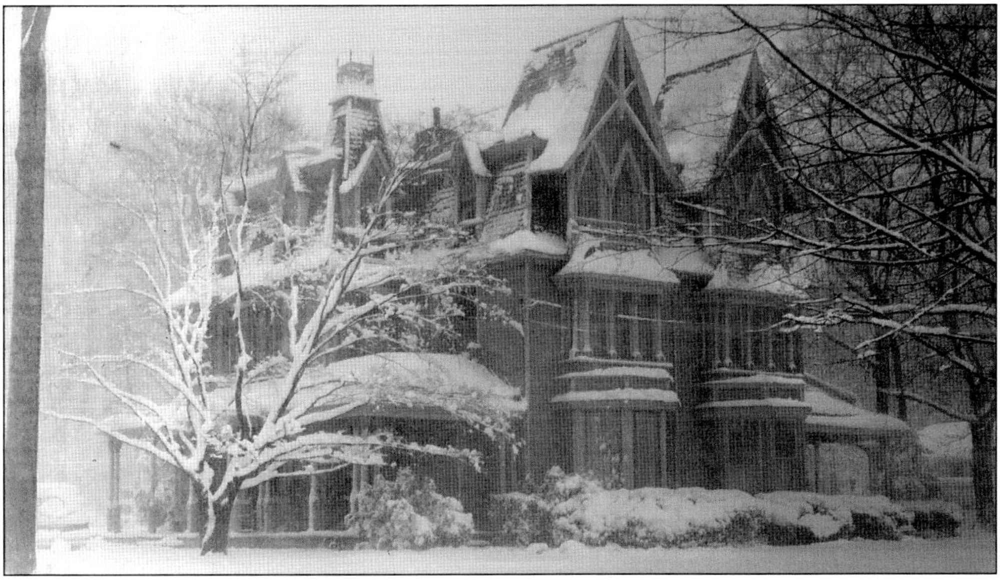

The Centennial House, a double dwelling at 17–19 East Chestnut Avenue, was assembled c. 1893. It arrived from Philadelphia in pieces by barge and train. Both John Dorrance and young George Arthur Crump lived briefly at 17 East Chestnut. Records show the transfer of land on which the Centennial House stands from George Crump to his brother Henry J. in 1884, then to George Arthur in 1893. The Centennial House is significant because of its outstanding architectural composition and detail. It still remains to this day. Richard N. Hollingshead, founder of the R.N. Hollingshead Corporation, lived at 19 East Chestnut Avenue. (Maureen McLoone.)

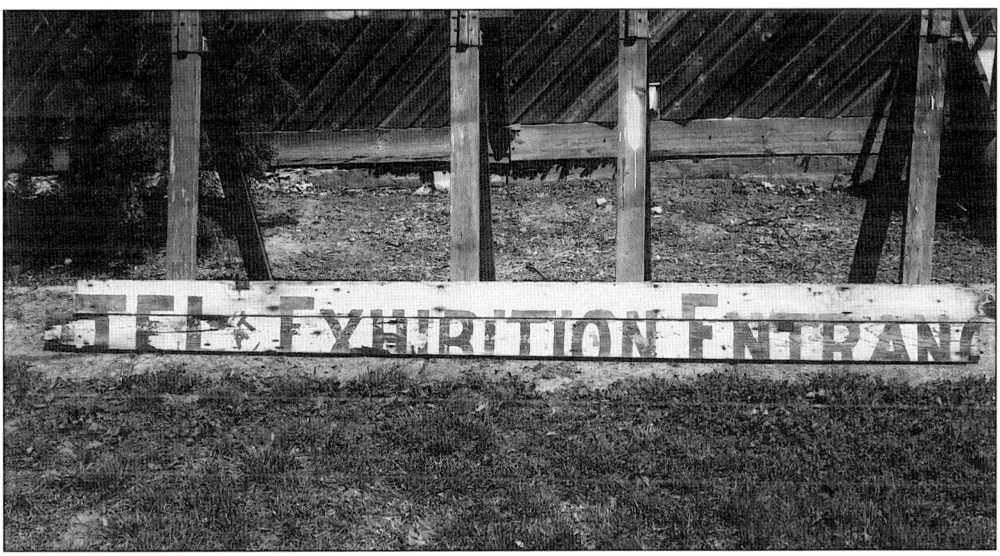

While tearing apart a doorjamb at 17 East Chestnut Avenue, parts of a sign were found. Positioning the two pieces of wood revealed the phrase "tel at Exhibition Entrance." The World's Fair of 1876 was called the Centennial Exhibition, and the sign might have read, "Hotel at Exhibition Entrance." When the structure came to Merchantville, additional lumber may have also been transported for the rebuilding. This would explain the presence of the pieces of wood. (Maureen McLoone.)

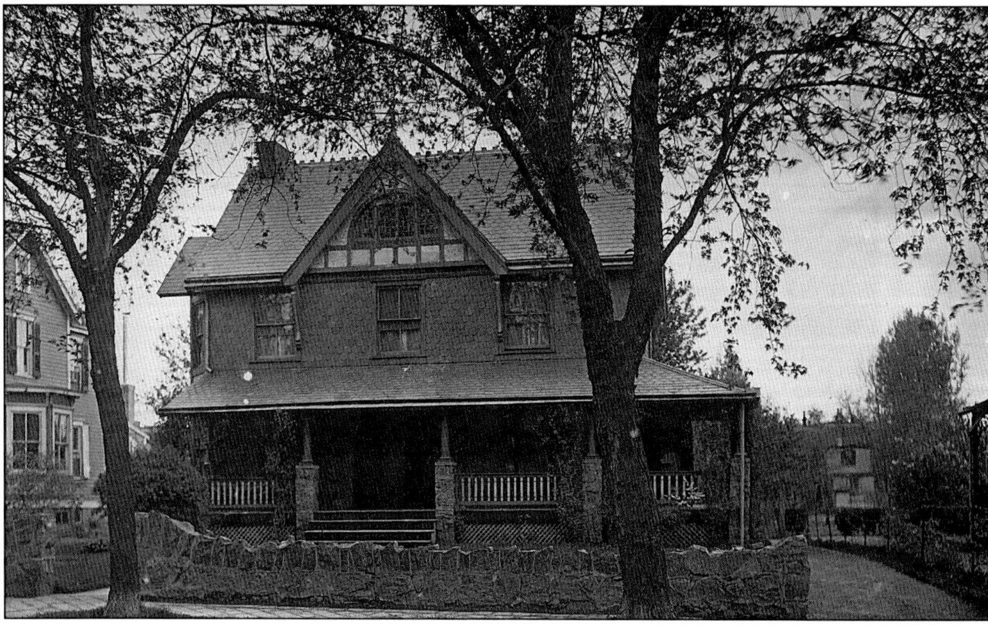

William McAllister and his wife, Mary, lived at 20 West Walnut Street, as listed in the 1911 directory. McAllister was elected president of the borough council in July 1910. He was one of the first appointees to the Merchantville-Pennsauken Water Commission. His profession was recorded as a treasurer. (Vernon Collins.)

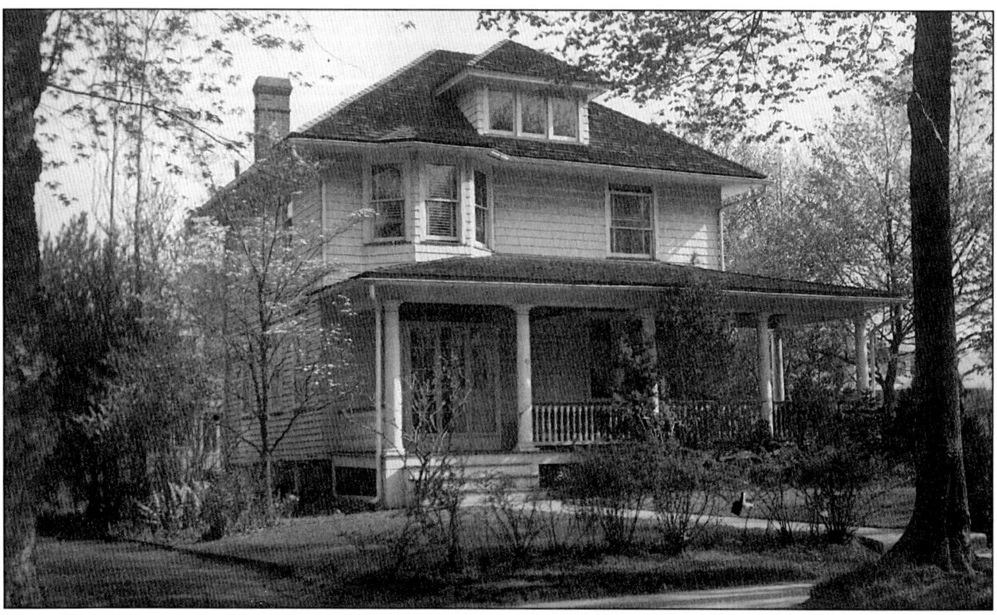

Not all the houses built in the early history of Merchantville were as large and imposing as those of the founders. Two, on West Walnut Avenue, were originally built for summer occupancy and for years were referred to as "the cottages." In the late 1880s, West Walnut lots were selling for $400 and $500. (Vernon Collins.)

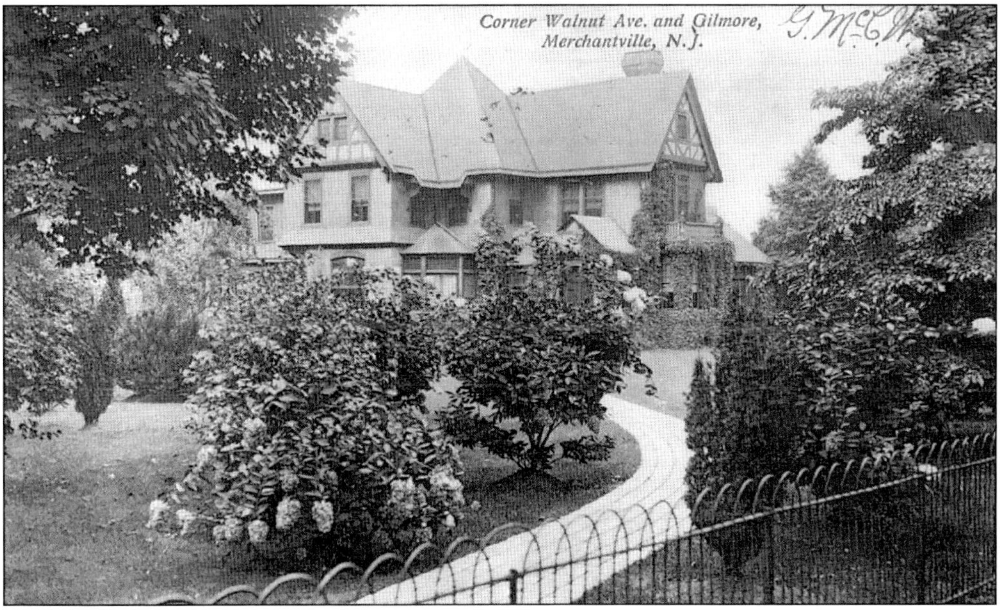

Buildings designed by professional architects were uncommon in the Cattell Development. One of these rarities is 101 East Walnut, on the northeast corner of East Walnut and Gilmore Avenues. The Harned-Parvin House was designed *c.* 1881 by and for Issac Pursell. This is an excellent example of Old English and Queen Anne style and may have been described in the popular magazine *Godey's Lady's Book*. (Bobbi Stagliano.)

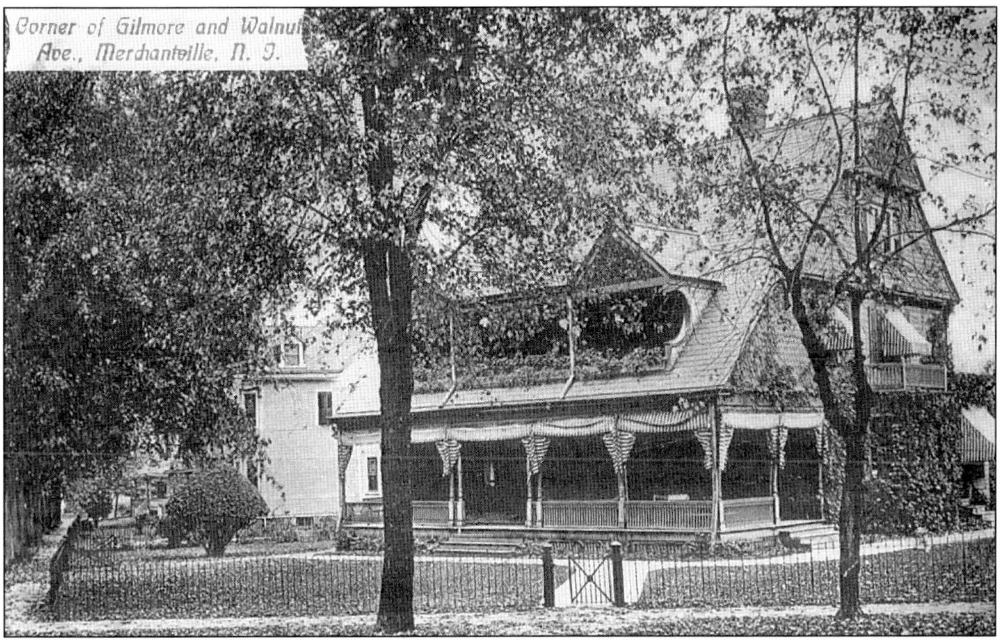

The other rarity attributed to Issac Pursell is at 100 East Walnut Avenue. This residence is on the southeast corner of East Walnut and Gilmore Avenues and combines the picturesque Queen Anne and Stick styles. The second-floor balcony provides a quiet place to watch the world go by. Architectural commissions, in the late 19th and early 20th centuries, commonly occurred along Maple Avenue where the upper class lived. (Tina Schmidt.)

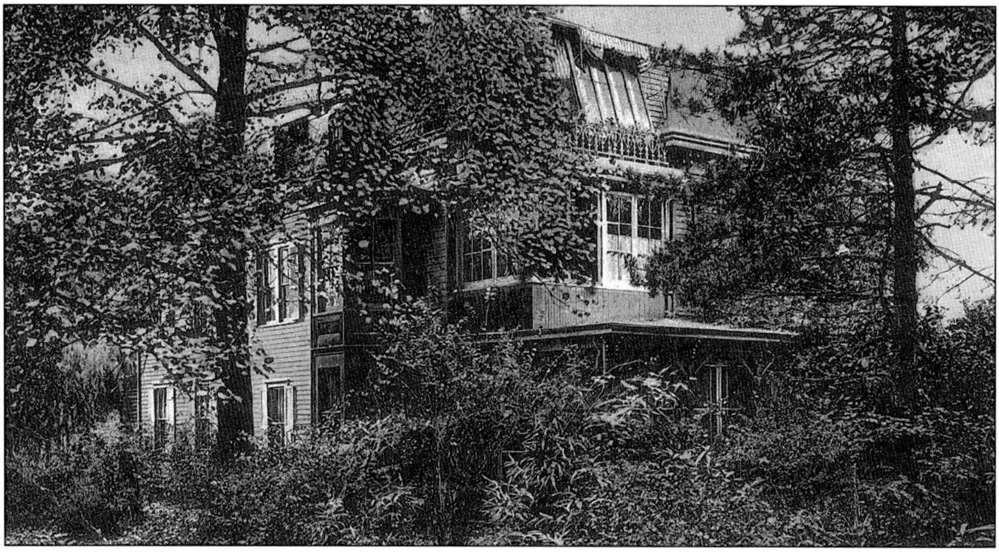

The famous towering hedge that surrounded the estate of Charles G. Garrison, New Jersey Supreme Court justice, extended along the west side of Cove Road from East Walnut to East Cedar Avenues. He was the borough solicitor and a councilman for many years prior to his death in 1924. The hedge was one of the prides of its owner, who derived great satisfaction from the seclusion it afforded him. (Maureen McLoone.)

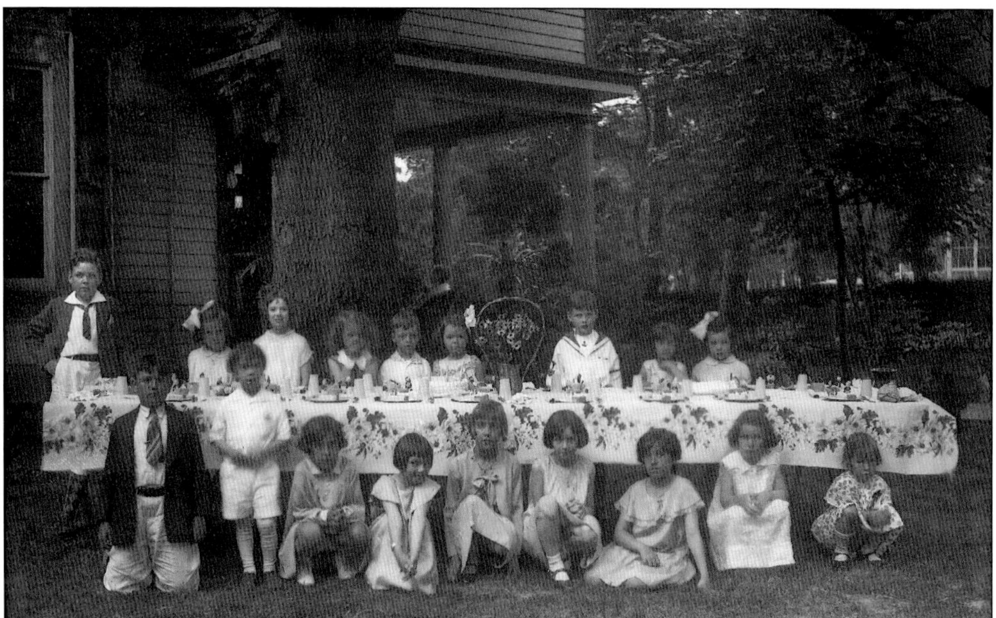

In 1929, the former Garrison home was the scene of a birthday party for Elizabeth Newell. Her father was Dr. Charles Newell. Much of the tree-rich gardens were still in existence at 117 East Walnut Avenue at the time this picture was taken. (Bob Hanna.)

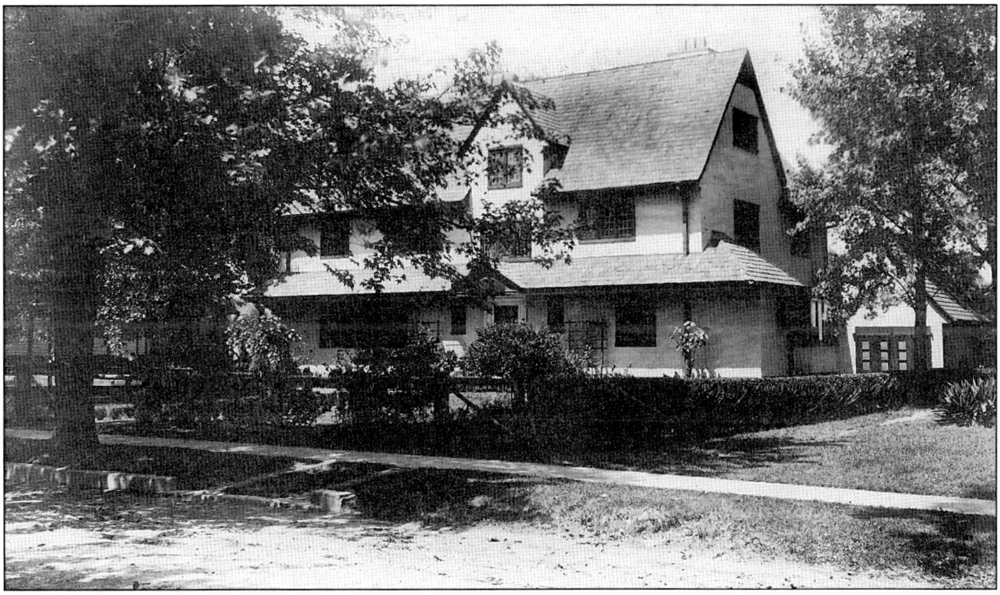

Tudor Revival in style, this home was built for the astronomical sum of $37,000. Samuel H. Rous, vice president of Victor Victrola (later RCA) in charge of cabinetry, used the finest woods throughout the home. The garage boasted of a turntable for the car, similar to that of a record player. (Tina Schmidt.)

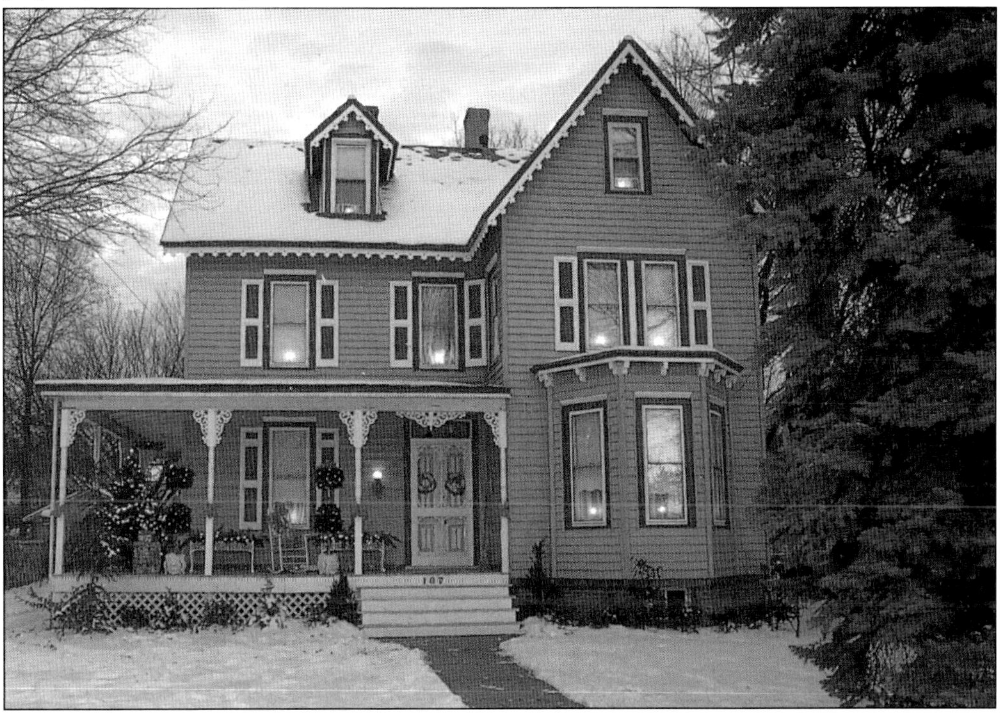

Anna M. Traute, a widow, was shown as living at 137 East Park Avenue in the 1911 directory. This home was positioned near the commercial area of Merchantville, which consisted of sections of Centre Street, Maple Avenue, and Park Avenue (formerly Jordantown Avenue). This home stands today in all its restored splendor. (Mark Thellman.)

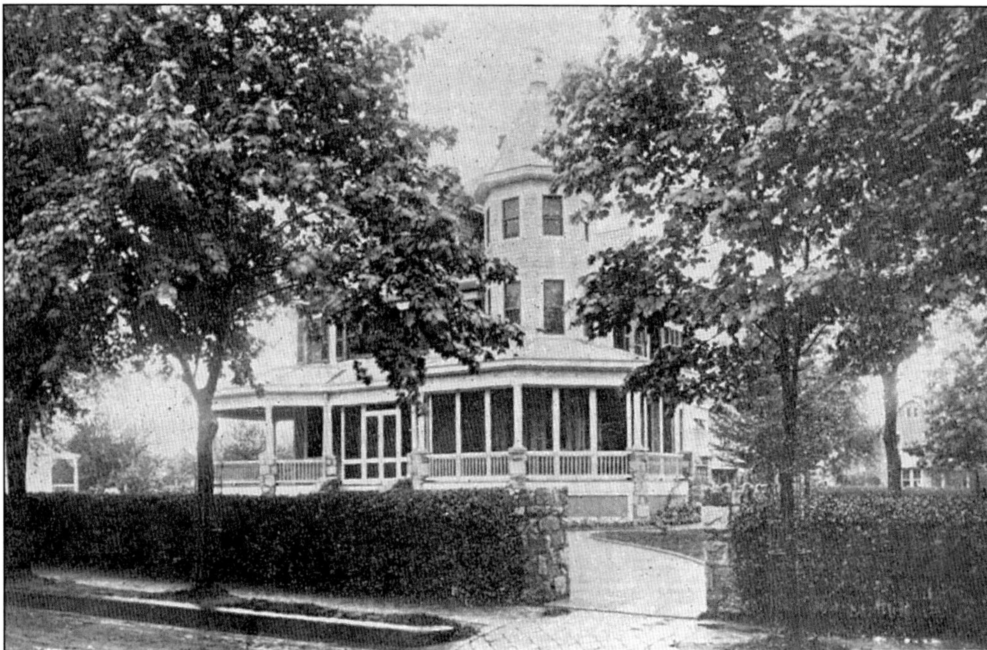

FRED. A. DOWNE'S RESIDENCE, Cor. Cove Road and Cedar Ave., MERCHANTVILLE, N. J.

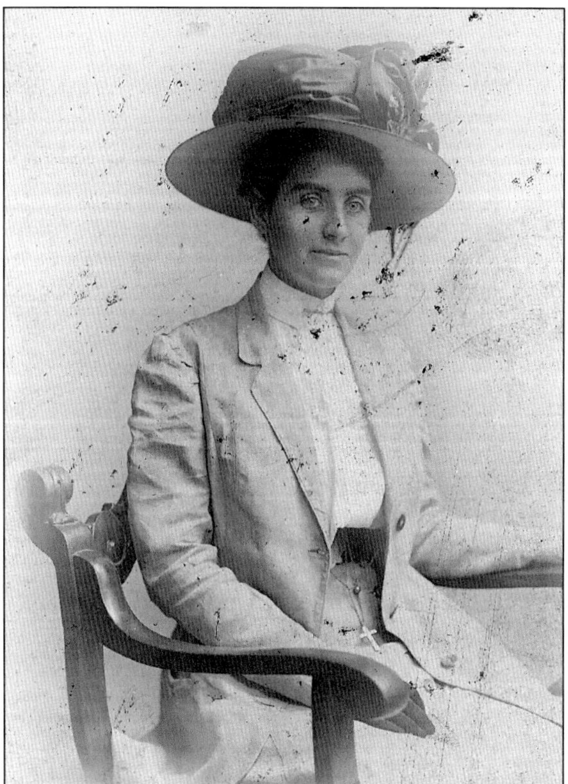

On the corner of North Cove Road and East Cedar Avenue was the Frederick A. Downe residence. Catherine A. (Marr) Downe poses here for a portrait. The "Mrs. Merchantville" of 1874 wore hats of many styles, with or without veils, often with plumage, over coiffures of swirls of curls. Her high-styled boots would have been side-laced or buttoned. Note the cross (near her waistline) that Catherine is wearing. Her day apparel is of a conservative styling. (Tina Schmidt; Merchantville Historical Society.)

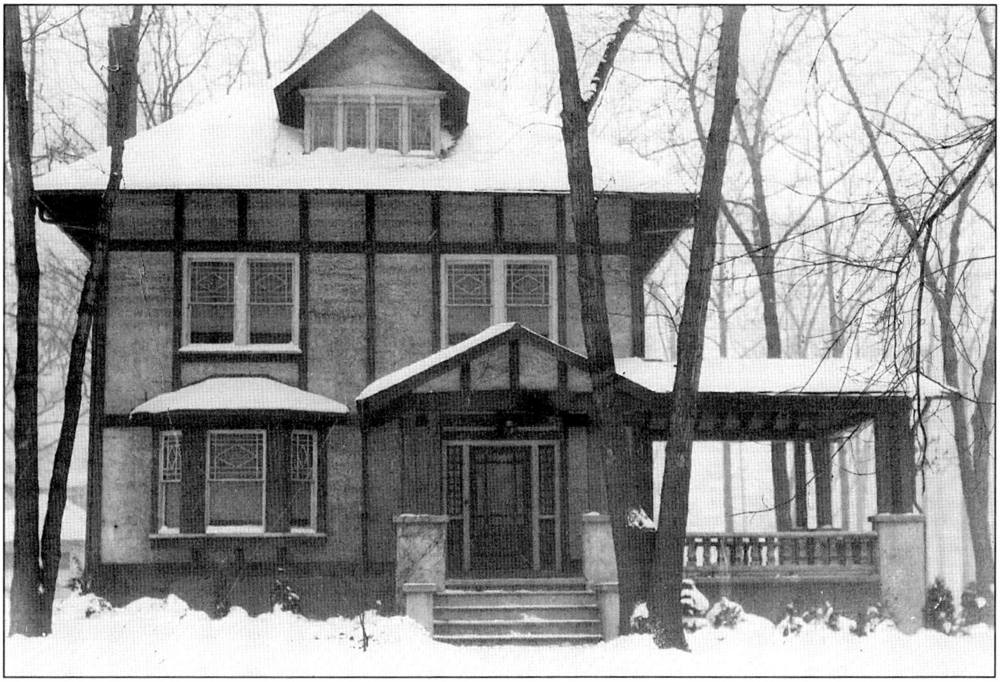

According to the Merchantville directory of 1911, Louis Lothridge and his wife, Grace N., made 10 Morris Street their home. Lothridge is listed as a chemist. Morris Street ran north from 100 West Maple Avenue. (Merchantville Historical Society.)

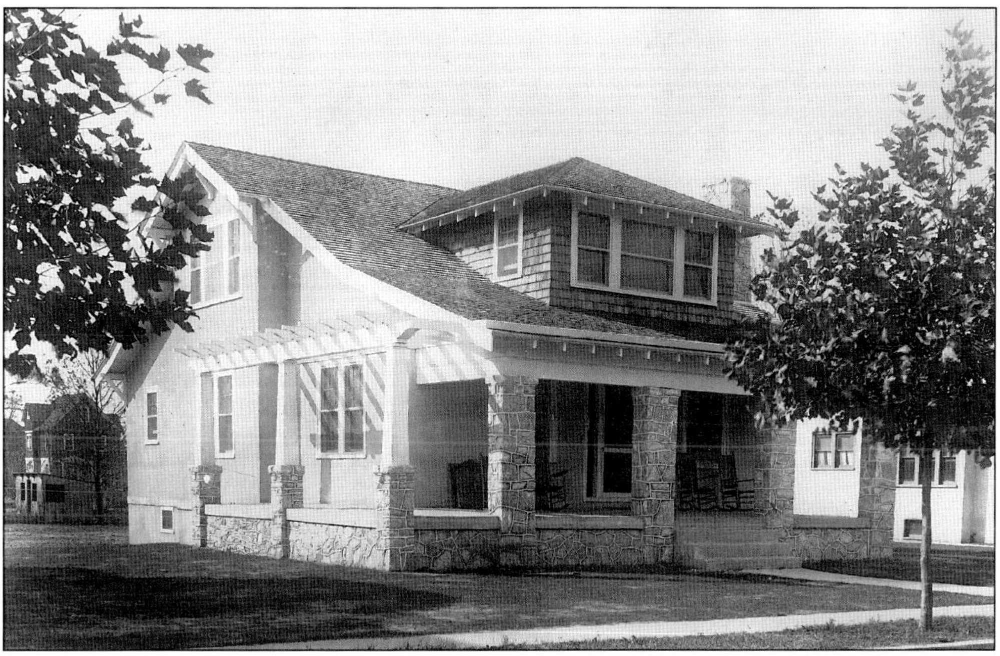

Leslie Avenue, perpendicular to the main streets of the Cattell Development, was divided into lots in 1915 and lined with bungalows. The bungalow designs were part of Gustav Stickley's movement to simplify housing and furnishings. In this photo postcard is the residence of J.E. Ohl at 126 Leslie Avenue. (Merchantville Historical Society.)

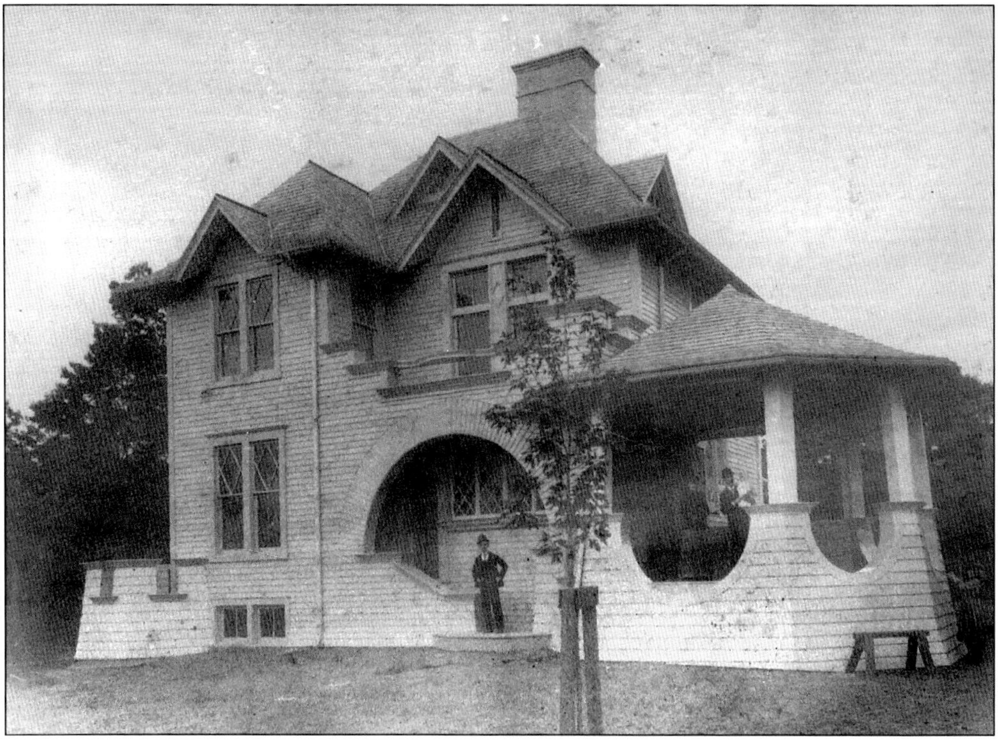

Architectural sophistication in Merchantville is seen most convincingly in this Richardsonsian Shingle–style residence designed and occupied by architect Arthur Truscott. This dwelling at 19 Springfield Avenue is the only example of Truscott's work in Merchantville and demonstrates the architect's proficiency and the influence of high-style design upon suburban architecture. (Joy Perry.)

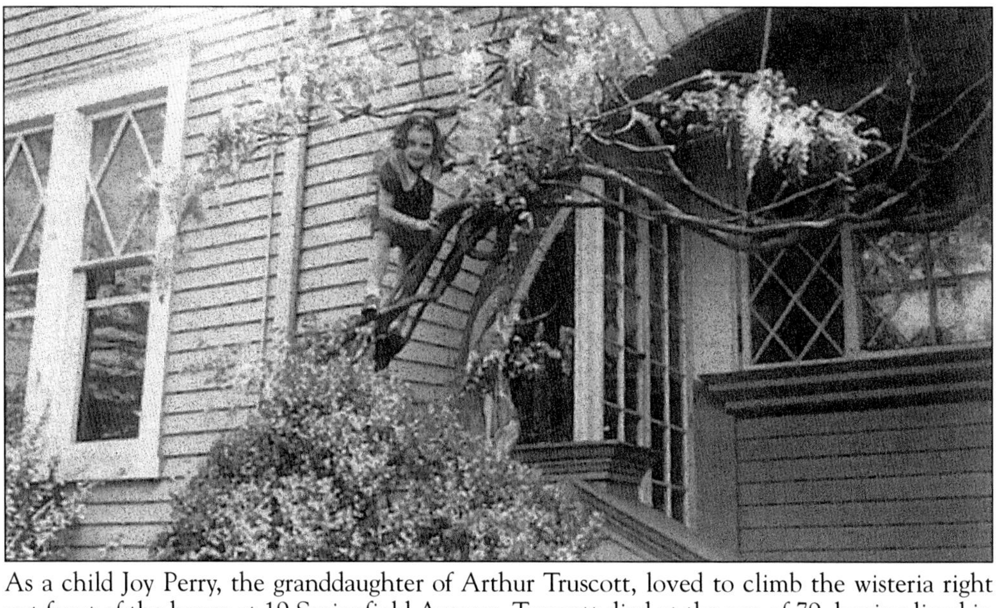

As a child Joy Perry, the granddaughter of Arthur Truscott, loved to climb the wisteria right out front of the house at 19 Springfield Avenue. Truscott died at the age of 79, having lived in Merchantville for nearly 50 years. (Joy Perry.)

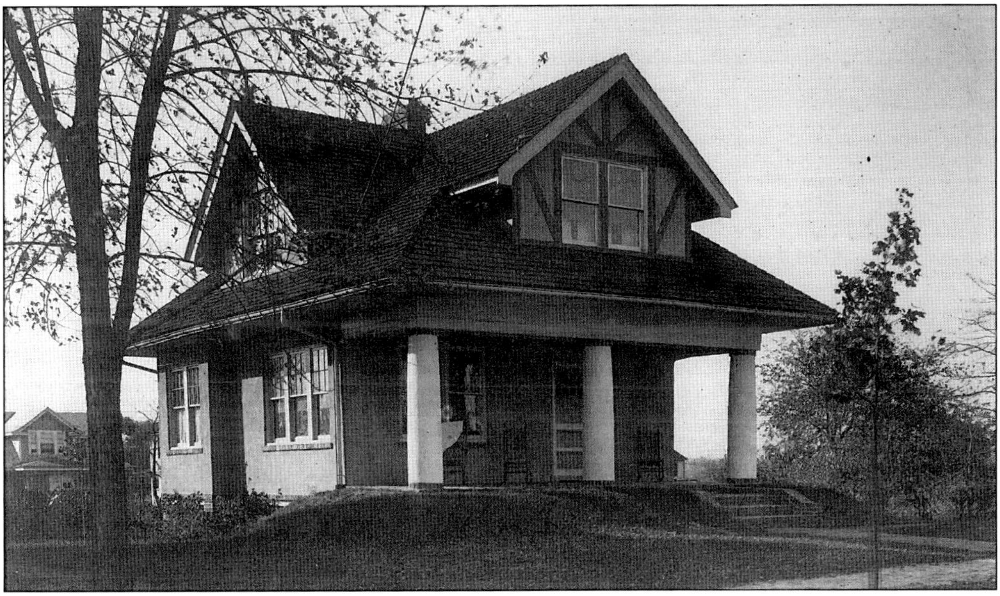

Clinton Avenue does not appear as a residential street in the 1911 directory. It is situated in the vicinity of what was known as West Merchantville. This bungalow belonged to H. Osborne at 18 Clinton Avenue. The two rocking chairs on the porch were a welcoming sight at the end of the day. (Merchantville Historical Society.)

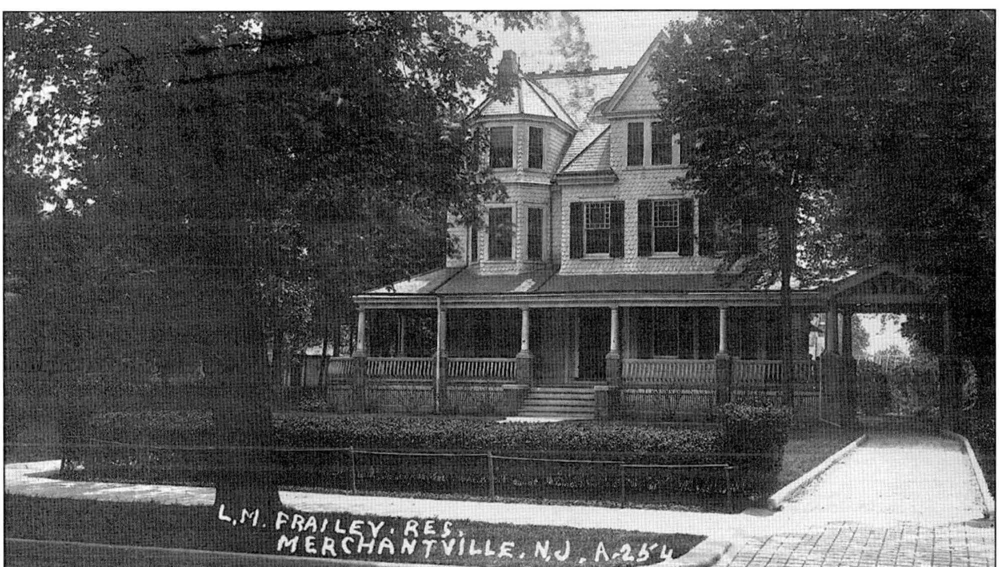

The Frailey family occupied the stately home at 8 East Maple Avenue. Mr. and Mrs. Len M. Frailey were initial members of the congregation of St. Peter's Roman Catholic Church. Katherine P. Frailey performed a solo in one of the last minstrel shows of 1909, entitled *A Field Club Dinner*. The Fraileys named the estate Kathetlen. (Bobbi Stagliano.)

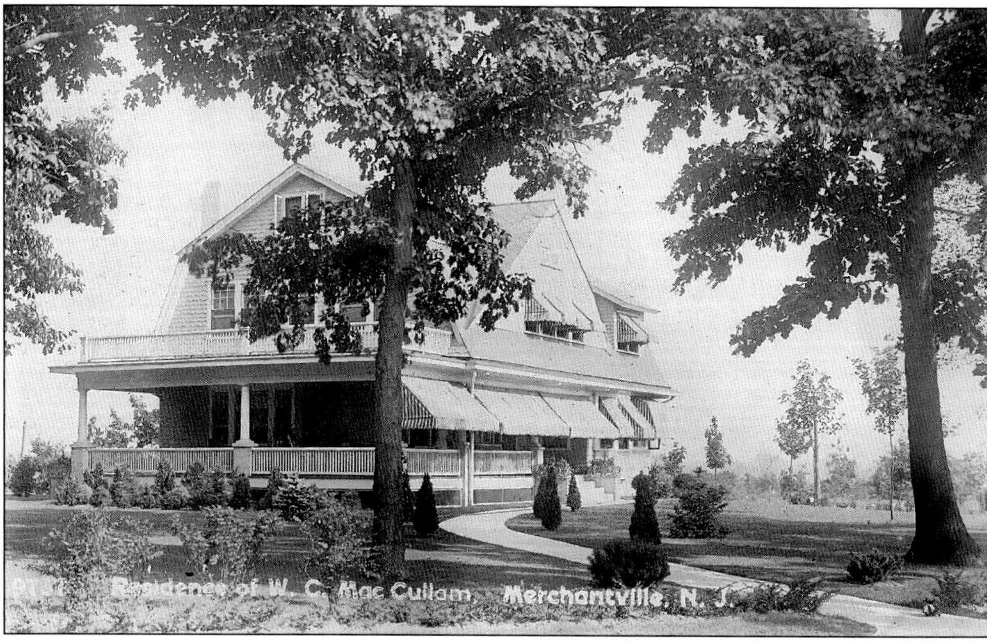

This postcard indicates that the house pictured is the residence of W.C. MacCullam. The Alexander MacCullam family lived at 111 Wellwood Avenue in an estate called the Oaks. George Rhedemeyer, a landscape architect, was largely responsible for transforming the Oaks into a very attractive section of Merchantville. He organized the Oaks Realty Company. (Bobbi Stagliano.)

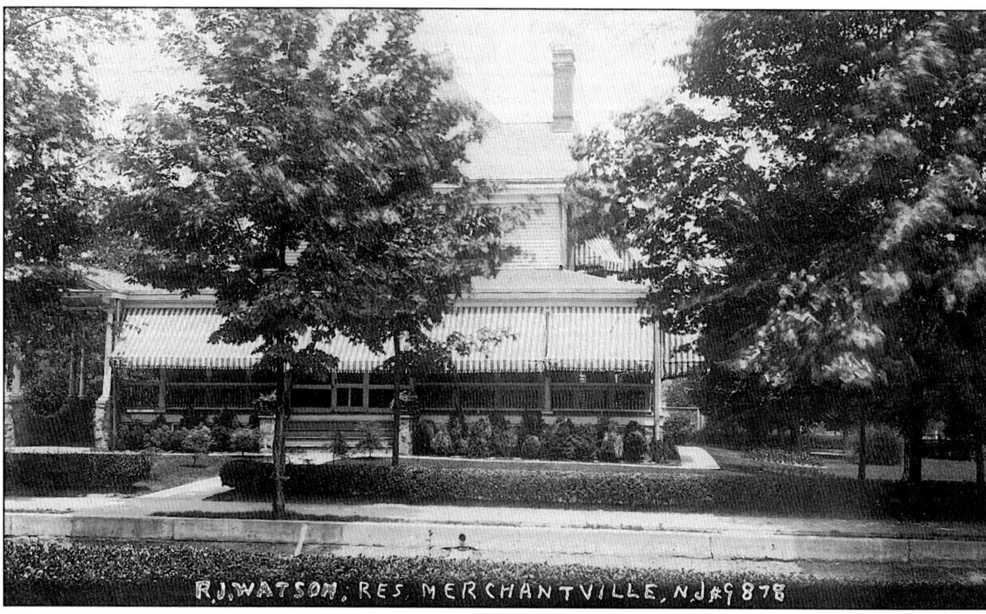

Richard J. Watson and his wife, Ella, made their home at 37 North Cove Road. Watson's profession was listed as manager in the 1911 directory. In 1924, Watson was a vice president of the Home Building & Loan Association of Merchantville. Emma Watson, his daughter, was also included in the household. The directory listed all adults, male and female, and all those engaged in any business or occupation. (Tina Schmidt.)

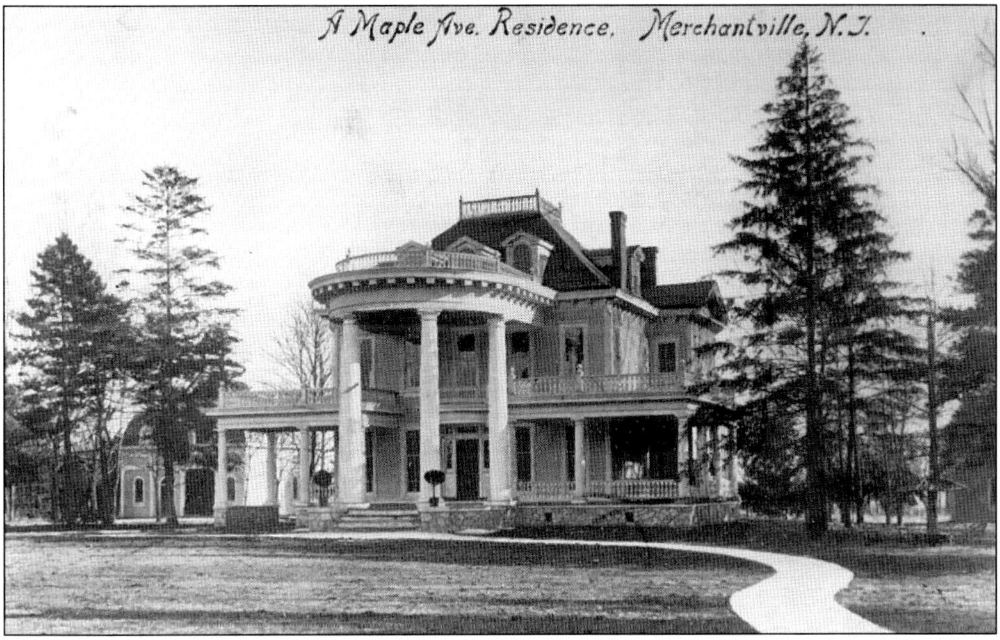

Walter J. Staats, an executive of the Victor Talking Machine Company, purchased the home of William Kempton, which was built in 1869. In 1874, the *Beacon*, the local newspaper, announced that Kempton was having an addition built to his estate's handsome stable. The apartments at 56 West Maple Avenue now occupy the grounds of the former Kempton-Staats residence. (Merchantville Historical Society.)

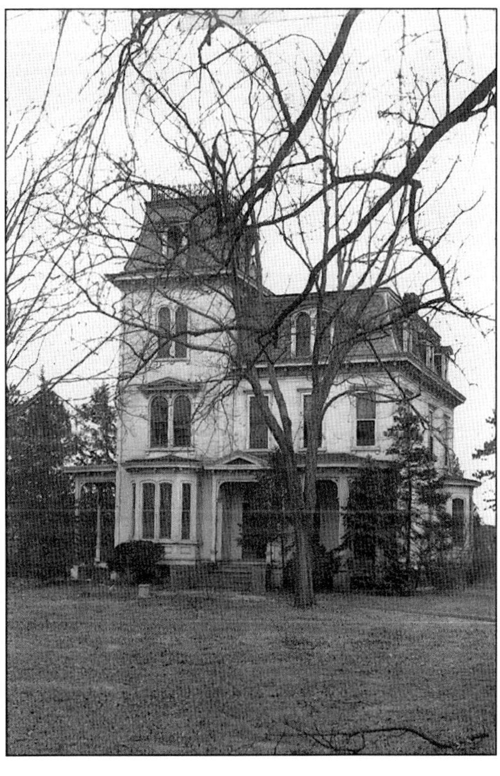

Originally, it was said that the D. Tenney Gage house was identical to the Kempton home. In later years, the houses bore no resemblance to each other. The setting of the Gage-Nevin house was a large plot of ground on the south side of West Maple Avenue, east of where Morris Street was later cut through. Gage was a Philadelphia manufacturer. When his daughter, Mrs. Edwin Nevin, took over the home, it became the Nevin Estate. The home was lost in a fire in 1946. Morris Court Apartments are now located here. (Merchantville Historical Society.)

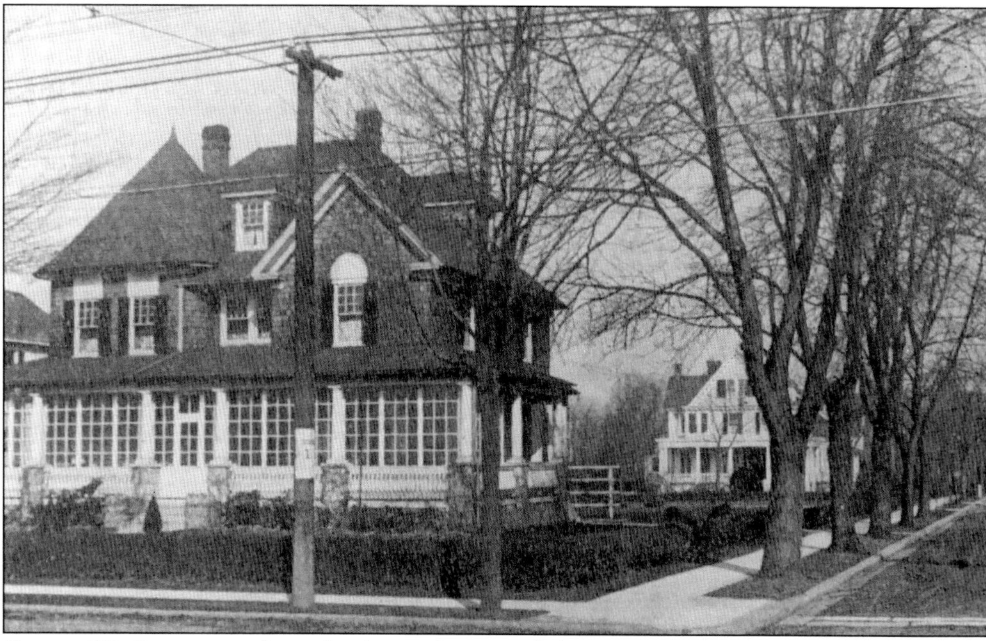

George W. Carey served on the borough council from 1908 to 1910. Three months after Carey's resignation, in May 1910, the Citizens League gained control of the borough council. The home was located at 201 West Maple, which was at the northwest corner of Springfield Avenue. (Vernon Collins.)

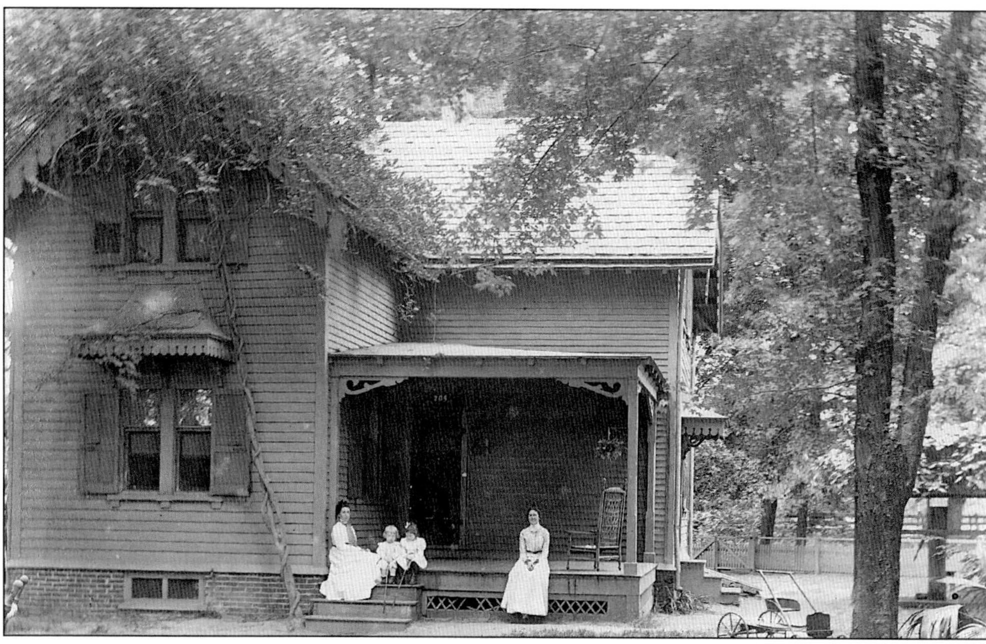

Henry Alexander Macomb built a large residence at 105 West Maple Avenue in 1888. However, before designing that home, Macomb resided at Myrtle Avenue and Browning Road. He continued to own his former home while living along the more fashionable West Maple Avenue. Macomb was responsible for shaping much of the town's architecture and designed the town flag. (Merchantville Historical Society.)

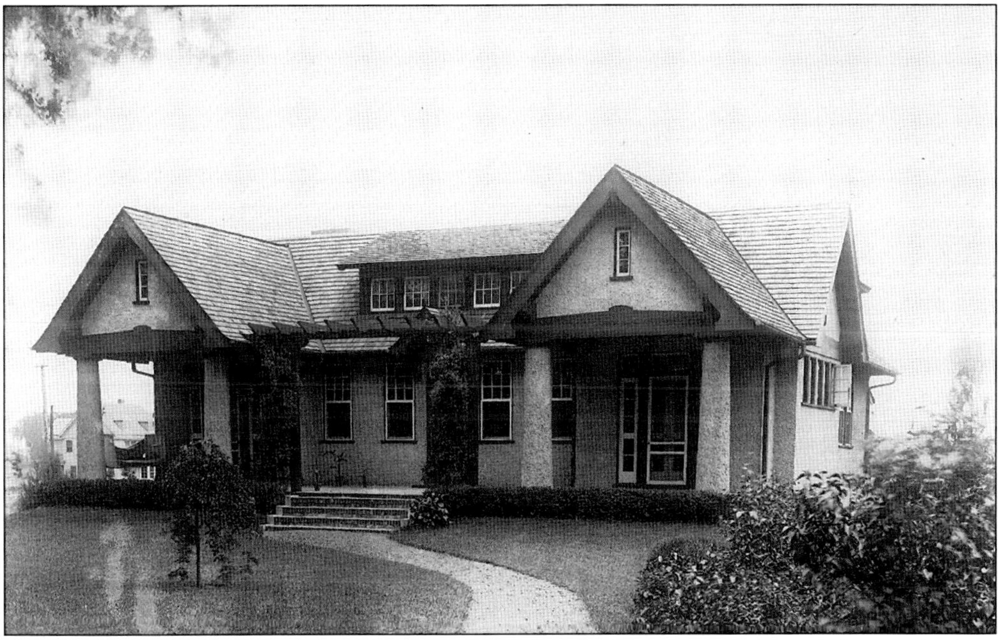

The Rowes' bungalow was located at 10 Church Road. Church Road ran southwesterly from 300 East Maple Avenue. The 1911 directory shows a common situation where more than one family lived in the home. Mrs. J.M. Rowe was a widow. Her son, a merchant, and daughter-in-law, John M. and Helen, also resided in the home. (Merchantville Historical Society.)

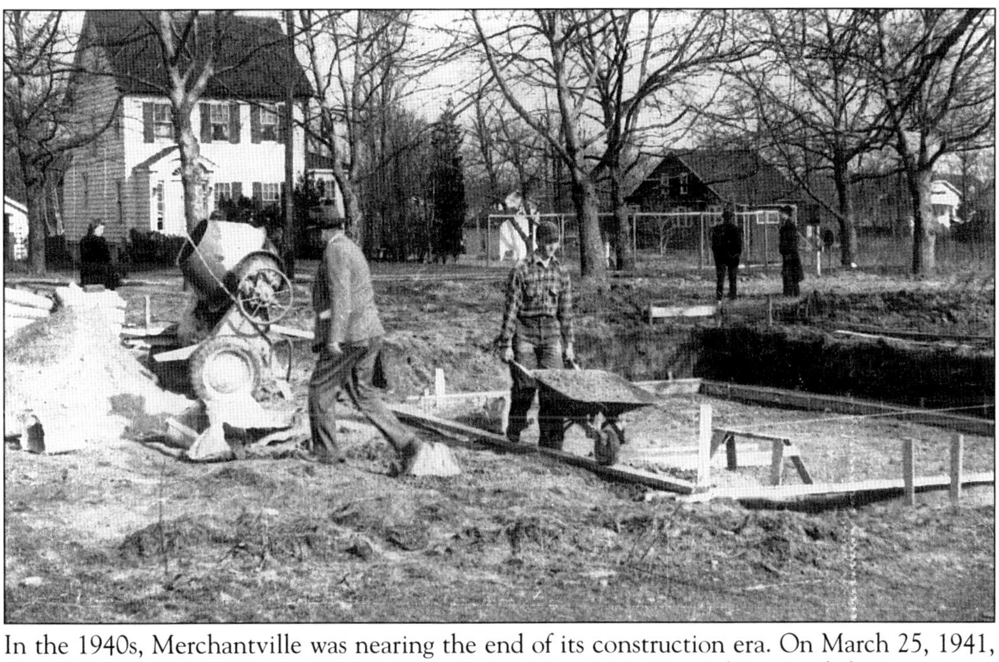

In the 1940s, Merchantville was nearing the end of its construction era. On March 25, 1941, ground was broken for the building of 300 St. James Avenue. Clearing of the overgrown lot of land expanded the residentially occupied area of Merchantville to its outer limits. (Ruth Curran Neild.)

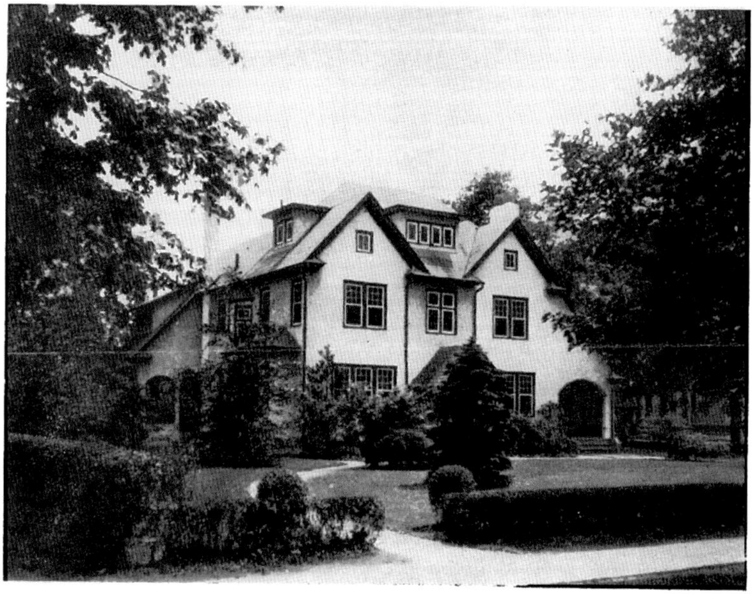

$12,500

IN ORDER to close an estate a real bargain is available to anyone desiring a charming home in an established residential area. 100 East Maple Avenue designates a corner property with spacious landscaped grounds in the smart section of Merchantville.

OLD TREES cast their shadows over the surrounding hedge. A curved walk of red cement laid in small squares winds to the entrance doorway.

THE FRONT DOOR opens onto a 3′ x 7′ entry of small red tiles with a roomy entrance hall beyond. The stairs begin about seven feet back, with clear vision made certain by light from the windows at the turn of the open stairway.

TO THE RIGHT is the living room, 22′ x 12′8″. In the long wall opposite is the fireplace. The beamed ceiling harmonizes with the Flemish colored woodwork. On either side of the fireplace double French doors lead to a cement floored porch, completely screened in for comfort in summer. At the rear of the living room, opposite the porch is the entrance to the book-room. A rear exit leads from this room to the garden and garage. By leaving open this door as well as the one from the book-room into the entrance hall, a clear view of the garden can be had from the front entry.

ON THE OTHER SIDE of the entrance hall is the dining room. The delicate blue wallpaper of the upper walls is shown off to great advantage by the high white wainscoting of the base and again the beamed ceiling. At the far end of the dining room and beyond an archway eight feet high is an alcove, its three windows enabling a clear view of the trees and shrubbery, planted for picture effect.

CHAS. R. MYERS & CO., Inc.
12 NORTH 7th STREET
CAMDEN, N. J.

Phone, Camden 5958

This real estate advertisement dates to the 1930s.

Six

Commemorative Celebrations

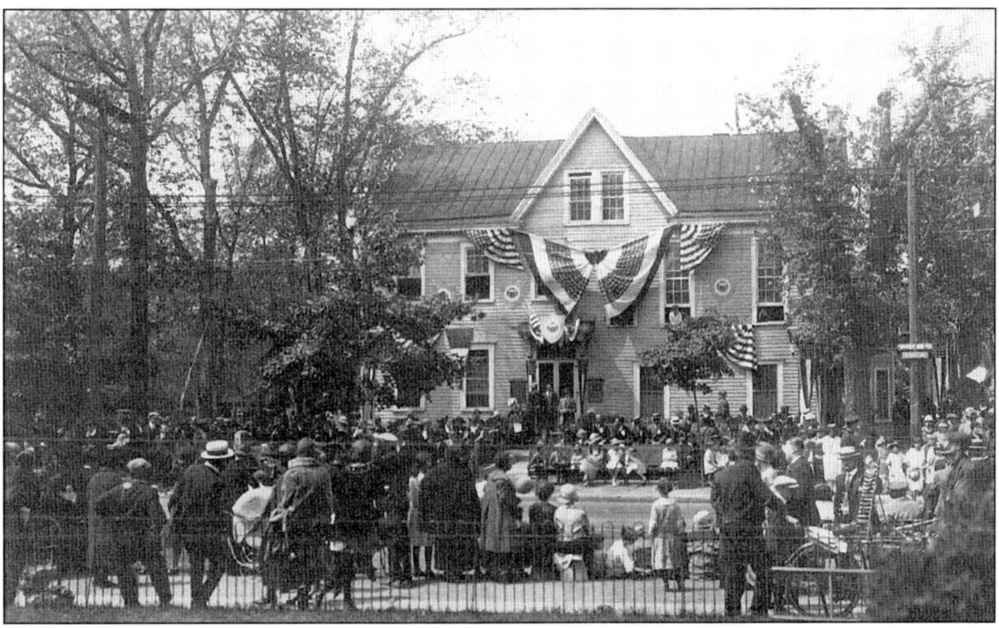

Merchantville held a grand 50th anniversary celebration in May 1924. Frederick L. Holman, the 14th mayor of Merchantville, presided. The pageant parade formed in the Wellwood section, west of Poplar Avenue, and then headed east down West Maple Avenue. Mrs. William J. Adams oversaw the committee activities. This scene shows the parade passing the borough hall. (Merchantville Historical Society.)

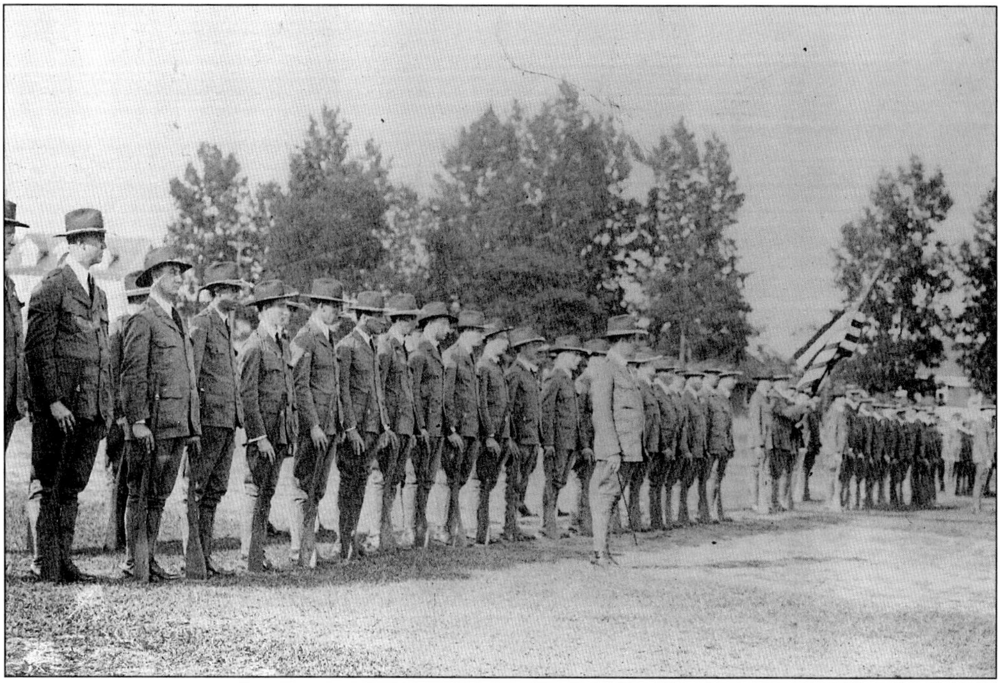

A call to enrollment in the Merchantville Home Guards was issued for April 4, 1917. Two companies were formed, designated Company A under Capt. Mahlon F. Ivins Jr. and Company B under Capt. William F. Frazee. There were two drill nights a week. A successful minstrel show was staged as a fundraiser to outfit the men in cotton khaki and campaign hats. Ranks were depleted by enlistments in the regular service. The company was mustered out on April 19, 1919. (Merchantville Historical Society.)

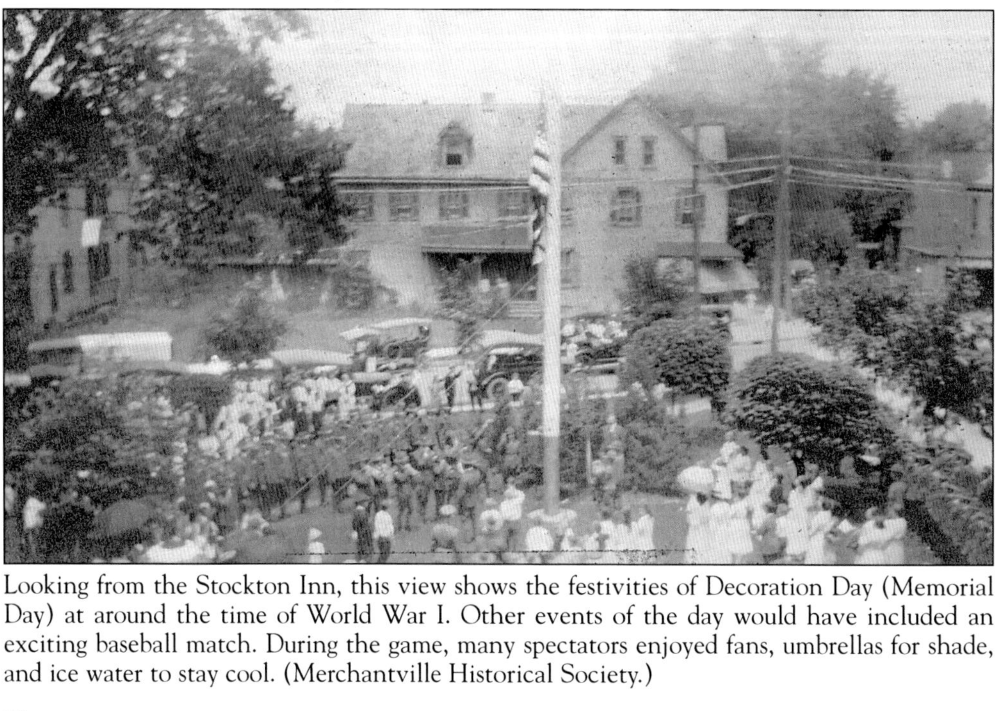

Looking from the Stockton Inn, this view shows the festivities of Decoration Day (Memorial Day) at around the time of World War I. Other events of the day would have included an exciting baseball match. During the game, many spectators enjoyed fans, umbrellas for shade, and ice water to stay cool. (Merchantville Historical Society.)

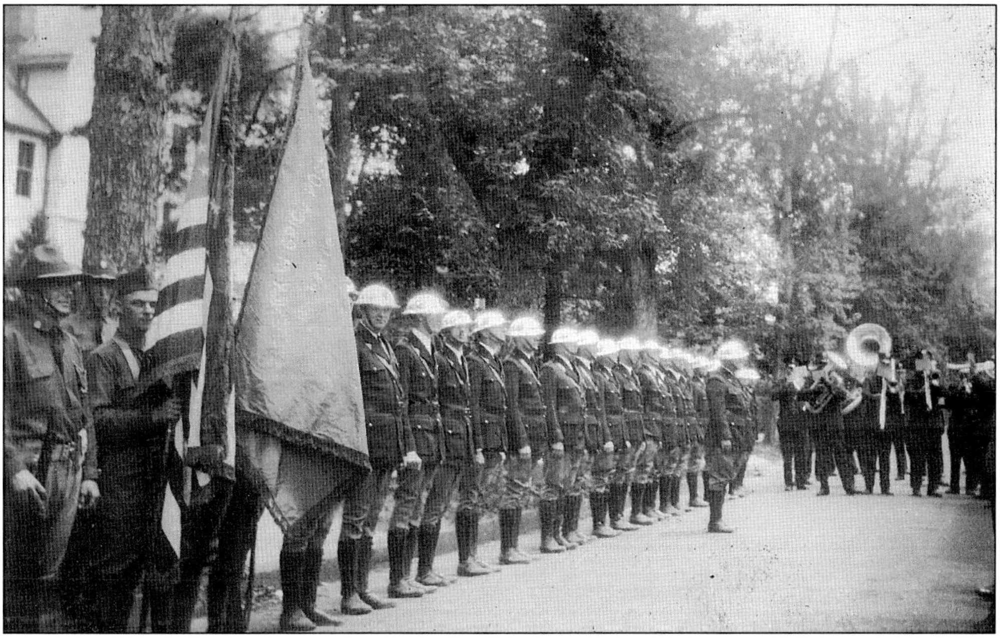

The question of adopting a distinctive uniform for the Frederick W. Grigg Post No. 68 members was brought up on November 12, 1926. The uniform selected was a legion blue, single-breasted, military-style coat with rolled collar, light tan breeches with black puttees, and a Sam Browne belt and aluminum helmet. Shown here is the post uniform line. (Tony Repice.)

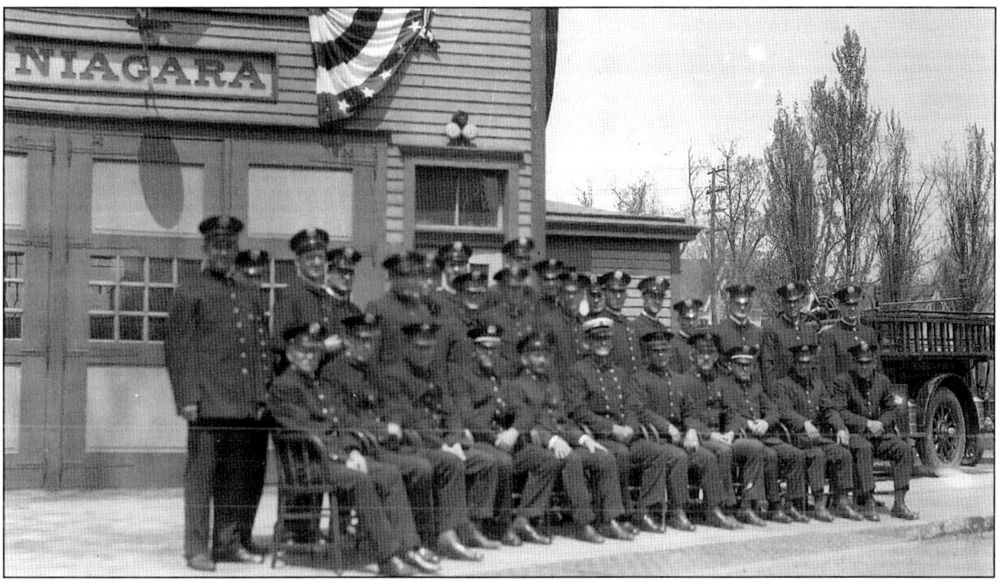

The first firehouse, built in 1888 at 19 East Park Avenue, is shown during the 50th anniversary celebrations. In May 1924, the Niagara Fire Company members pose for a photograph. From left to right in the front row are Fred Johnson, John Plasket Jr., Dan Carr, Harold Watson, Richard Neumann, Chief Edward F. Rudderow, Harry Simon, John Plasket Sr., Bill Simon, Jim Carr, and Bill Strong. In the back row (positions unknown) are Leonard Smith and Bill Williams. The president of the company in 1924 was D. Walter Bayne Jr. (Merchantville Historical Society.)

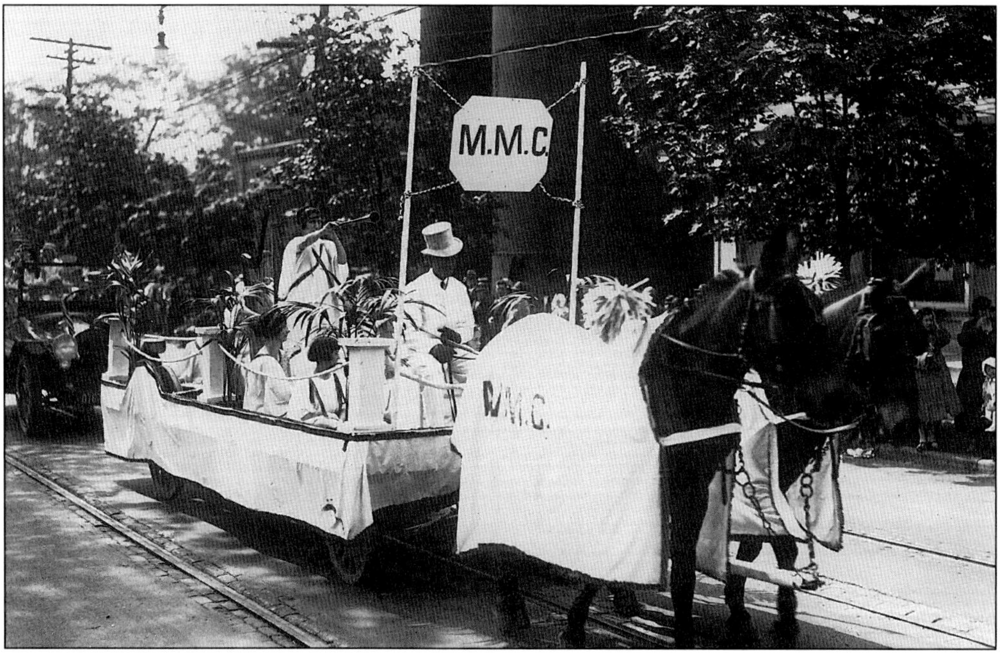

The Merchantville Music Club, founded by Julia E. Williams, was organized on September 28, 1910, with 17 charter members. The membership had 136 active, 145 associate, and 65 junior members in 1924. On May 23–24, 1924, *Pinafore* was being presented. Julia Williams, honorary president and president of New Jersey Federation of Music clubs, was active president from 1910 to 1922. Pictured are club members on their 50th anniversary parade float. (Maureen McLoone.)

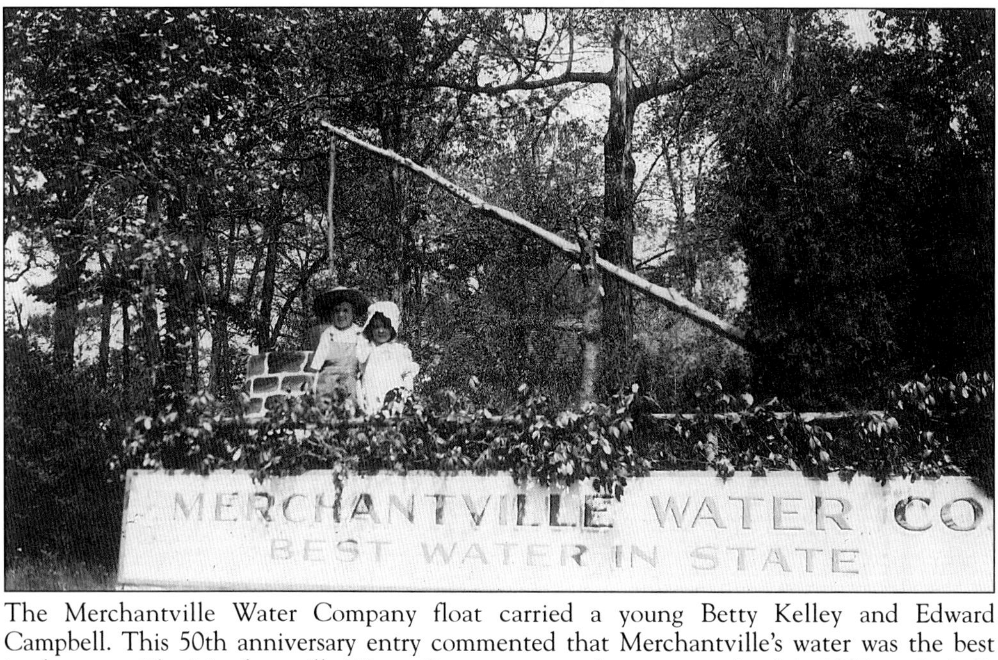

The Merchantville Water Company float carried a young Betty Kelley and Edward Campbell. This 50th anniversary entry commented that Merchantville's water was the best in the state. The Merchantville Water Company started service on April 1, 1887, with A.G. Cattell as its first consumer. The standpipes on West Maple at West Park held the water. (Merchantville Historical Society.)

Stella Fryer, whose slogan, "Merchantville, the Borough Beautiful," won the publicity committee's prize of $25, unselfishly presented her prize to the Camden County Society for the Prevention of Cruelty to Animals, which had active representation in Merchantville. Here in the 50th anniversary parade, Elizabeth Partridge (left) and Dorothy Reitz (right) flank Stella, who carries the banner bearing her slogan. Stella was the daughter of author Jane Eayre Fryer. (Merchantville Historical Society.)

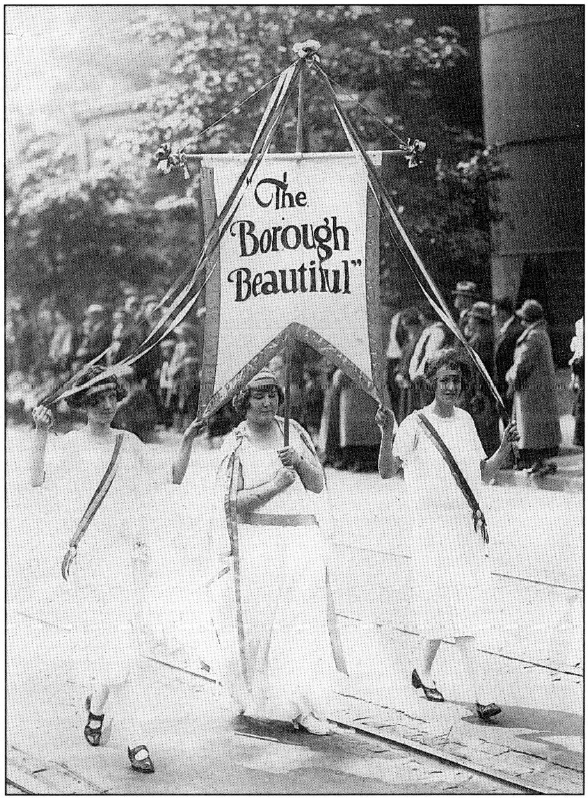

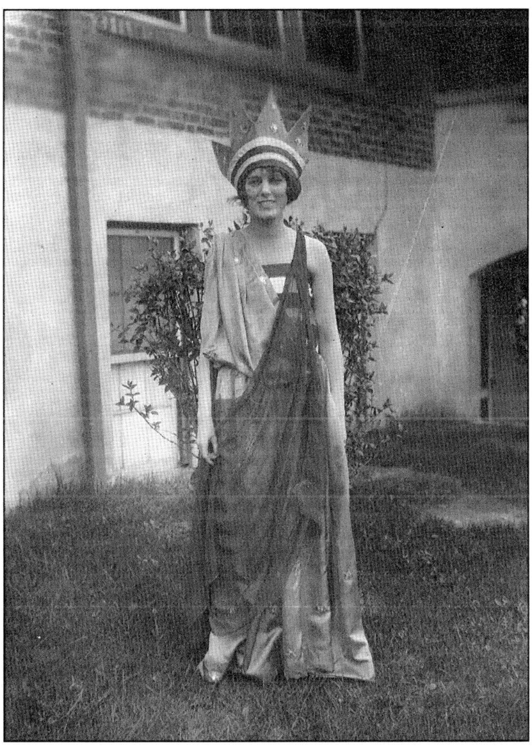

The Pageant of Nations on Friday, May 16, 1924, on the Merchantville Country Club grounds attracted more than 6,000 spectators. A series of tableaux and dances, representative of all countries, preceded the crowning of Elizabeth Cross as Queen of the May. Here, Maxine Atkins poses as "Miss Columbia" outside the Merchantville Country Club (now the community center). (Merchantville Historical Society.)

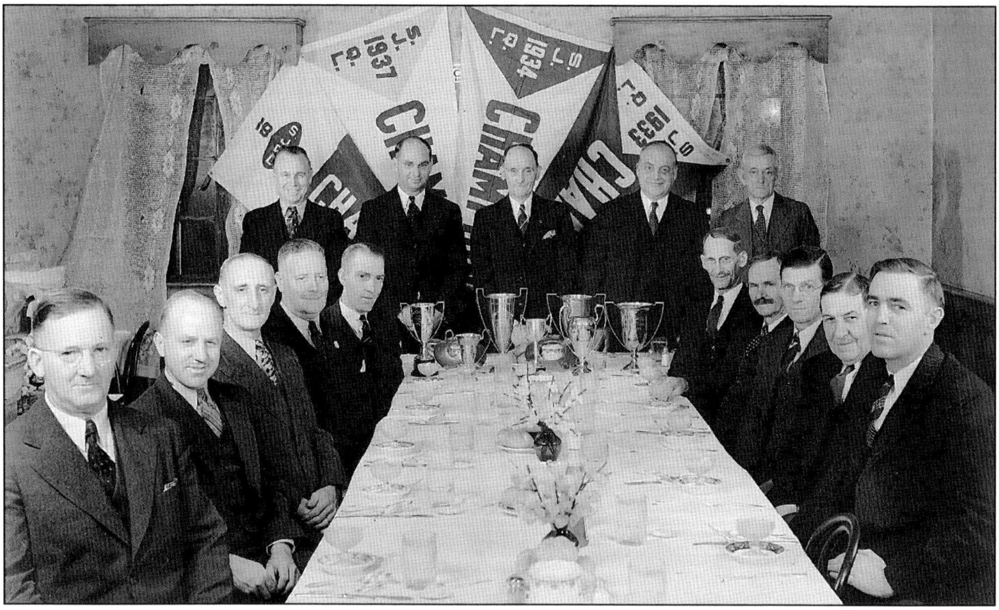

The Merchantville Quoit Club took many championships in the 1930s. In the background are at least three banners bearing the South Jersey Quoit League title for 1933, 1934, and 1937. Quoits is a game in which flattened rings of iron or rope are thrown at an upright pin in an attempt to ring the pin. Shown from left to right are the following: (left side) unidentified, Russell James, Walter Richards, Arthur Cooper, and Ray Price; (back row, standing) Fred Crawford, Ray Hoffner, Joseph Lund, Alvin Pitman, and William Russel; (right side) "Pop" Hoffner, Joseph Rudderow, unidentified, Benjamin Robb, and Harry Ditmhier. (Merchantville Historical Society.)

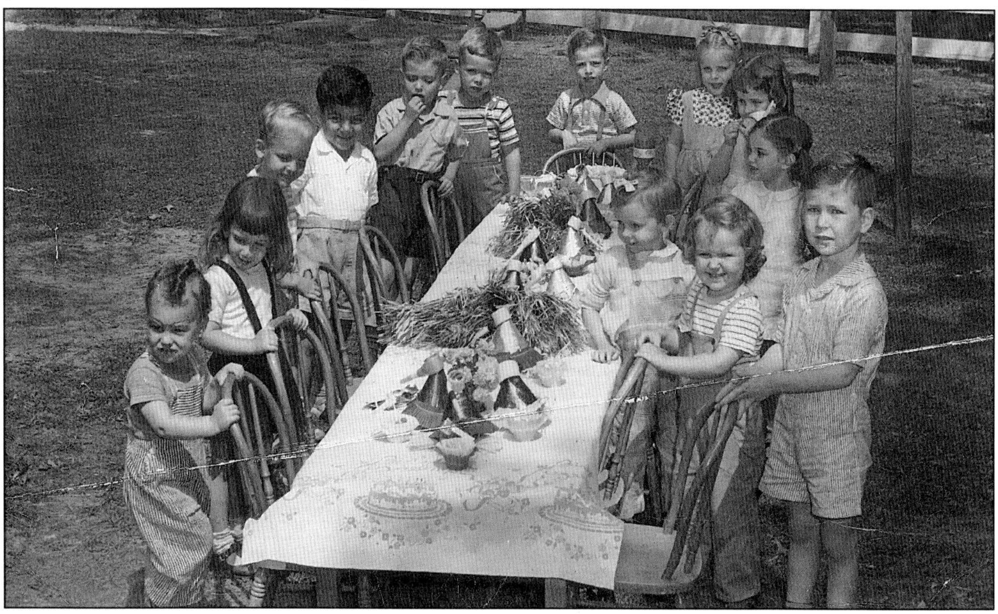

This children's birthday party was held at the Bo-Peep Day Nursery at 16 Morris Street. Dottie Mutschler, a registered nurse, ran the nursery school in order to remain home with her children. Bobbi Mutschler Stagliano is the last little girl in the back on the right side. (Bobbi Stagliano.)

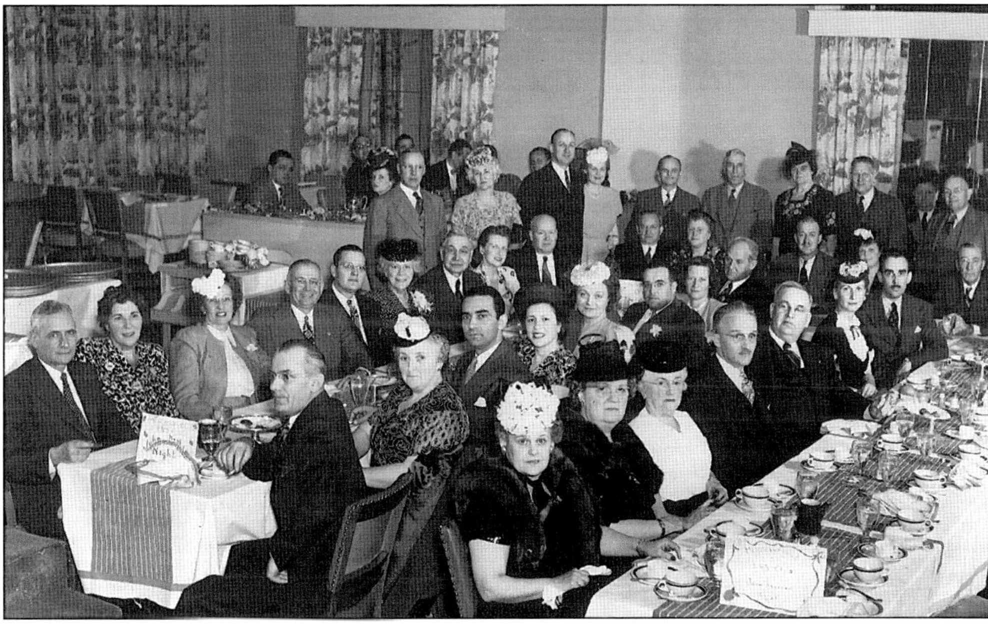

The Lions Club celebrates John W. Kratzer Night. Kratzer was the supervising principal of Merchantville School. Feeling that there was a need for a service club in the borough, 25 residents headed by Maurice B. Rudderow met on July 26, 1926, and joined the International Association of Lions Clubs. (Aunt Charlotte's.)

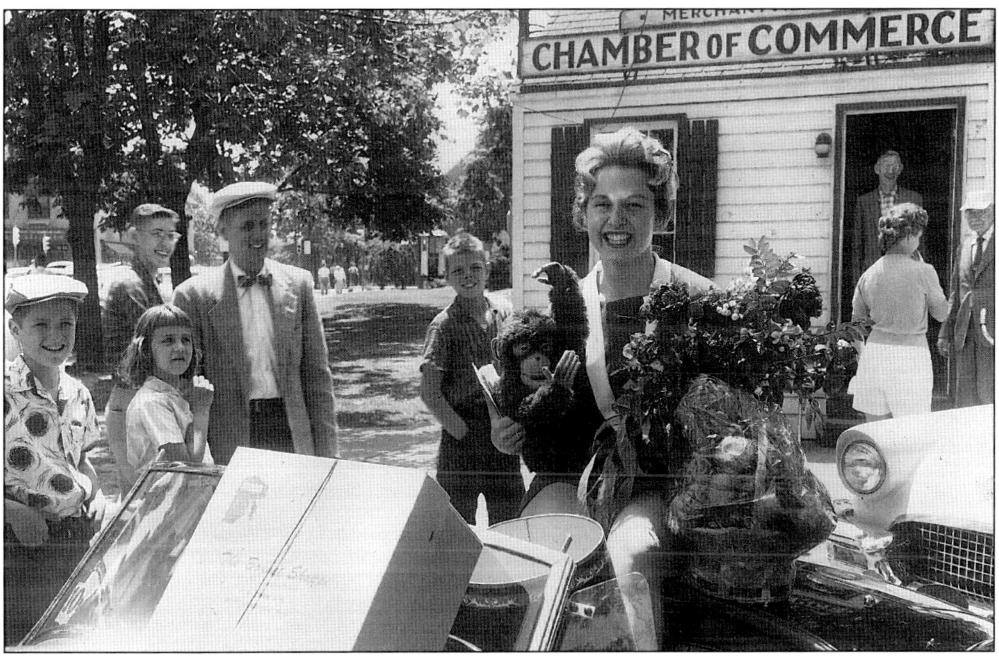

The Merchantville Chamber of Commerce held a Miss Sports Car contest. In 1960, Gwen Browing held the title. Note the many gifts she received. In particular, notice that the hat box is from the Bonnet Shoppe at 19 East Park Avenue. Near the doorway are Francis Plasket (just inside the door) and John Kratzer (outside the door). On the left are Brooks Oakford and Candy Oakford. (Aunt Charlotte's.)

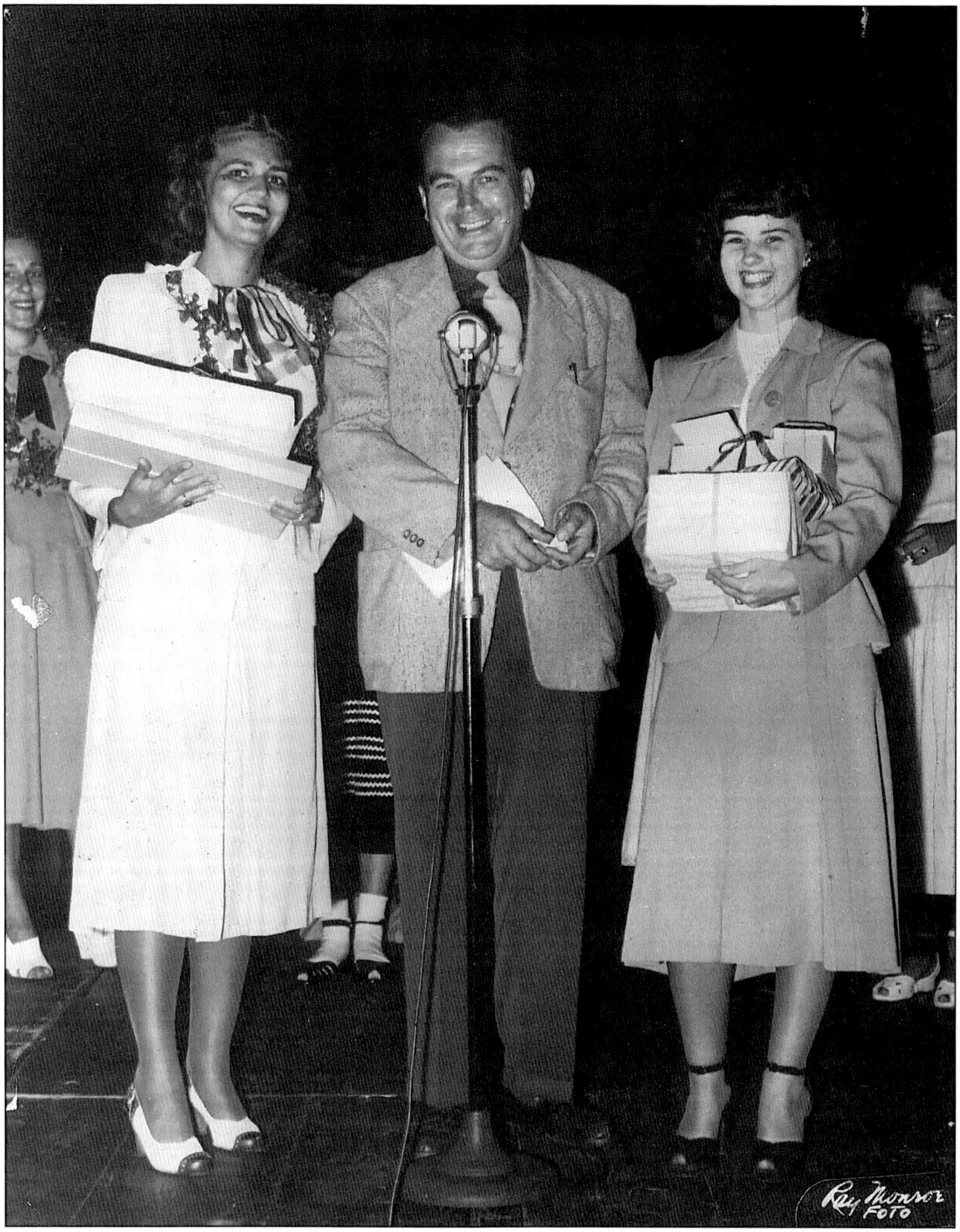

The Merchantville-Pennsauken Business Association sponsored the Mrs. and Miss Merchantville contests in the early 1950s. Shown here are Bunny Oakford, who won the Mrs. Merchantville title, and Janet Rice, winner of the Miss Merchantville crown. Jack Ludlam was the president of the chamber of commerce. (Aunt Charlotte's.)

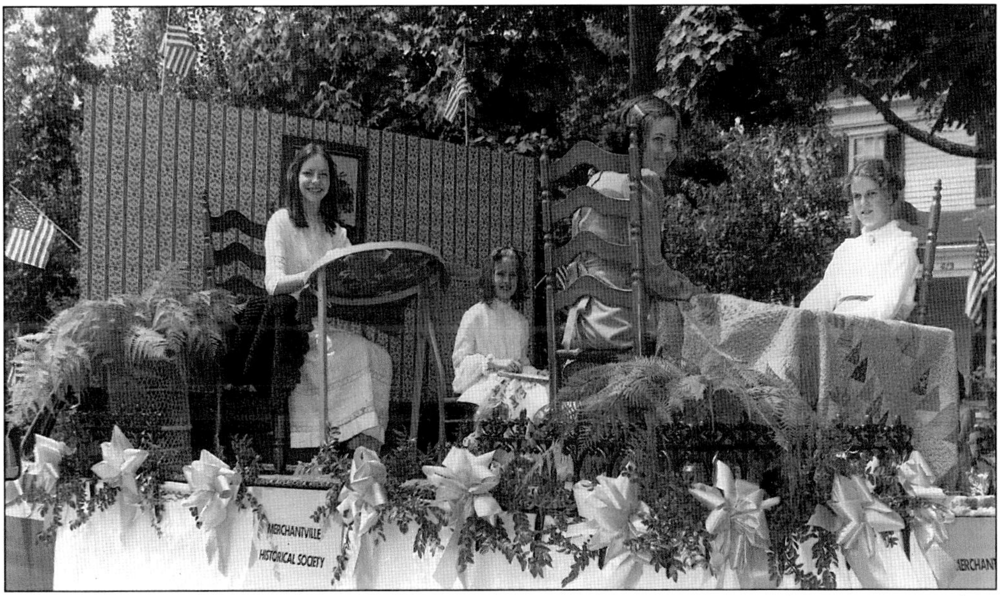

On May 18, 1974, the centennial parade celebrated Merchantville's 100th anniversary. Alice Creedon, Cathy Cunningham, Hope Hughes, and Lynn German ride the Merchantville Historical Society float. The historical society came into being just before the centennial year as the historical research group within the centennial celebration committee formed by the townspeople. (Merchantville Historical Society.)

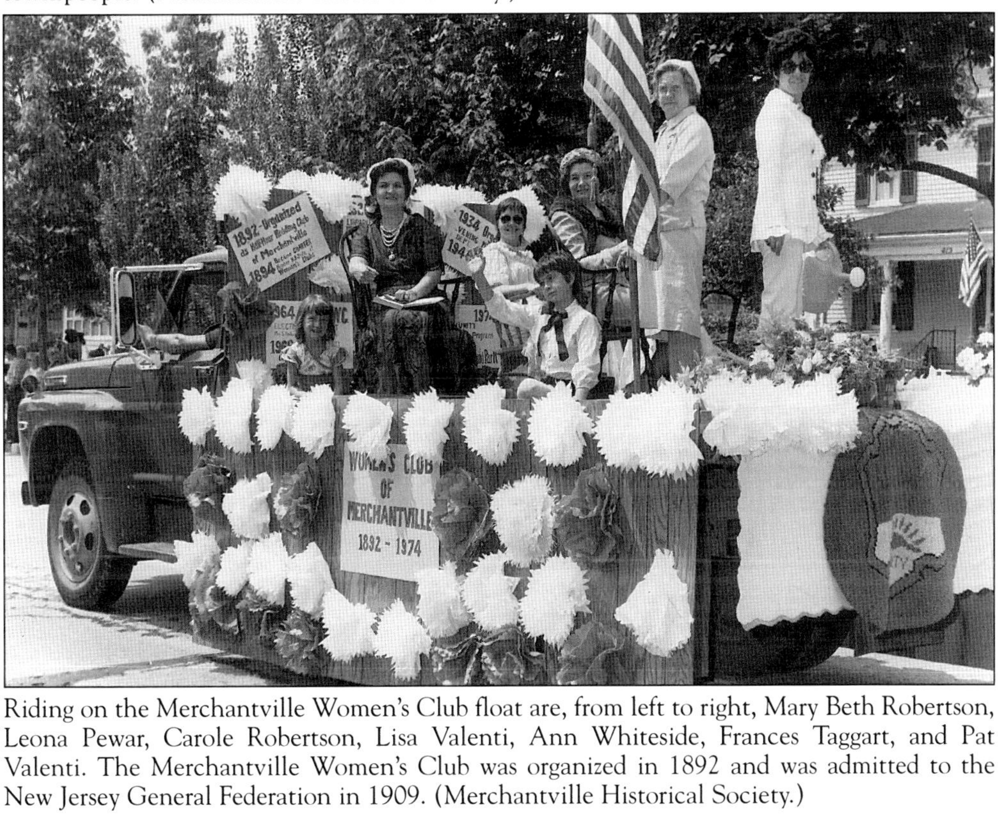

Riding on the Merchantville Women's Club float are, from left to right, Mary Beth Robertson, Leona Pewar, Carole Robertson, Lisa Valenti, Ann Whiteside, Frances Taggart, and Pat Valenti. The Merchantville Women's Club was organized in 1892 and was admitted to the New Jersey General Federation in 1909. (Merchantville Historical Society.)

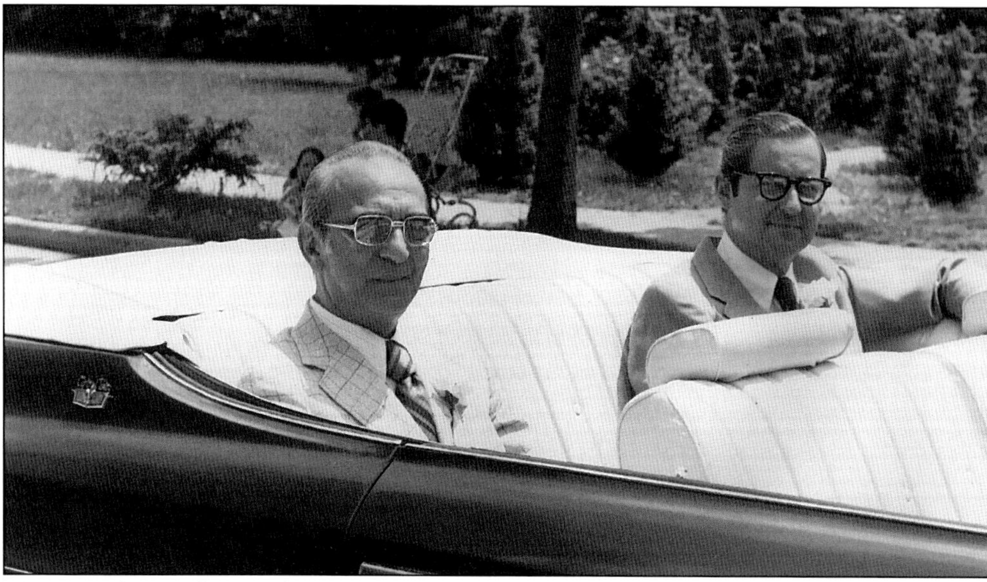

Mayors Walter Kurkian and G. Burton German ride in the centennial parade. Walter V. Kurkian assumed the office of mayor on January 29, 1962, following the death of Mayor J. Weer Chew. In 1954, Kurkian received the F.W. Grigg Post American Legion Citation as Citizen of the Year. G. Burton German Jr. had been mayor for seven years at the time of the centennial. Mayor German was named Centennial Man of the Year, in recognition of his dedication and service to the borough. (Merchantville Historical Society.)

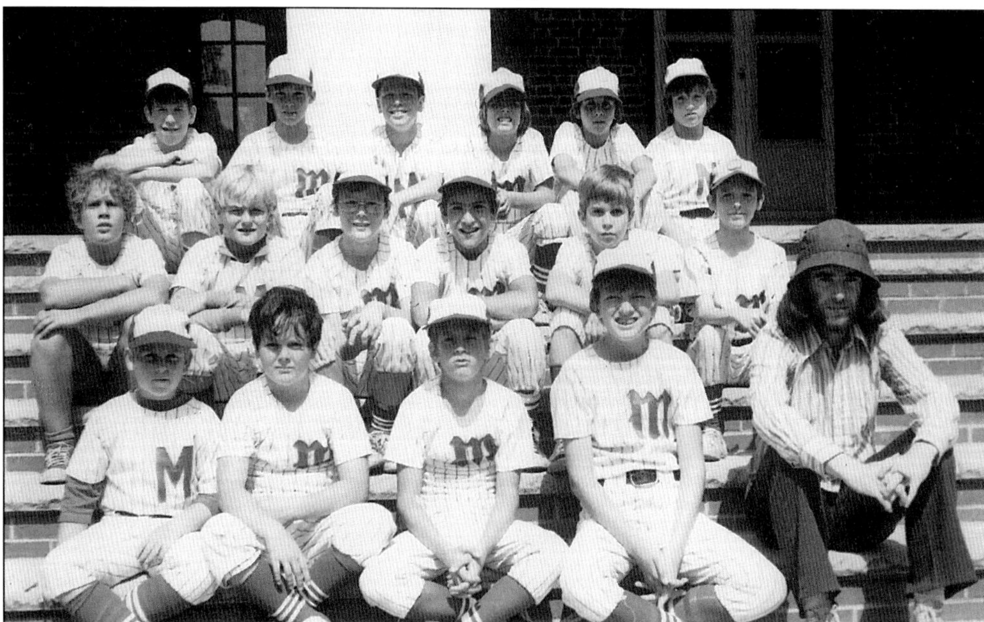

The Merchantville Boys Baseball League Champions for 1974 were the Phillies. They are, from left to right, as follows: (front row) Michael Huttonan, Paul Batdorff, Joe Loperfida, Brian Gorman, and manager John Curran; (middle row) Doug Barber, John McCoy, Matt Stehm, Jeff Selverian, Steve Frett, and Peter O'Connor; (back row) Jack Swinderman, Tony Abbewitz, Tom Gamon, John Bundick, Michael Ricci, and George Bordi. (Merchantville Historical Society.)

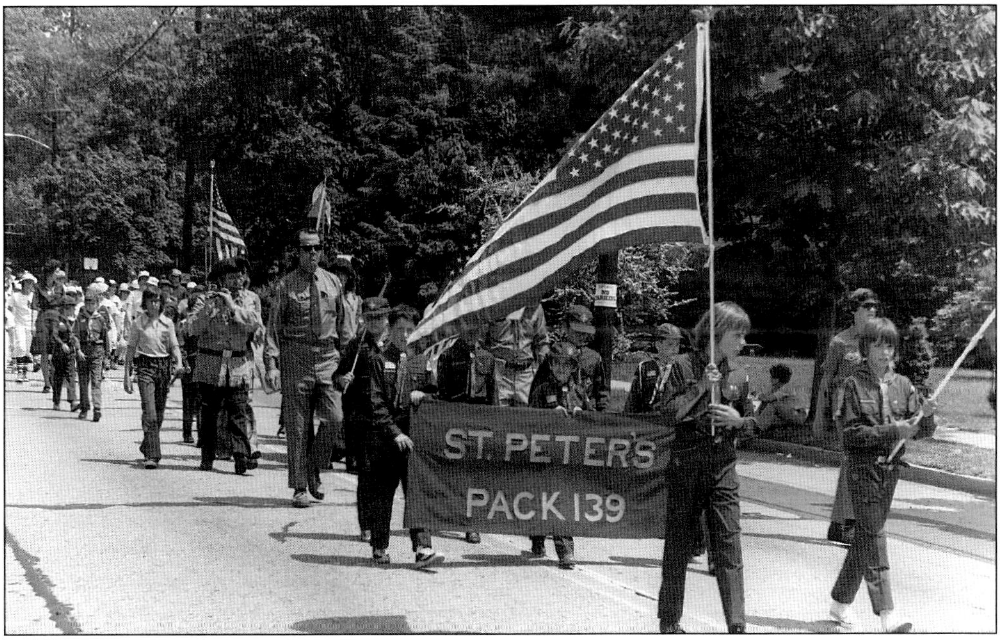

The centennial parade began at noon from East Maple Avenue and Church Road and continued for two hours down Maple Avenue to Wellwood Park. Three chairpersons made this day a huge success. They were Jack Plasket, Jeff Brown, and Len Pikulski. The scene included high school and private bands, antique cars, floats, the Cunard clowns, and Scout groups. In this photograph, Scout Pack No. 139 from St. Peter's is marching in the parade. (Merchantville Historical Society.)

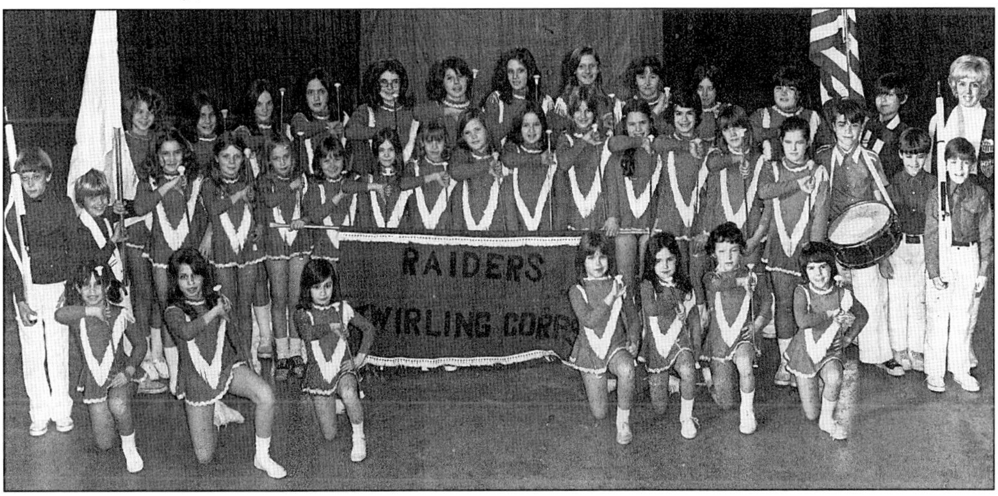

The Raiders Twirling Corps was founded in 1972 by Lorrie Dell, who was the director during the centennial year. Shown from left to right are the following: (front row) T. Lamborn, T. Viggiano, B. Donlan, D. Petitta, J. Clements, S. Solomon, and G. DiPietro; (middle row) R. Solomon, S. Dell, C. Frank, A. Button, K. Beam, K. Werner, M. Donlan, L. Hammill, K. McDermott, P. Werner, A. Householder, L. Behlau (captain), D. Larusso, D. Petitta, K. Morrissey, R. Hart, J. Rogers, and T. Massey; (back row) D. Donovan, M. Rogers, M. O'Sullivan, L. Pedrick, D. Wall, K. Conner, T. Sikorski, J. Sudbrink, M. Henkel, J. Goetz, K. Hewitt, D. Wall, and Laurie Dell. (Merchantville Historical Society.)

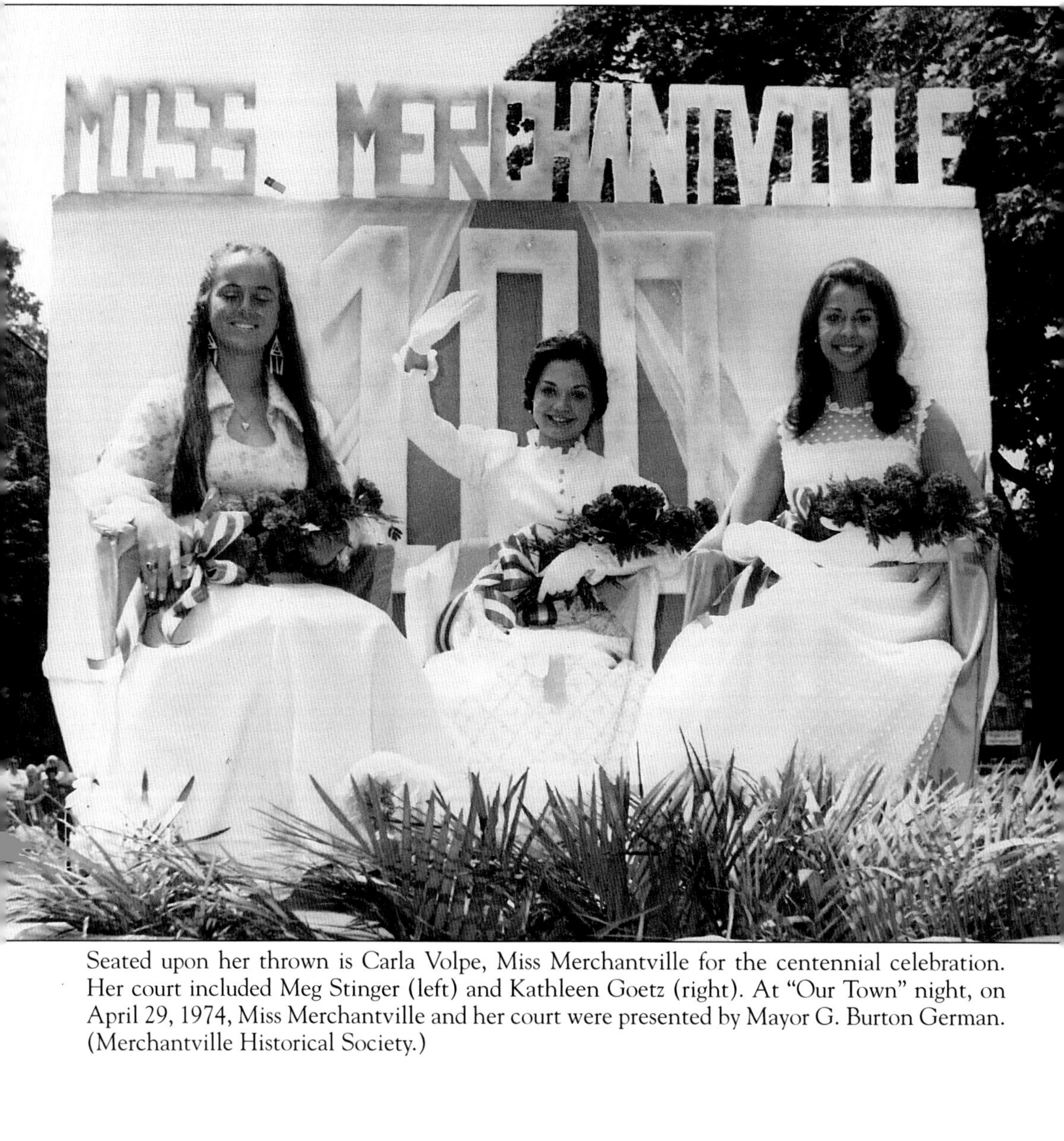

Seated upon her thrown is Carla Volpe, Miss Merchantville for the centennial celebration. Her court included Meg Stinger (left) and Kathleen Goetz (right). At "Our Town" night, on April 29, 1974, Miss Merchantville and her court were presented by Mayor G. Burton German. (Merchantville Historical Society.)

Seven

Destination Downtown

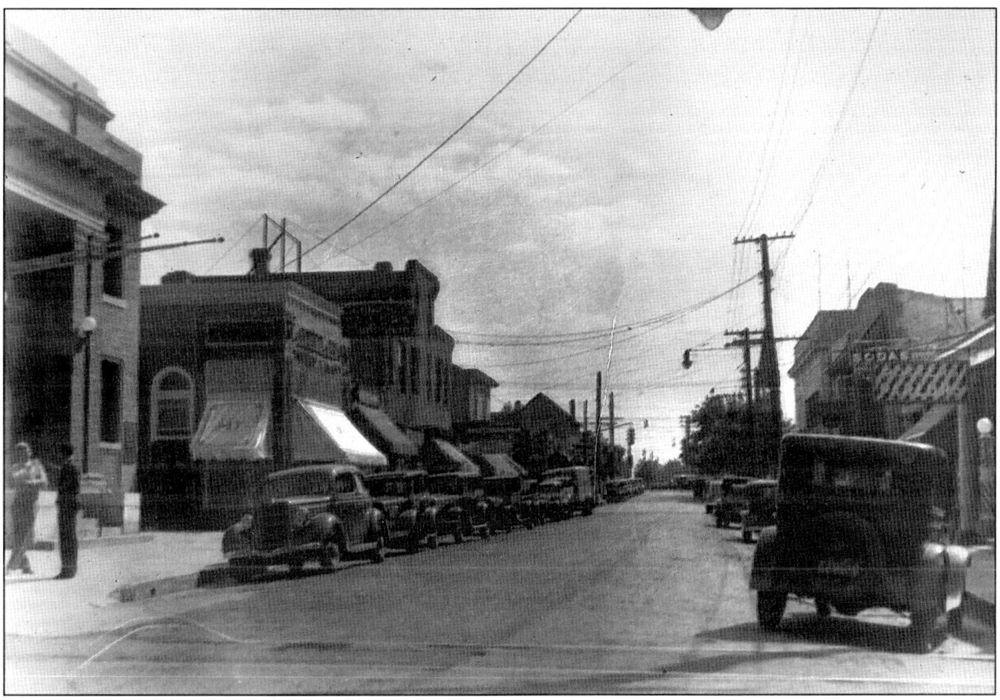

The heart of a town is its downtown. This is the legacy bonding the past, present, and future. All the contributions of yesterday are recognized and cherished and are built on to fuel the future of the town center. Here is a scene of the downtown, earlier in the 1900s, on South Centre Street, looking from the railroad tracks toward Park Avenue. (Vernon Collins.)

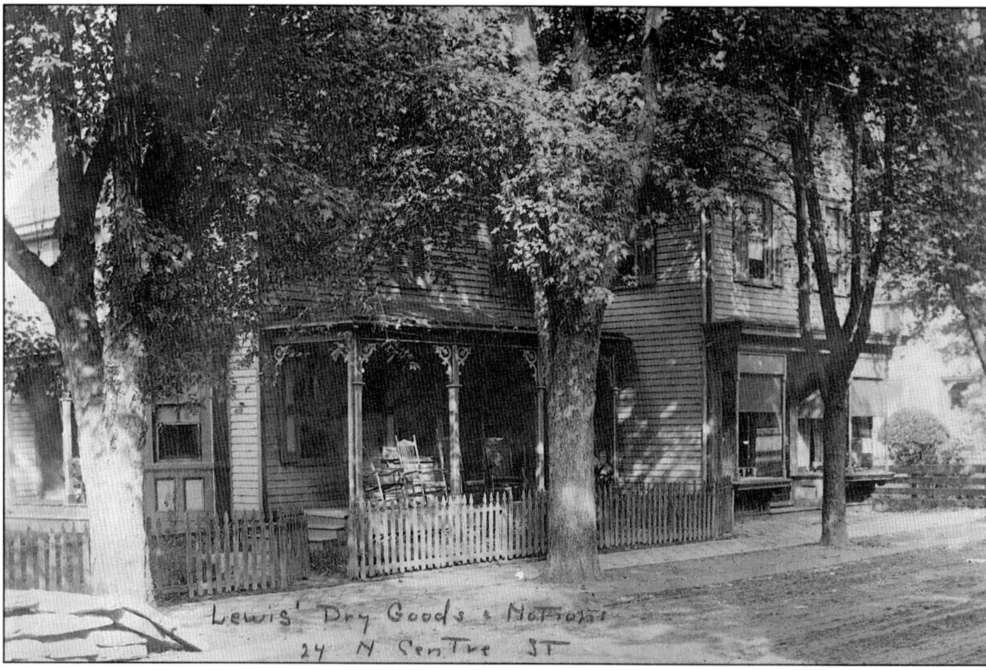

In the late 1800s, Samuel W. Lewis decided to go into business for himself. He swapped land with Dr. John Marcy and opened his store at 24 North Centre Street. Merchantville residents affectionately called it John Wanamaker's of Merchantville. Three of his four daughters, Beth, Reita, and Catherine, assisted in running the business. After Lewis's death, at the age of 75, his daughters continued to run the business until 1949, the 50th anniversary of the Lewis Dry Goods Store. (Merchantville Historical Society.)

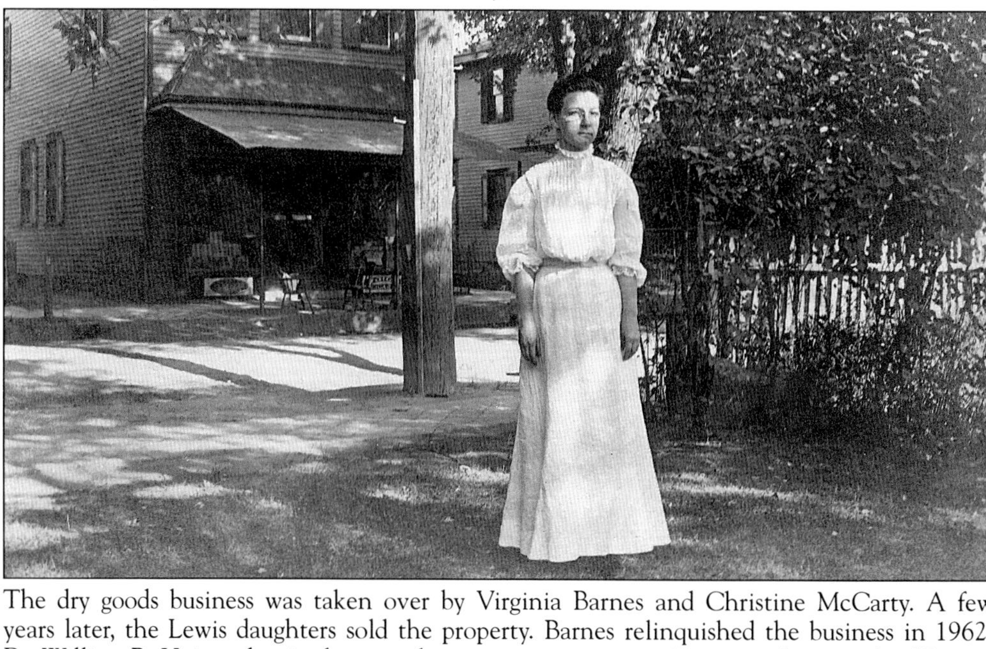

The dry goods business was taken over by Virginia Barnes and Christine McCarty. A few years later, the Lewis daughters sold the property. Barnes relinquished the business in 1962. Dr. William R. Haig, a dentist, became the new property owner. Here is a photograph of Barnes in front of the store before she took over the business. (Tina Schmidt.)

Aunt Charlotte's Candies is a sweet story of success. Over its 80-plus years of operation, the business has been located at Leslie Avenue (in the kitchen, 1920), 6 Linden Avenue (in the basement, 1923), 16 South Centre Street (1926–1931), 16 North Centre Street (1931–1971), and 5 West Maple Avenue (1971–). The Oakfords bear the name of a family prominent in Merchantville since 1888. Charles Oakford started the candy business, and his son Brooks entered the business in 1945. Shown is an evening scene of the store at 16 North Centre Street. (Aunt Charlotte's.)

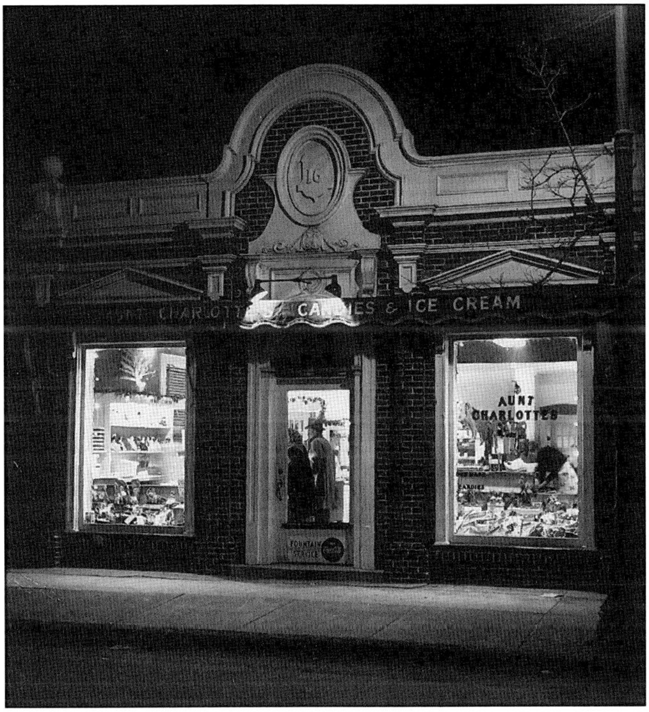

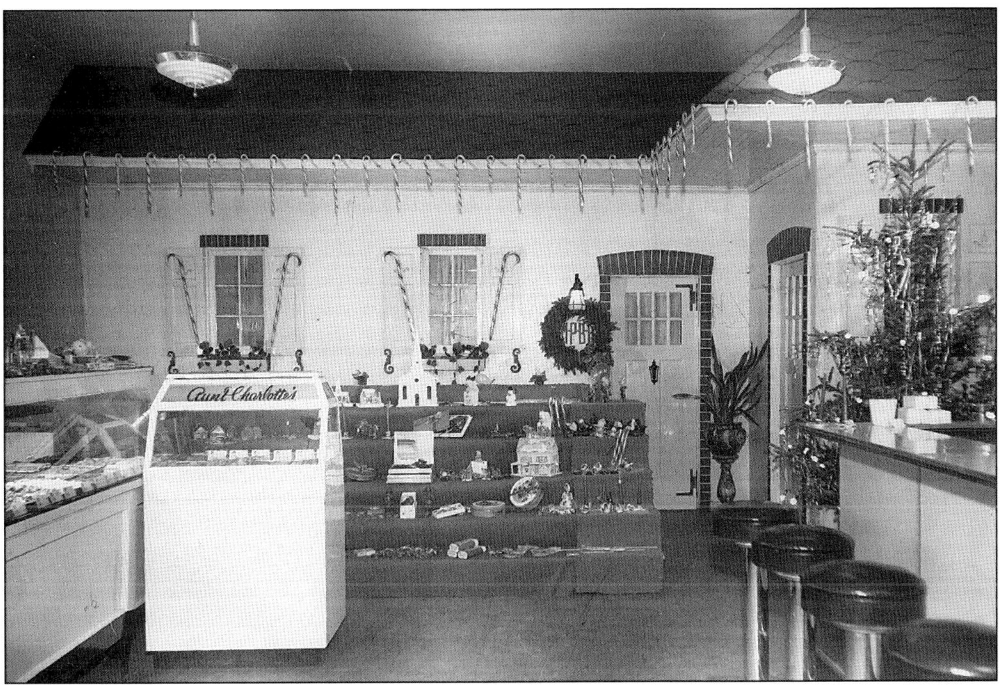

This scene of Aunt Charlotte's welcomed scores of customers at the 16 North Centre Street store. The business was named after Charles Brooks's Aunt Charlotte, his mother's sister. Many townspeople recall the delicious ice cream and confections purchased in the store. Those were the days when the slogan "Delight in Every Bite" was fast becoming a byword to all in the community. (Aunt Charlotte's.)

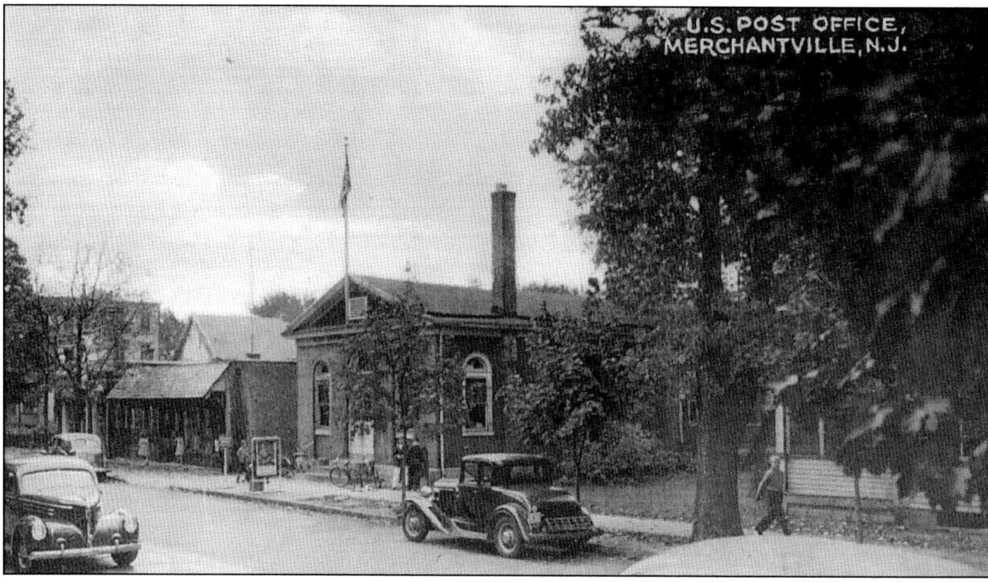

Charles W. Starn was the first postmaster of the new settlement. He operated the post office from his store at 28 West Maple Avenue. The next postmaster was Richard C. Schriener, son-in-law of the first burgess, Matthias Homer. Schriener established his rural emporium and post office in the newly constructed Merchantville Hall. Before the beginning of the 20th century, the post office moved to 9 West Park and then to the north side of Collins and Pancoast Hall at the southwest corner of South Centre Street and West Chestnut Avenue. On December 4, 1909, postmaster Walter Ball opened for business at 22 North Centre Street, which is pictured here. (Tina Schmidt.)

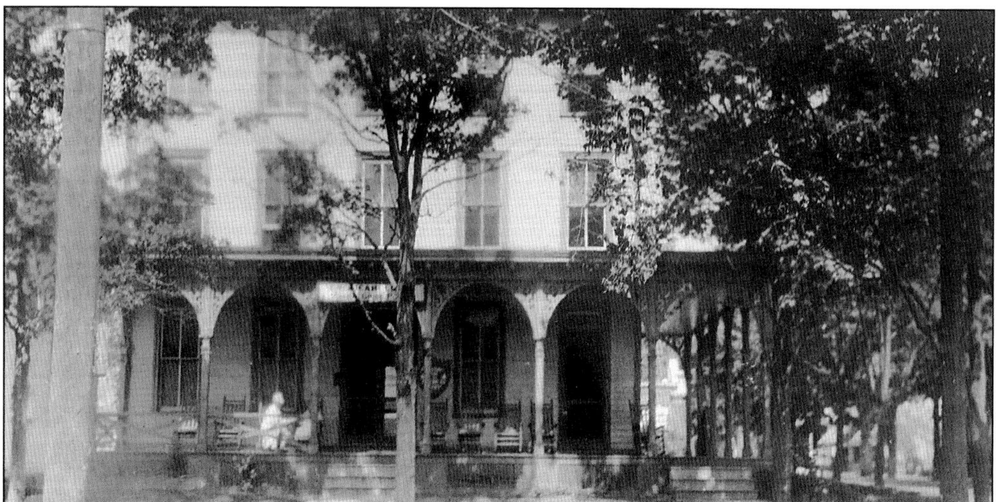

The Frederick W. Grigg Post No. 68 was organized in 1919. Members met at the "Club," William Prickett & Company, which served cigars and had pool and billiard tables at 19 North Centre Street, to discuss the formation of an American Legion Post. On July 26, 1920, Walter J. Staats proposed the purchase of Arthur E. Craig's property, which had sold confectionery and ice cream, at North Centre Street and West Chestnut Avenue. Frederick W. Grigg was killed fighting in World War I on October 12, 1918. The home has been demolished. (Merchantville Historical Society.)

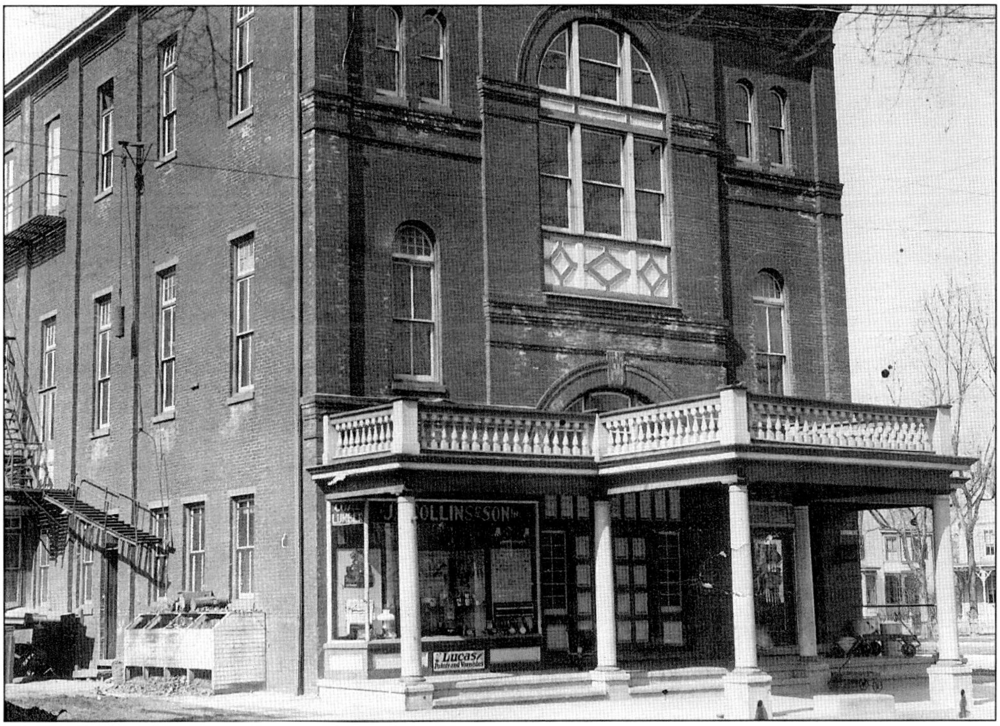

Collins and Pancoast Hall was built in the spring of 1893. The first entertainment there was by the St. Agnes Guild of the Grace Episcopal Church. It was largely used for fashionable entertainment around the beginning of the 20th century. The Merchantville Lodge of Free Masons No. 119 held its meeting the second Friday of every month. J. Collins & Sons sold coal, lumber, paints, and varnishes on the first floor of the hall. The post office was also located here for a short period of time. (Merchantville Historical Society.)

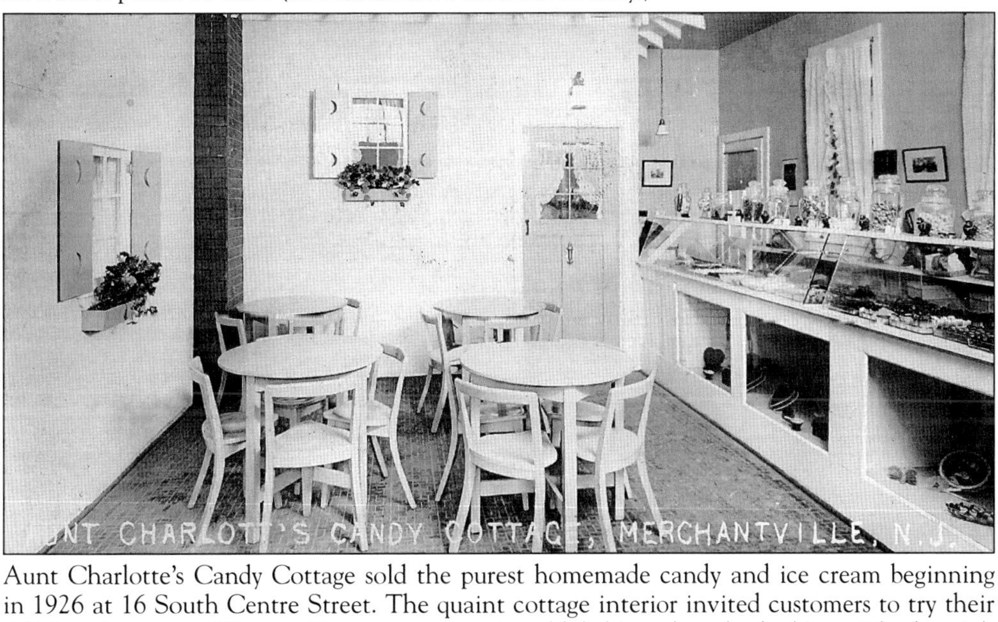

Aunt Charlotte's Candy Cottage sold the purest homemade candy and ice cream beginning in 1926 at 16 South Centre Street. The quaint cottage interior invited customers to try their delicious ice cream. The candies were made using old-fashioned methods. (Aunt Charlotte's.)

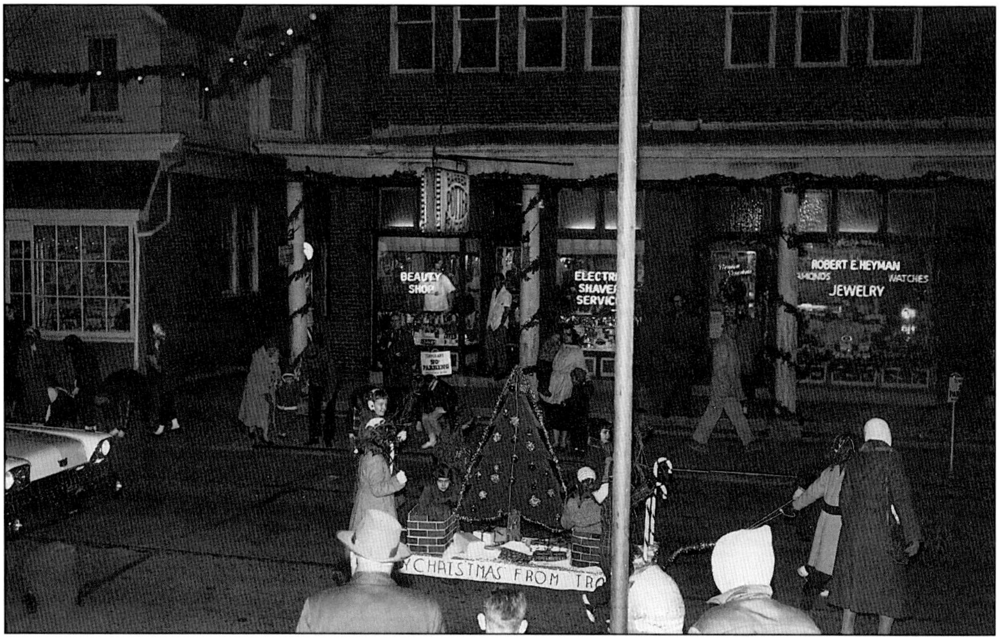

Holiday parades have been a longtime tradition in Merchantville. This particular Christmas parade, at the end of the 1950s, shows the community's involvement. In the background is the building known as Potter's Hall, containing the barbershop, beauty salon, and Robert E. Heyman's jewelry store. (Aunt Charlotte's.)

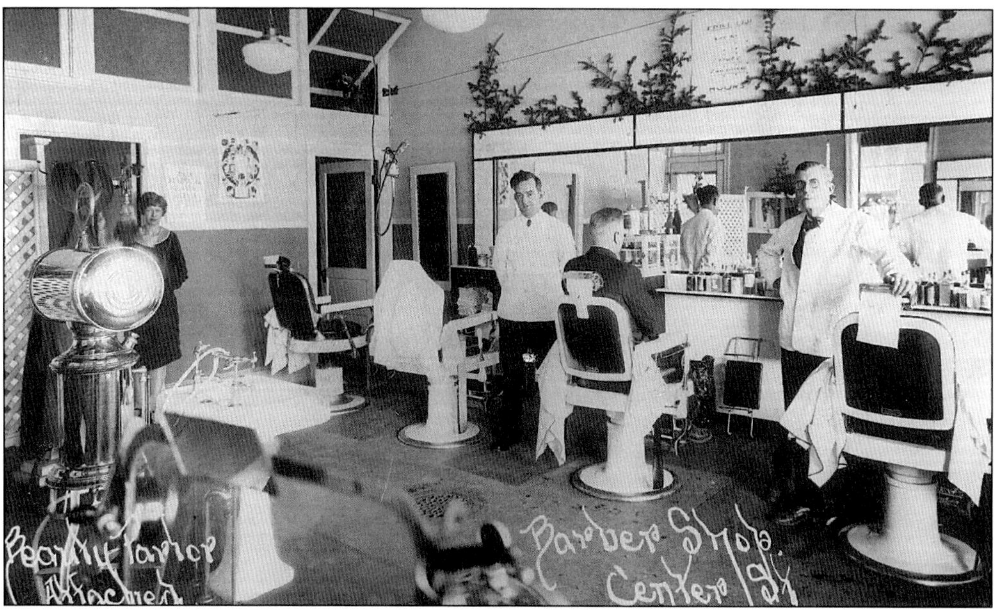

Potter's Barbershop, pictured here in the late 1920s, was located in Potter's Hall, which was built in 1919 at 14 South Centre Street. In the early 1900s, Whitelock's Barbershop was situated between 14 and 18 South Centre Street. Many barbershops operated here. Early records show that William Knehr's barbershop opened in 1898 and was advertised as "the practical haircutter." On the wall of the shop is the 1928 fishing and gaming license. (Merchantville Historical Society.)

Richard E. Neumann's Upholstery Store operated at 20 South Centre Street. In the Merchantville directory of 1898, Neumann advertised carpets filled and laid, furniture and mattresses reupholstered, and window shades and window awnings made to order. Prior to being on South Centre Street, Neumann is listed on Chapel Avenue in the 1891 Presbyterian church cookbook. (Merchantville Historical Society.)

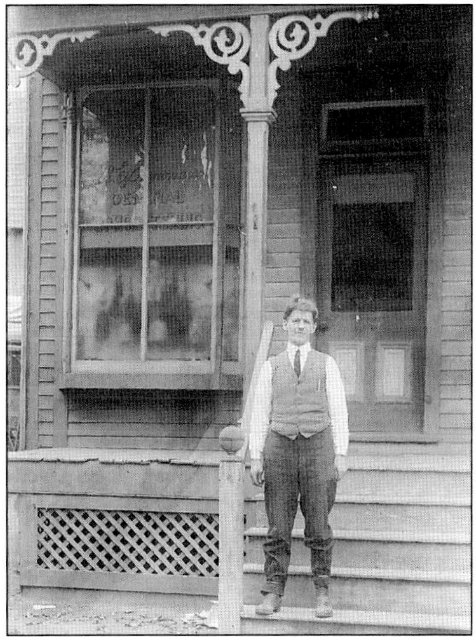

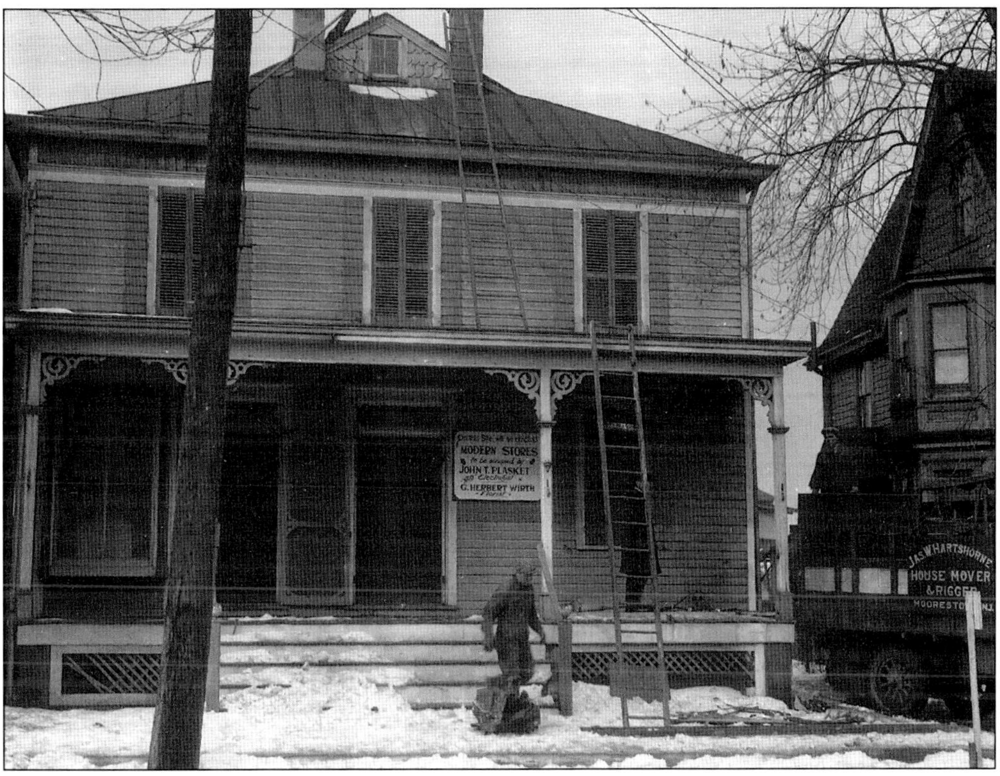

The house at 20–22 South Centre Street is being demolished to make way for a new building. A modern building was erected on the site and occupied by John T. Plasket and G. Herbert Wirth, florist. Neumann Upholstery had occupied the 20 South Centre Street portion of the house. This relocation of businesses took place in 1927. Wirth had previously been located at 37 South Centre Street. (Merchantville Historical Society.)

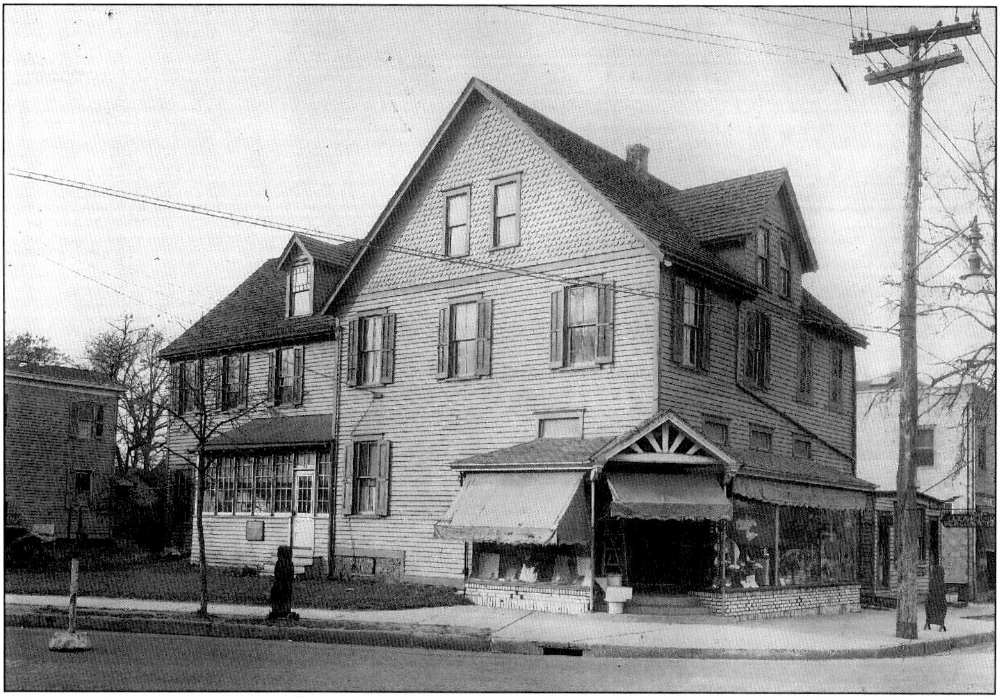

The People's Store, opened in 1908 by Louis Feinberg, had been operated previously as a dry goods store by the family of Feinberg's wife. Situated on the corner of South Centre Street and West Park Avenue, the store sold dry goods, children's clothing, hats, shoes, trunks, and more. Daughter Fanny Feinberg played piano accompaniment at the movie house at 15 South Centre Street. Feinberg was in business until 1925. The building was then torn down and replaced by the Merchantville Trust Company. (Merchantville Historical Society.)

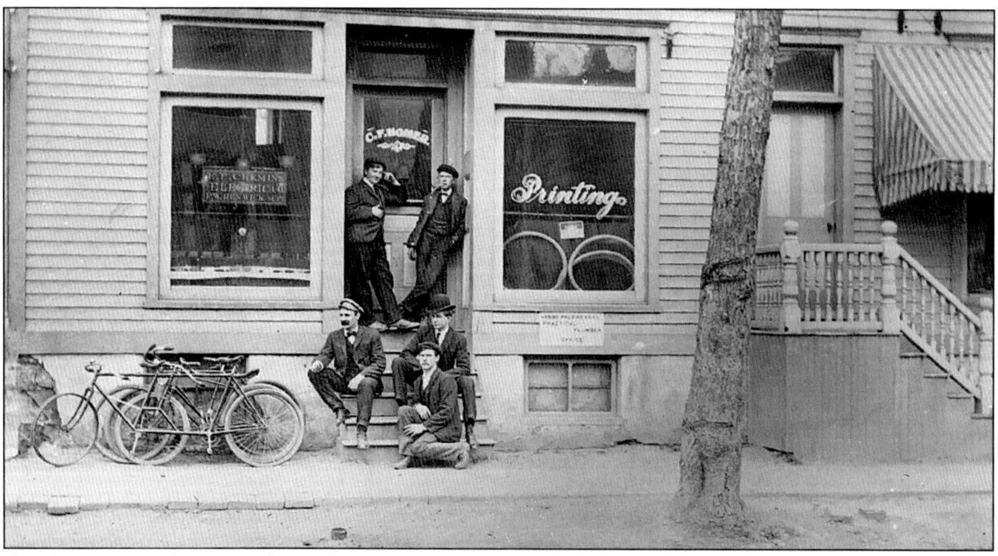

At 5 West Park were the offices of C.F. Homer Printing, F.W. Renwick Realty, and H. Palfreyman, plumber. The building was adjacent to Feinberg's Dry Goods. After the demolition of this office building, the Straub Building was constructed and is still standing. (Merchantville Historical Society.)

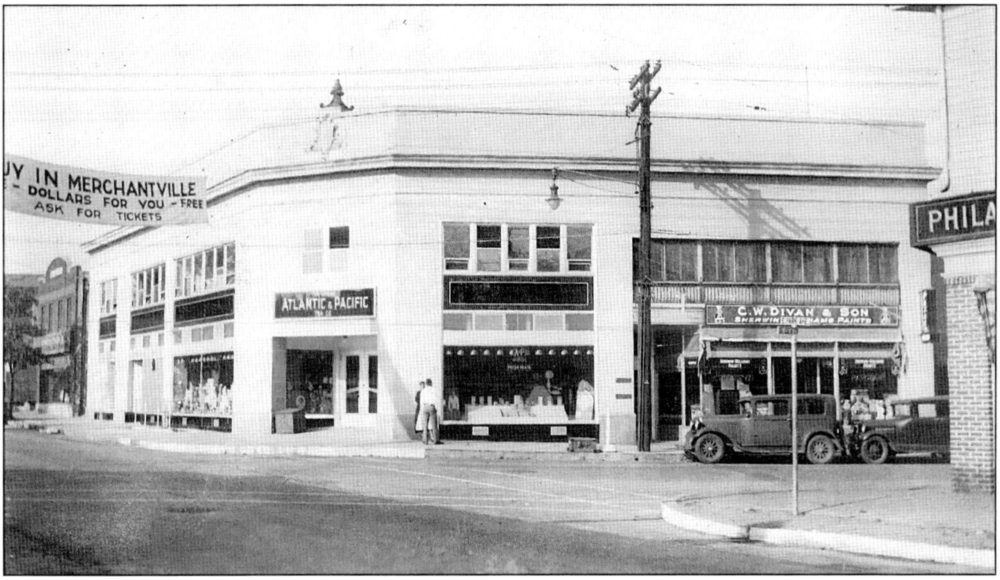

In 1931, as a result of the stock market collapse, Merchantville Trust Company merged with the First National Bank and moved to 9 South Centre Street. The Atlantic & Pacific Tea Company (A & P) took over the bank's former location at the corner of South Centre Street and West Park Avenue. C.W. Divan & Son is shown next to the A & P. Note the banner over West Park Street. It advertises the "free dollars" campaign, which encouraged shoppers to buy the goods in Merchantville. In the far left of the photograph is the Straub Building, at 5 West Park Avenue. Across South Centre Street is the Philadelphia Fruit Market. The Merchantville 5 & 10 operated at this location for many years after the A & P. (Merchantville Historical Society.)

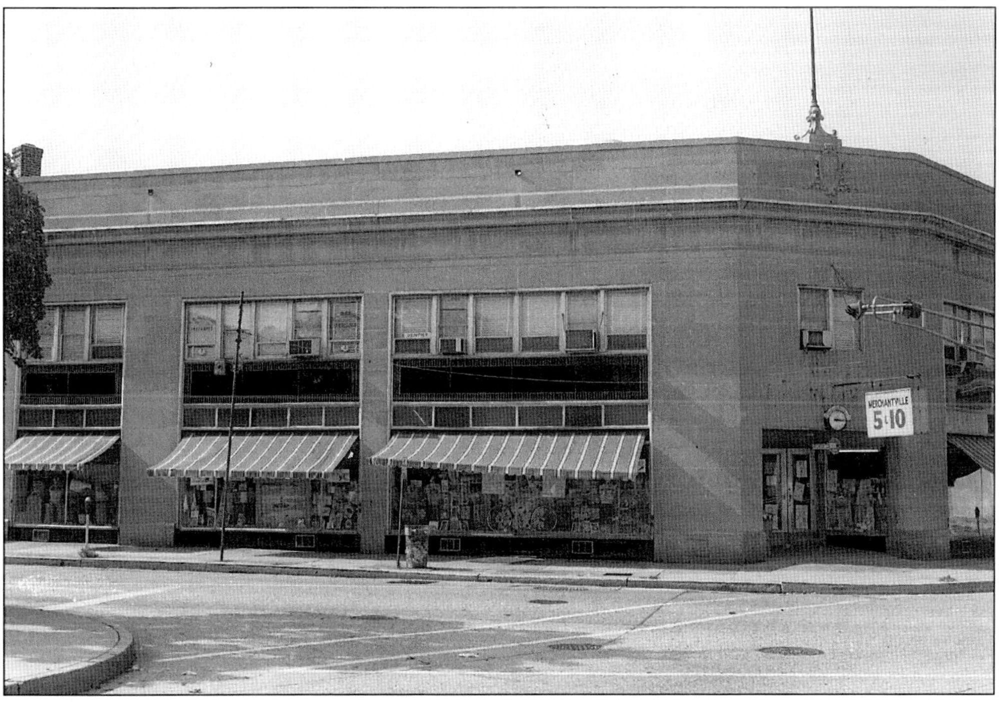

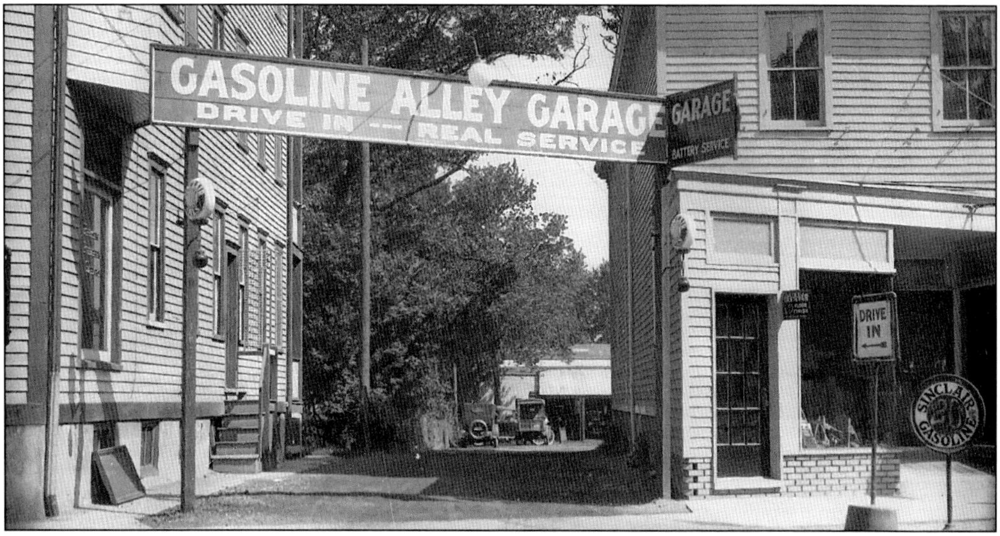

Next to the Kurkian Building, on West Park Avenue, was the Gasoline Alley Garage. With the increasing popularity of the automobile, providing gasoline, batteries, and other services on automobiles became very important. Sinclair Gasoline was sold for 20¢ a gallon. Over the entrance was a sign that read, "Drive in—Real service." (Vernon Collins.)

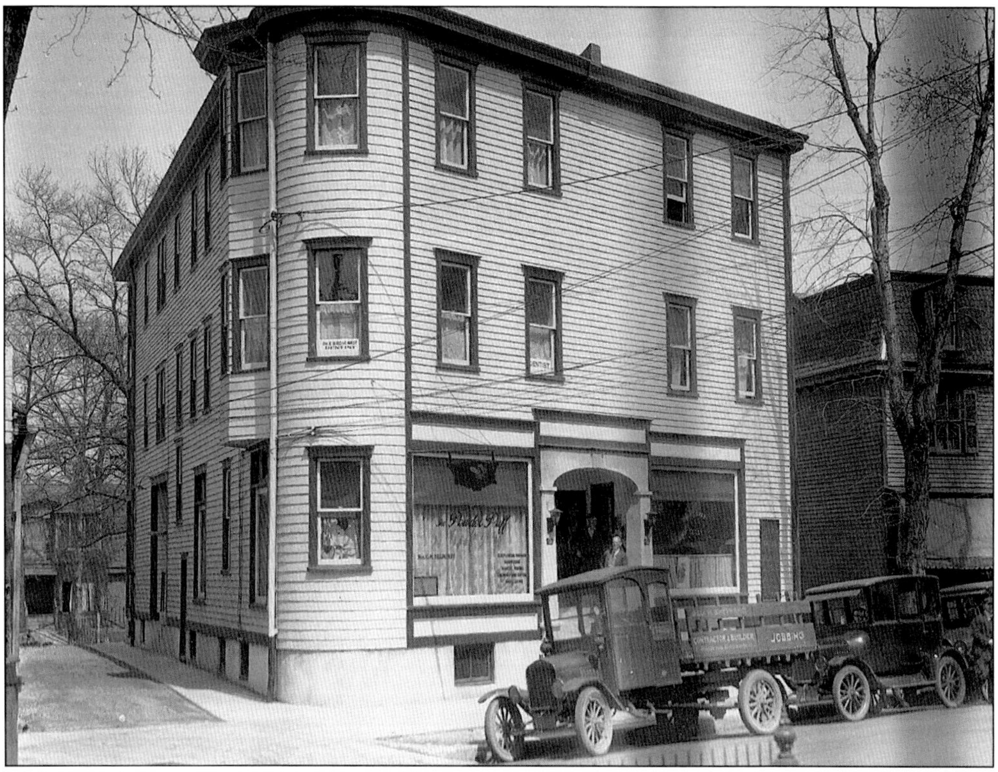

Walter Kurkian moved to Merchantville in 1926 and went into the dry-cleaning business. The business grew into a chain of four stores under his direction. The building was located at 17 West Park Avenue and advertised that for quality and dependable cleaning, pressing, repairing, and dying service, Kurkian Brothers was the place. (Merchantville Historical Society.)

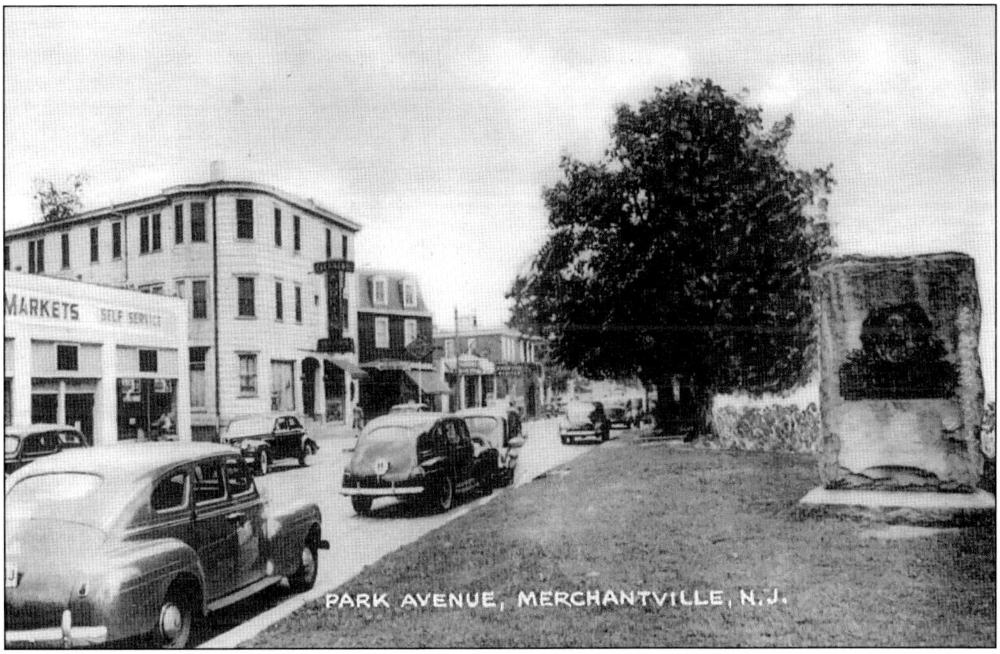

West Park Avenue housed stores on the odd-numbered side of the street and a small park area on the opposite side. A large block of granite sits in the triangular plot of grass. It is a tribute to a village doctor, David Hedding Bartine, born in 1841. In February 1866, he came to Merchantville and opened his first office. His fellow townspeople erected the monument in memory of the first guardian of their health. (Merchantville Historical Society.)

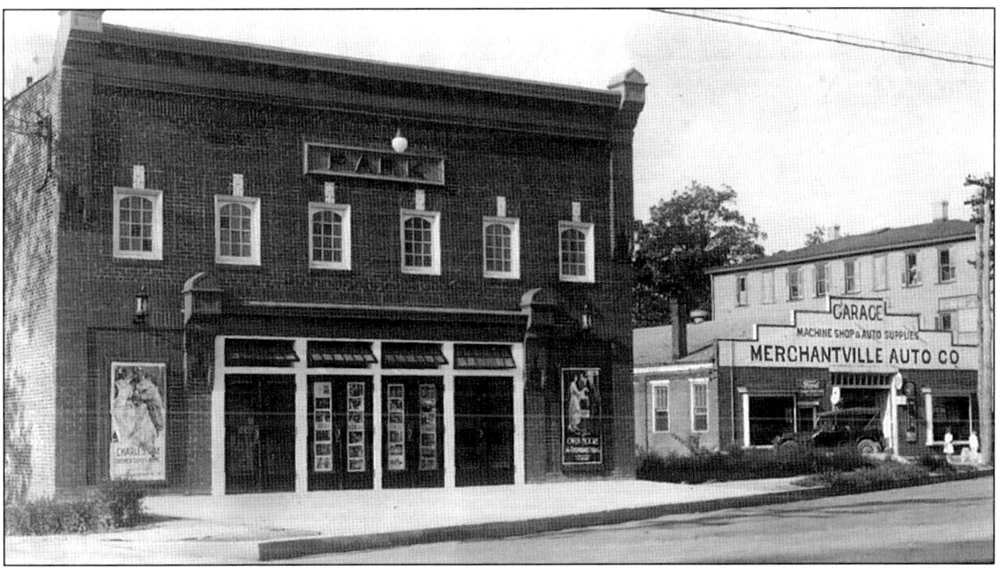

The Park Avenue Theatre, 31 West Park Avenue, the second movie house, was opened on August 20, 1920. It boasted a fine pipe organ, and the program was changed daily. Many residents recall that during the 1930s, pieces of china were given out during each performance. It took quite some time to accumulate a set of dishes. The theater was managed by Mark Bulifant. The old Park Theatre was discontinued as a movie house many years ago. Since that time, it has been used as a commercial property. (Merchantville Historical Society.)

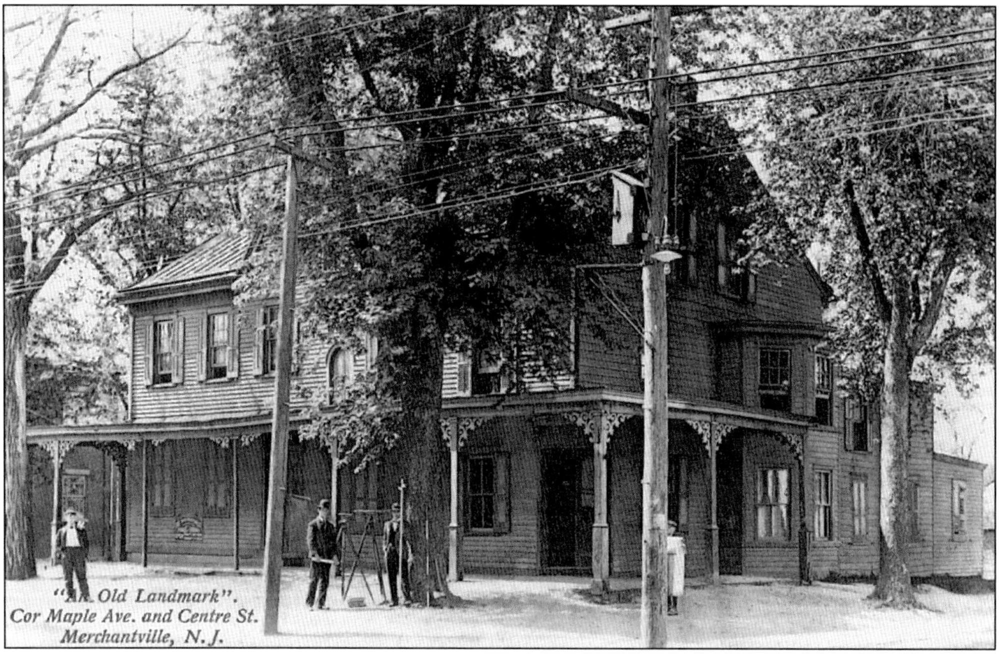

The Stockton House was originally a country inn built *c.* 1845. It was situated at the corner of West Maple Avenue and South Centre Street. The inn was sold to Benny Martin in 1856. The last proprietor was William Pancoast. The establishment advertised "board by day, week or month." A livery stable was attached. In November 1902, it was bought to be used as the municipal building and was demolished in 1928. (Tina Schmidt.)

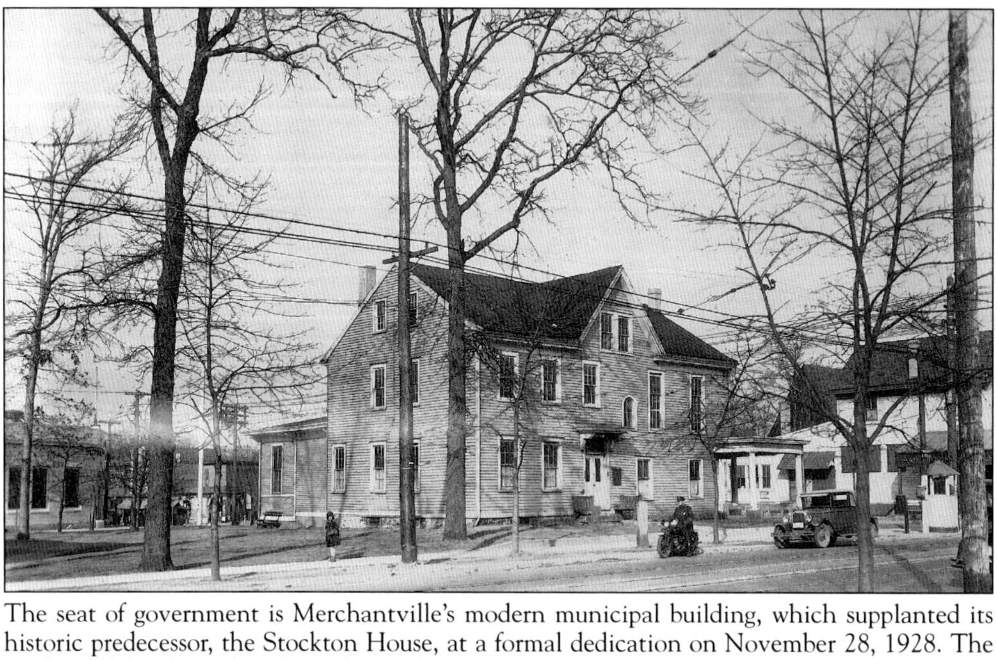

The seat of government is Merchantville's modern municipal building, which supplanted its historic predecessor, the Stockton House, at a formal dedication on November 28, 1928. The modern edifice fittingly reflects the public spirit of the community and sets a mark for many of the more populous boroughs of South Jersey. In its design and execution were combined simple, dignified beauty and lasting utility. (Merchantville Historical Society.)

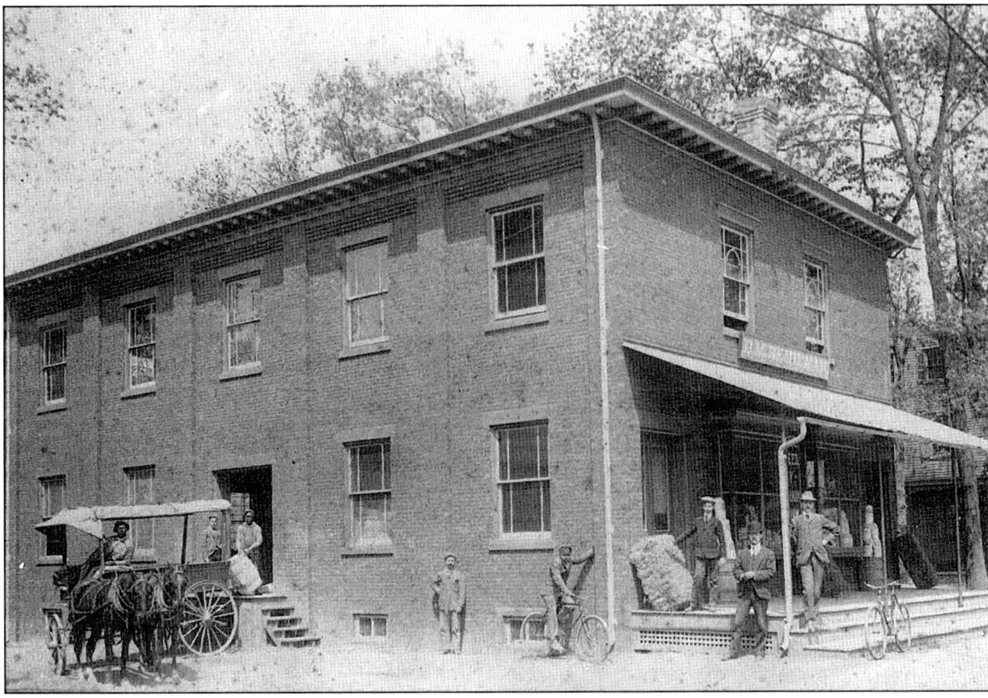

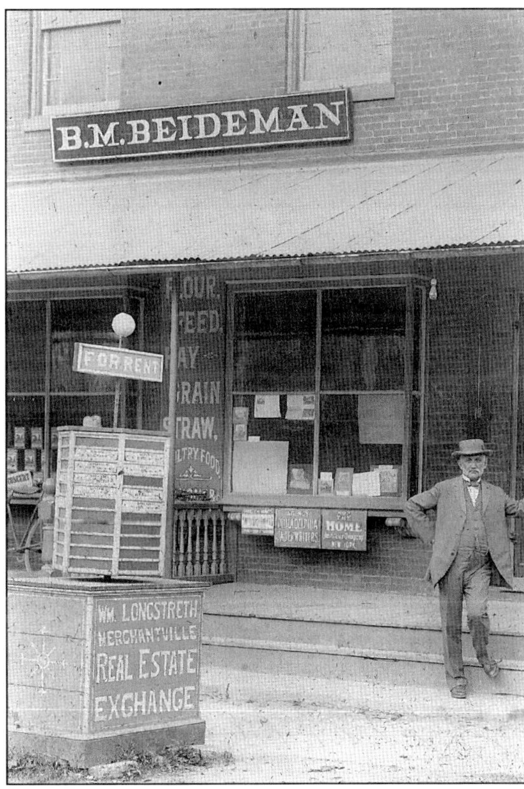

B. Melvin Beideman—dealer in flour, hay, and grain—started in business at the beginning of the 20th century. He originally rented a section of Merchantville Hall. In 1901, a brick section was added at 5 West Maple Avenue. The front was rented to William Longstreth, who was the 10th mayor, from March 14, 1904 to January 1, 1913. On the facade of the building are signs for the Home Insurance Company and the Philadelphia Underwriters. Casper Beideman had medical offices there between 1929 and 1936. In the 1960s, the building was used for Aunt Jean's Luncheonette and in 1971 became the home of Aunt Charlotte's Candies. (Merchantville Historical Society.)

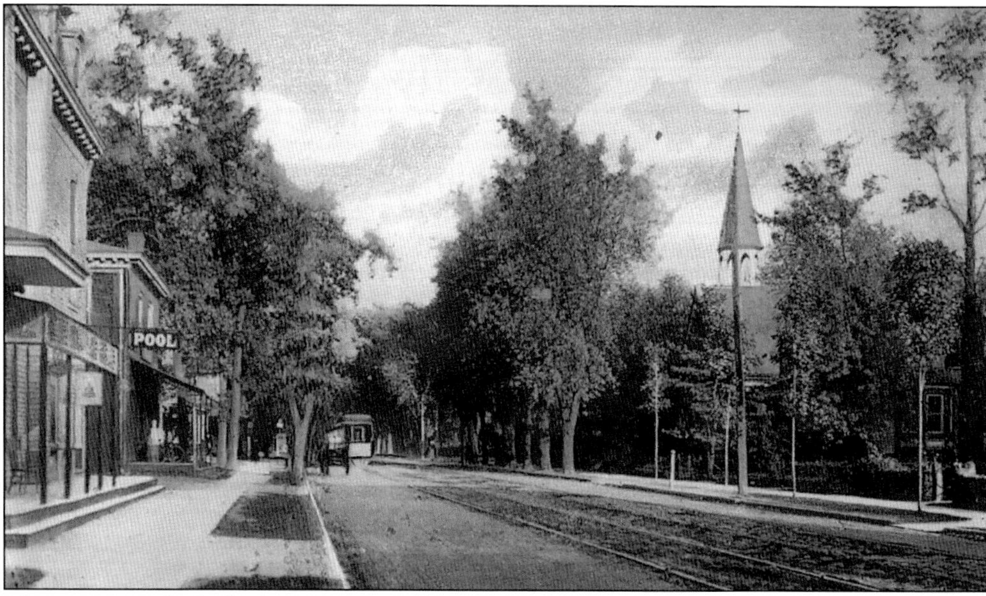

This scene is of Maple Avenue west of Centre Street. Merchantville Hall is on the left next to Beideman's. Hanging from the front porch of the hall is a pool and a telephone sign. The first switchboard in the borough, in 1874, was in the drugstore of Dr. Charles H. Jennings at 17 West Park Avenue. It moved to Blankenbush Pharmacy in 1893. In 1907, it came to the first floor of Merchantville Hall. Note the trolley and tracks on Maple Avenue and the First Presbyterian Church across the street on the right. (Tina Schmidt.)

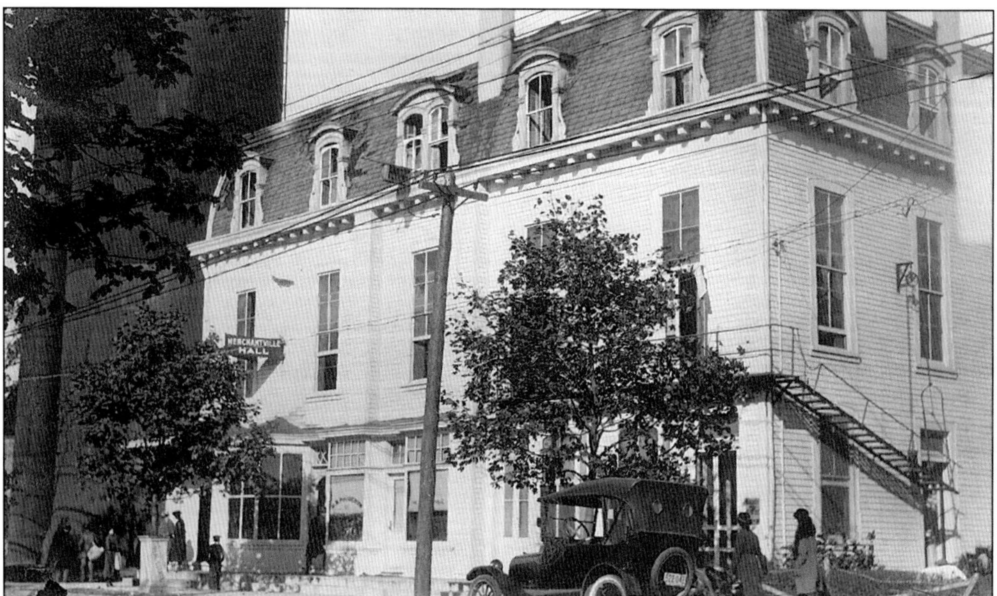

The three-story Merchantville Hall was completed in 1871. It housed a general store and post office at one time. The second floor had an auditorium, and the hall was used for meetings, dances, Masonic activities, and fraternal organization gatherings. From 1874 until 1902, the first floor was the municipal headquarters. The telephone company was there from 1907 until 1926. A fire destroyed the third floor in 1922. (Merchantville Historical Society.)

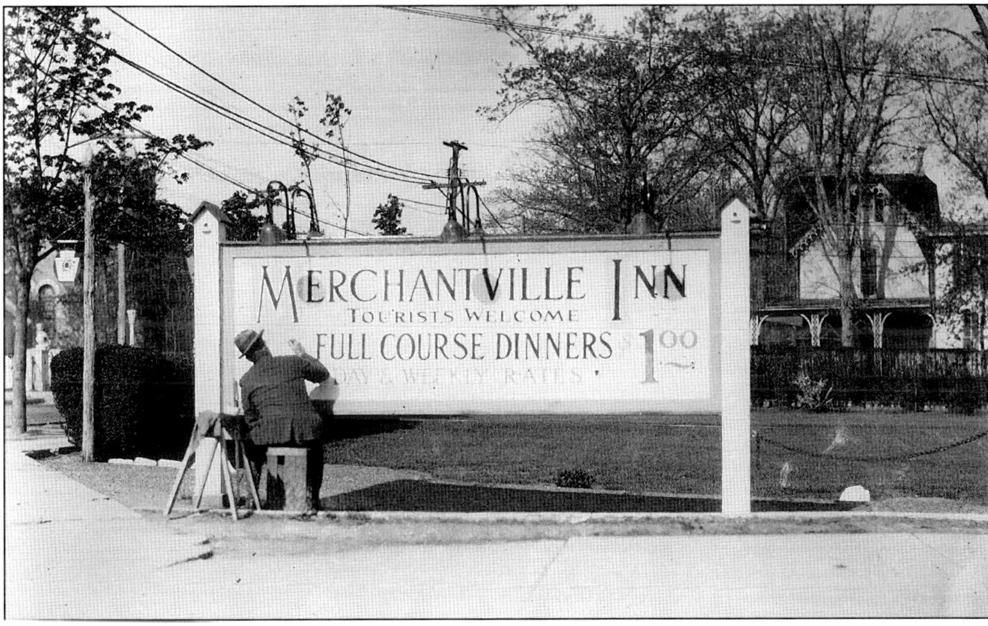

The Merchantville Inn, formerly the Oak Grove Inn, was located at the northeast corner of West Maple and Alexander Avenues. Built in 1868 by Elijah Cattell as a boys' school, it later became a summer boardinghouse. In 1900, William W. Pancoast purchased the building and moved from the Stockton Inn. The inn had the only liquor license in Merchantville. After 1919, it operated as a boardinghouse. Years after, residents recalled the delicious meals served there. (Merchantville Historical Society.)

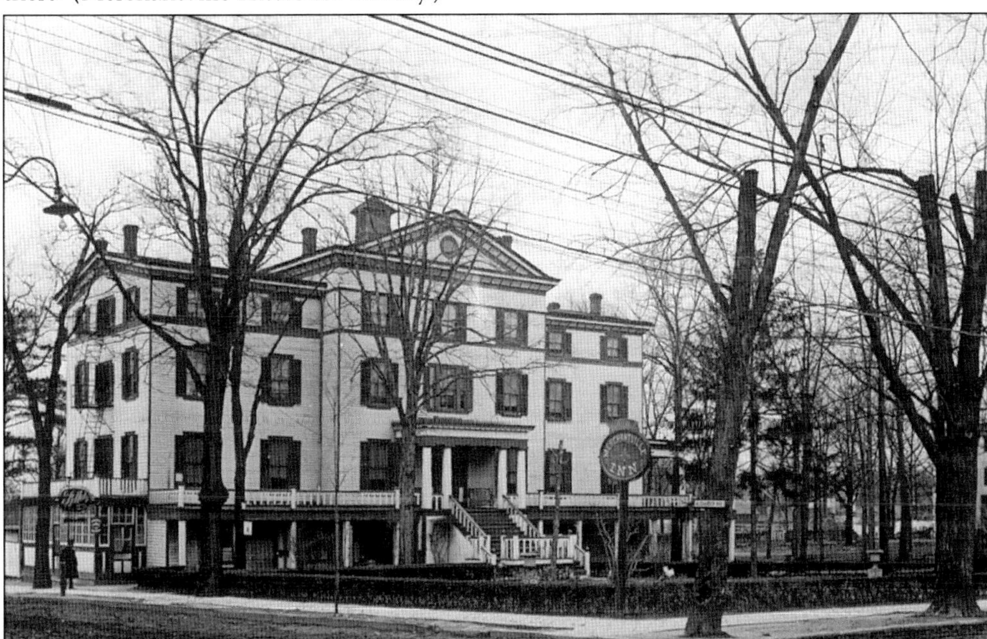

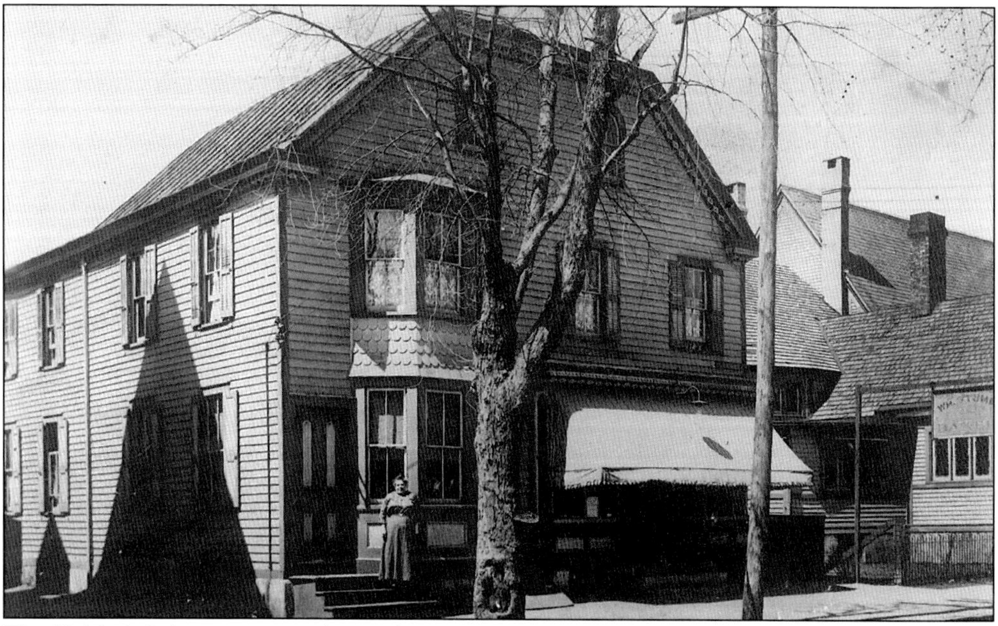

The Kohler's Bakery was once located at 112 South Centre Street but was moved when it was purchased by William Stumm in 1903. Stumm delivered both wholesale and retail goods by horse-drawn wagon as far as 30 miles from Merchantville. The business was sold in 1926 but, when the new owner did not succeed, the business returned to the Stumm family. In 1942, it converted to a grocery and a luncheonette. In the early 1950s, the First Presbyterian Church purchased the property. (Merchantville Historical Society.)

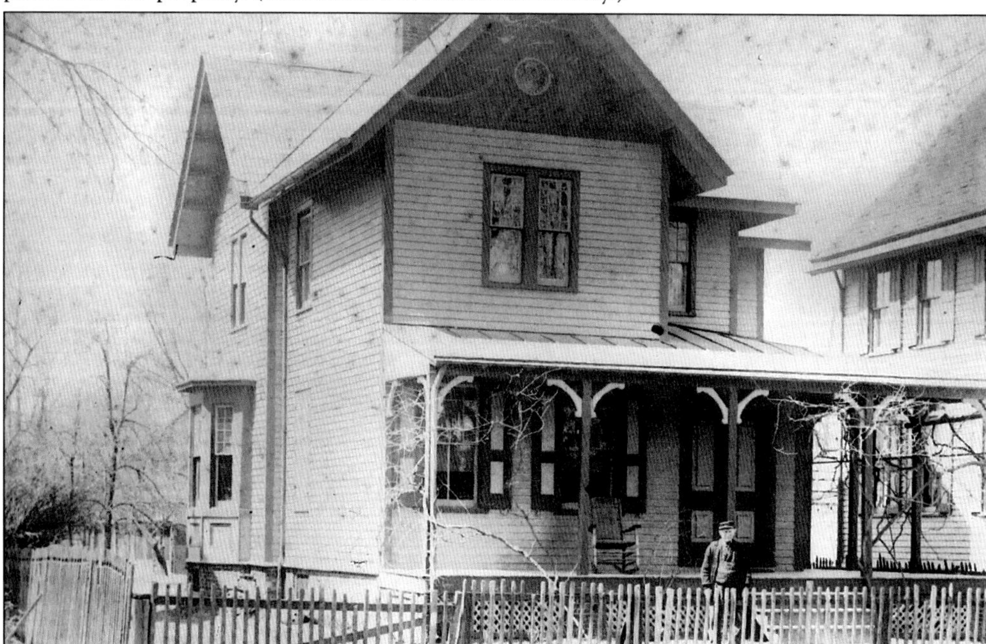

The home of Conrad Demmy stood at 120 South Centre Street at the present site of the Merchantville School parking lot. Demmy was a butcher in the winter and a farmer in the summer. (Merchantville Historical Society.)

On June 6, 1900, Anna Mae Clark (center) graduated from Merchantville School. In the beginning of the 1900s, the school housed elementary through the 10th grades. Later, Clark married florist Leonard Smith. (Merchantville Historical Society.)

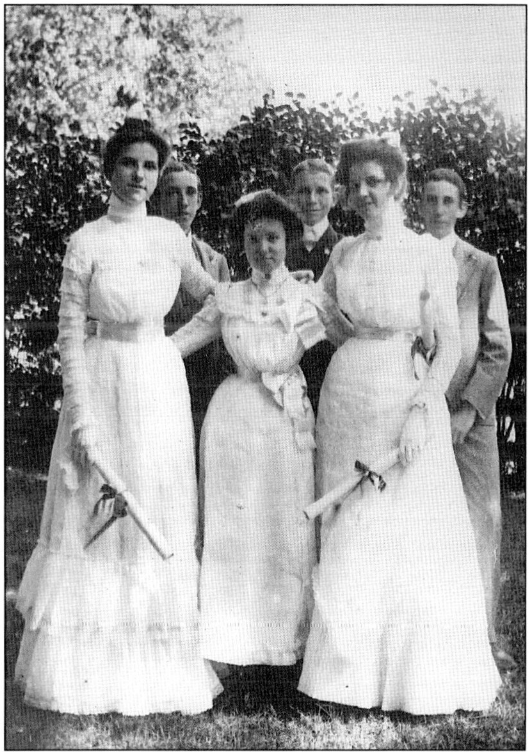

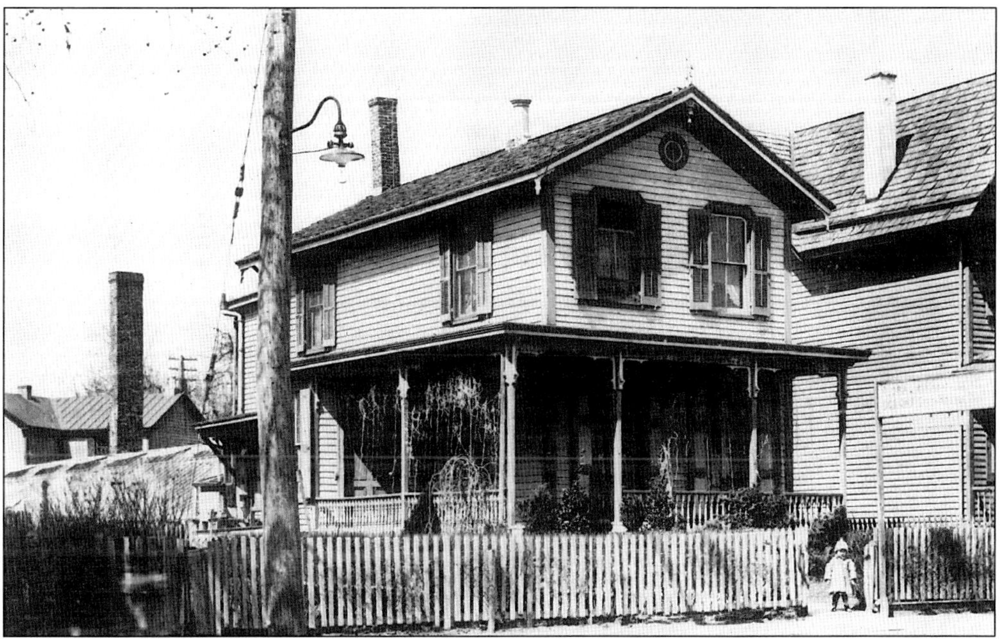

Smith Florists, 156 South Centre Street, began in 1903 and was operated by Leonard J. Smith, with the help of his family. Katherine and Harry Smith, his children, ran the shop after him. In addition to the greenhouse in the back, there was a nursery across the street. The Smiths specialized in "social decorations, wedding floral designs, hedges, trees and shrubs." (Merchantville Historical Society.)

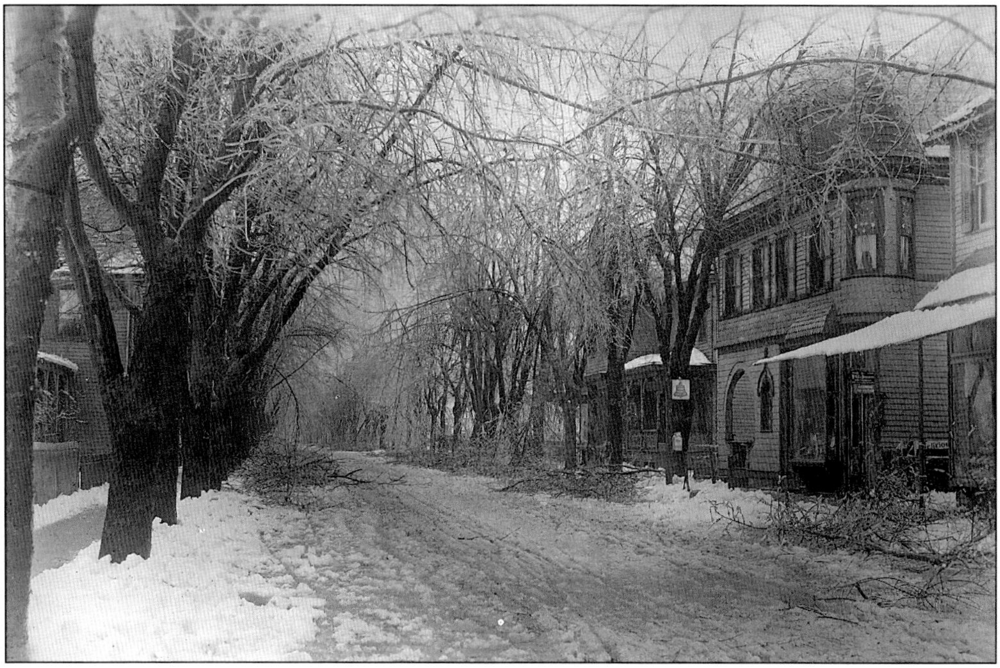

Kohlerman's Drug Store *c.* 1894 was operated by J. William Kohlerman at 21 North Centre Street. It also housed one of the early telephone exchanges. Kohlerman's sold powders that relieved neuralgic headaches in minutes. Bernard Blankenbush bought the store in 1924, and Milton Lev bought it in 1964. The building still stands today. (Merchantville Historical Society.)

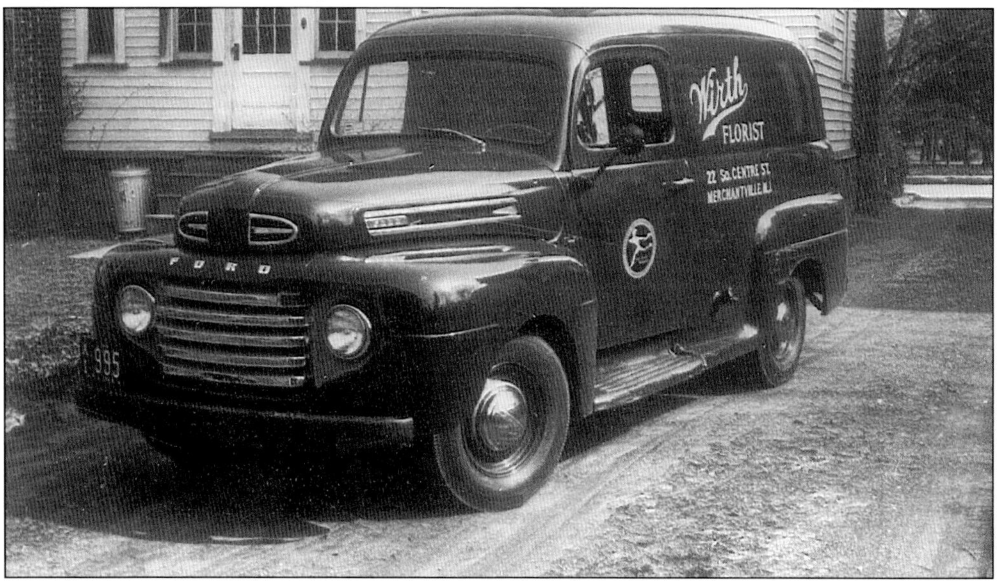

Wirth Florist is one of the oldest businesses in the borough. Herbert Wirth Sr. founded his shop in 1920 in the family home on Chestnut Street. It came to its current location at 22 South Centre Street in 1927. Wirth's son and daughter-in-law, Herb Jr. and Noel, took over. Then, the third generation, Karl, came to manage the business. The shop handles about 10,000 floral arrangements each year. This anchor store is what is so great about a small downtown. (Karl Wirth.)

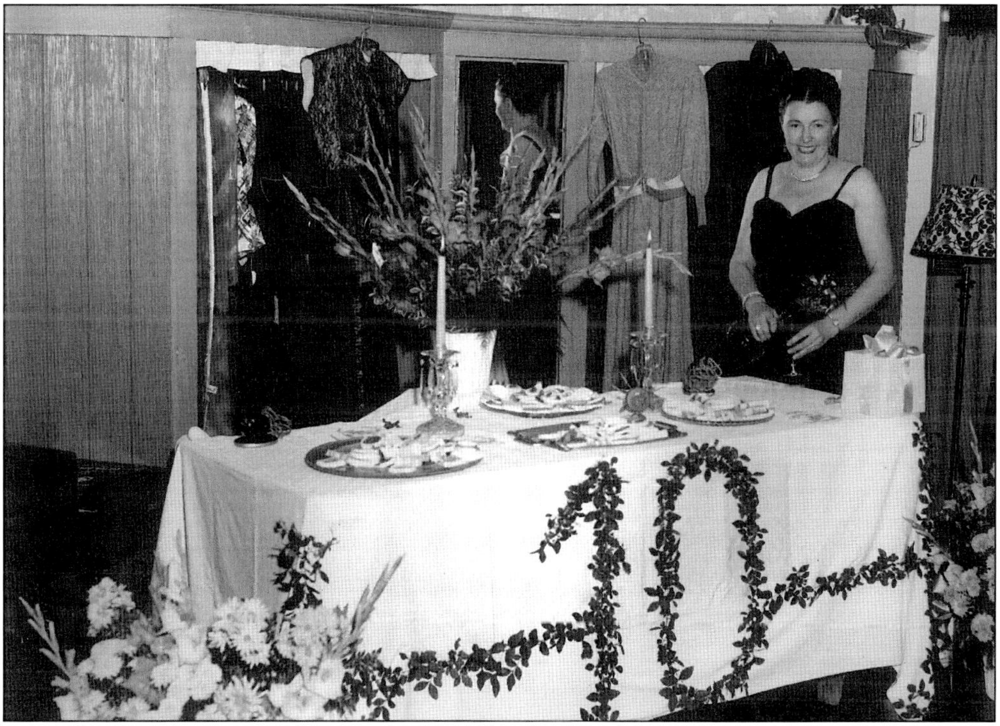

Benoit's Dress Shop was located at 19 North Centre Street. In the 1940s and 1950s, ladies could select from a lovely array of clothing for most any event. Young ladies were able to purchase special-occasion dresses for graduations, dances, or other events. Special attention was paid to all the details during the celebration of Anna Benoit's 10th anniversary in business. (Bobbi Stagliano; Aunt Charlotte's.)

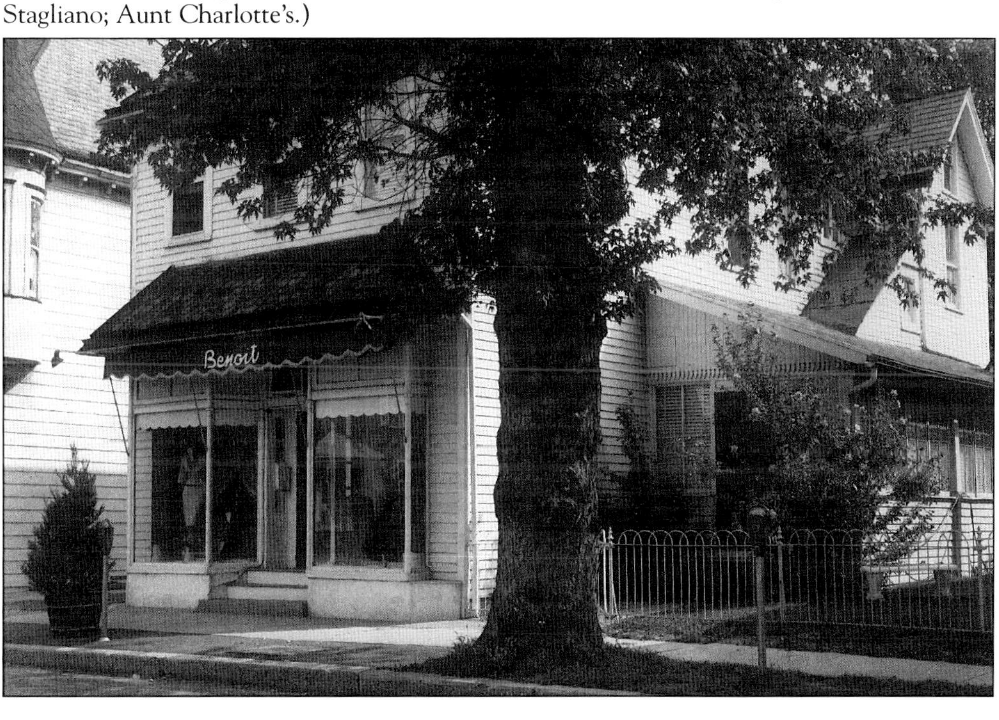

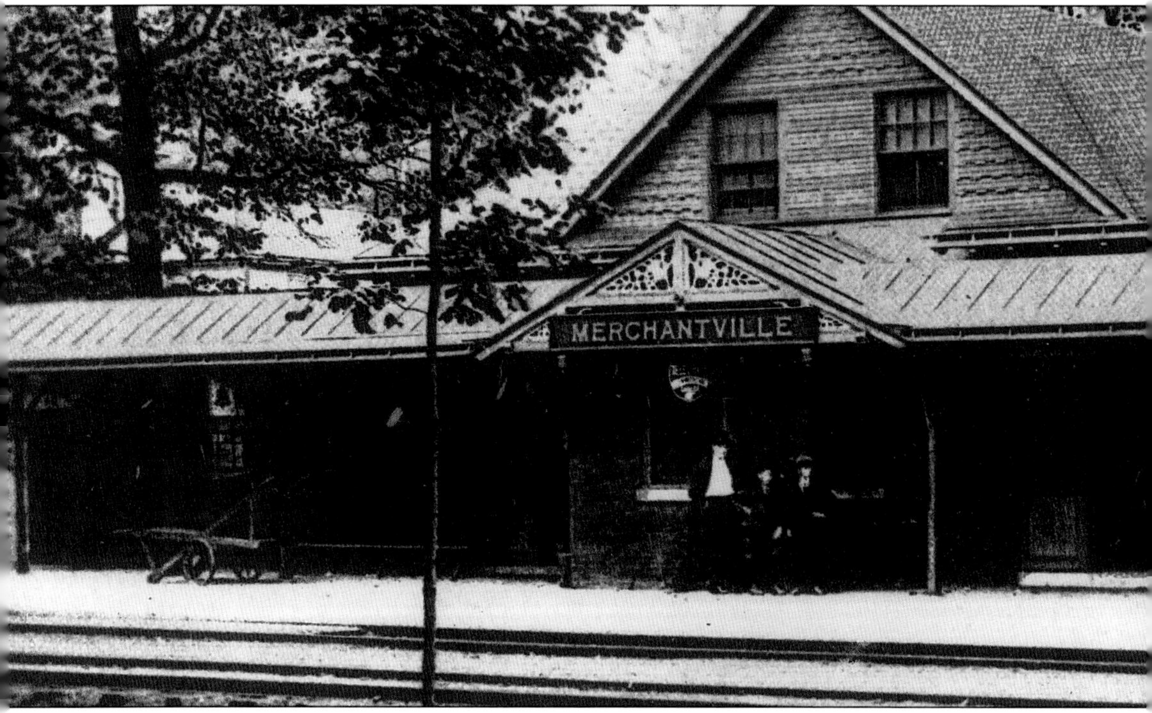

The development of Victorian Merchantville can be linked to the ease of transportation allowed by the railways. Philadelphians were able to live in a pleasant new development while commuting easily to the city for their business. The one-and-a-half-story train station was the center of life in the newly developed town. Its inviting porch provided protected areas for

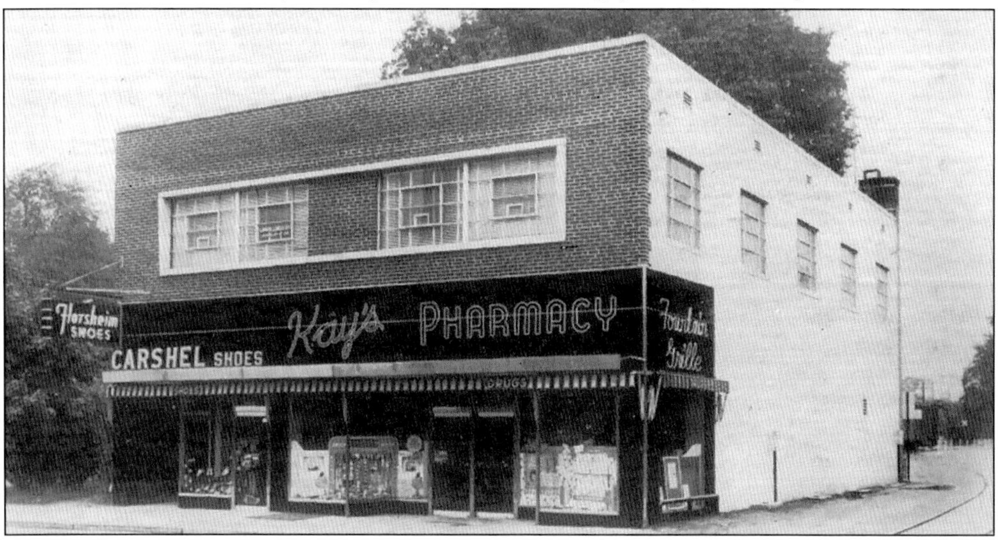

On the south side of the railroad tracks along the east side of South Centre was Kay's Pharmacy, located in the Kay Building, which housed the newest and most modern offices and stores. Also, at this location was Carshel Shoes, which carried the Florsheim line. Nothing could compare to sitting at the soda fountain and savoring a delicious chocolate ice-cream soda with whipped cream and a cherry. The building was extensively remodeled after it ceased to be Kay's. (Tina Schmidt.)

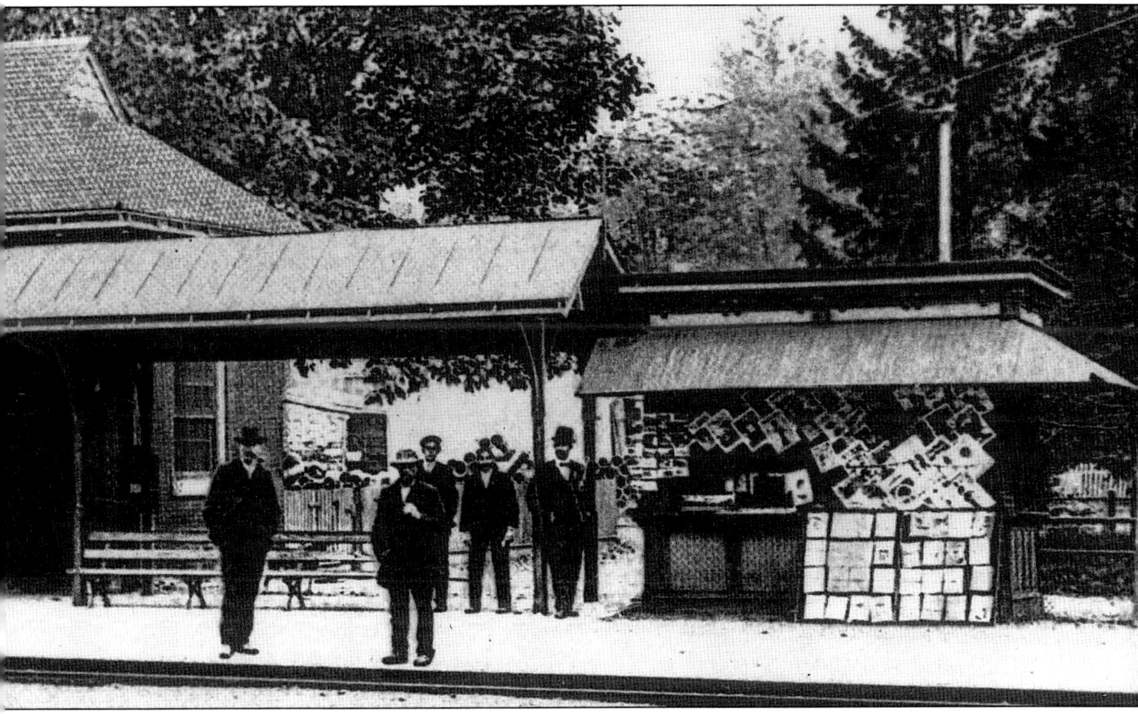

awaiting trains. The ticket office was located in the central area with freight and passenger waiting rooms on either side. At one time, the trainmaster lived on the second floor with his family. Note the carved griffins in the tympanum, a symbol of the Pennsylvania Railroad. (Merchantville Historical Society.)

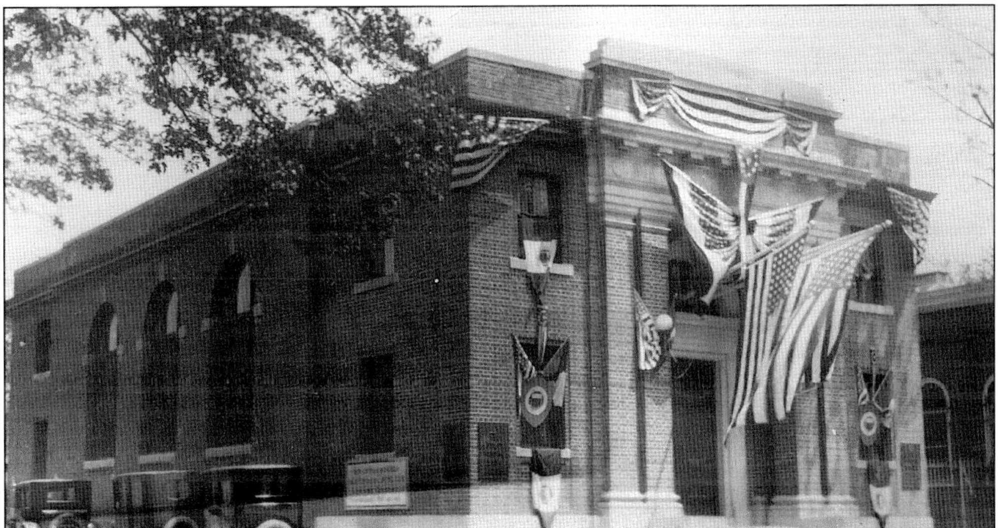

The First National Bank was established in 1906 and had deposits of $47,000 at the end of that year. The ground adjoined Ellis Parker's grocery at 11 South Centre Street. The bank prospered and, in the early 1920s, moved to a new brick building at 9 South Centre Street. After mergers with Merchantville Bank and Trust Company and Colonial National Bank, it became MidLantic Bank/South. Today it is PNC. (Merchantville Historical Society.)

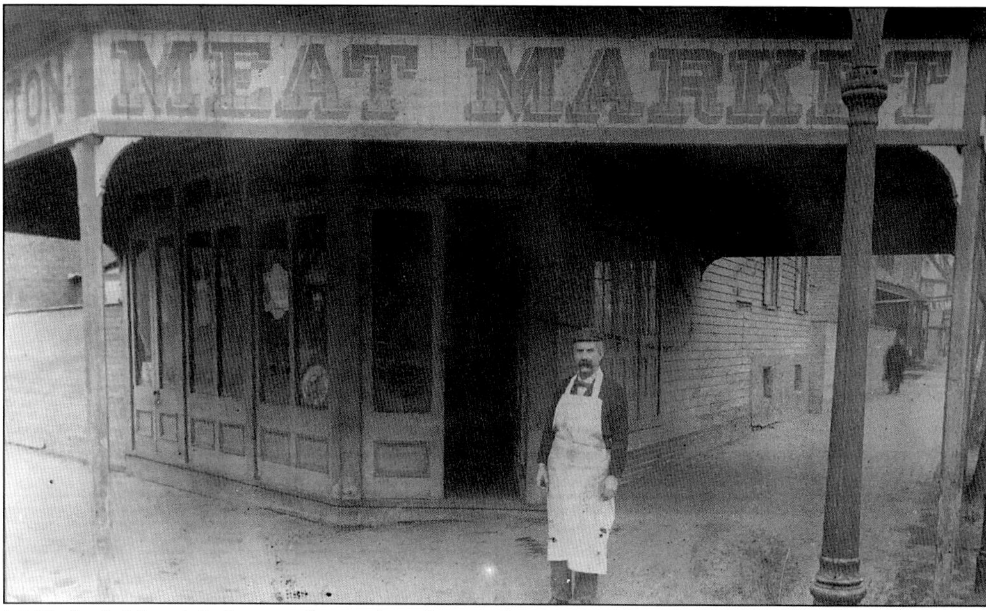

McFarlan's Meat Market was located at the northeast corner of Park Avenue and South Centre Street. William McFarlan was president of the Niagara Fire Company, the eighth postmaster, and a merchant. By 1911, MacFarlan had left his meat market and was a coal dealer at 27 North Centre Street. In the very early 1900s, Charley Linghing had operated a laundry at this corner. (Merchantville Historical Society.)

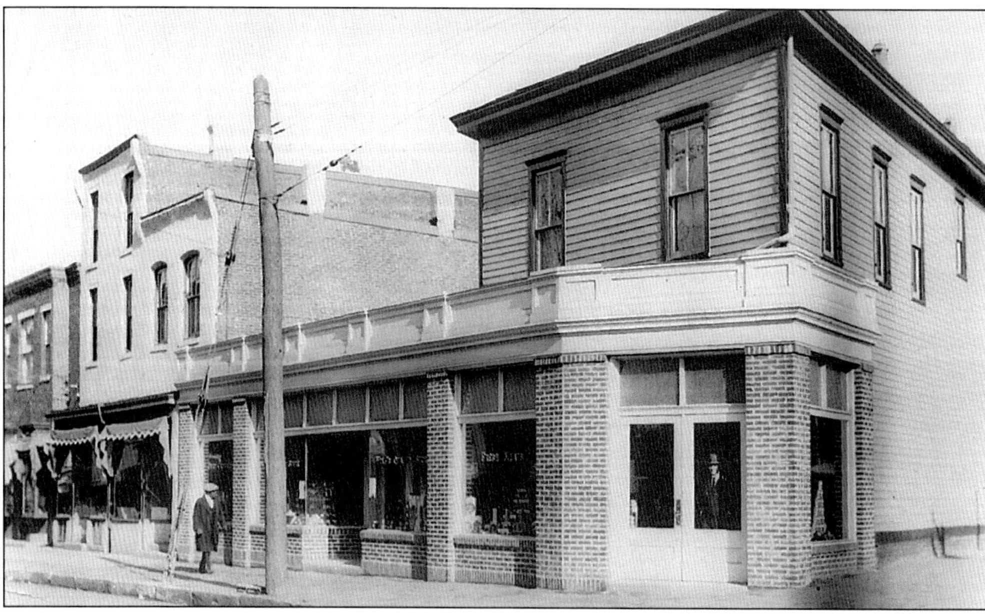

For scores of years, the Philadelphia Fruit Market has served the community at the corner of South Centre Street and East Park Avenue. In the 1950s, Herman and Al Rosen really made the market the institution that it is today. There were several owners over the years. The current owner, who has operated the store for 20 years, is Bob Hanna. The store is known for its selection of meats. Orders are still delivered. The interior is much as it was in years gone by. (Bob Hanna.)

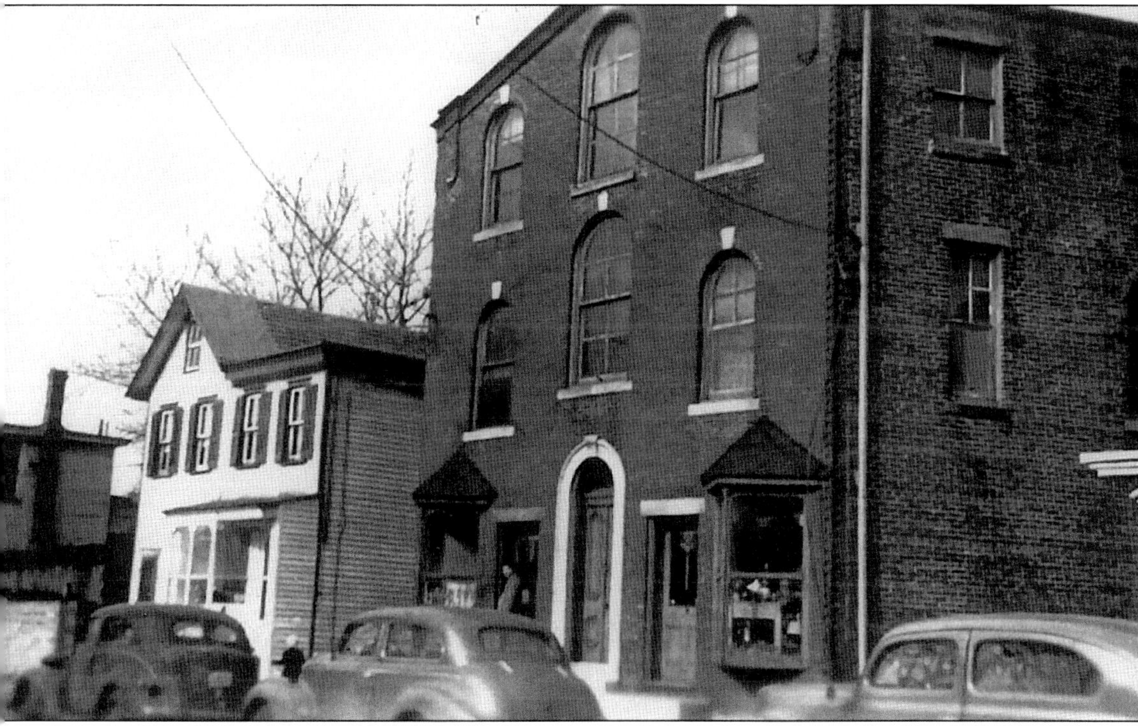

Just a short distance from the Philadelphia Fruit Market, on East Park Avenue, was the Davenport Building. The Friends had used the second floor of the Davenport Hall for their first meeting. This building contained offices and stores as well. There was a laundry on the first floor (left side). After the building was razed, it became the parking lot for the bank on South Centre Street. (Merchantville Historical Society.)

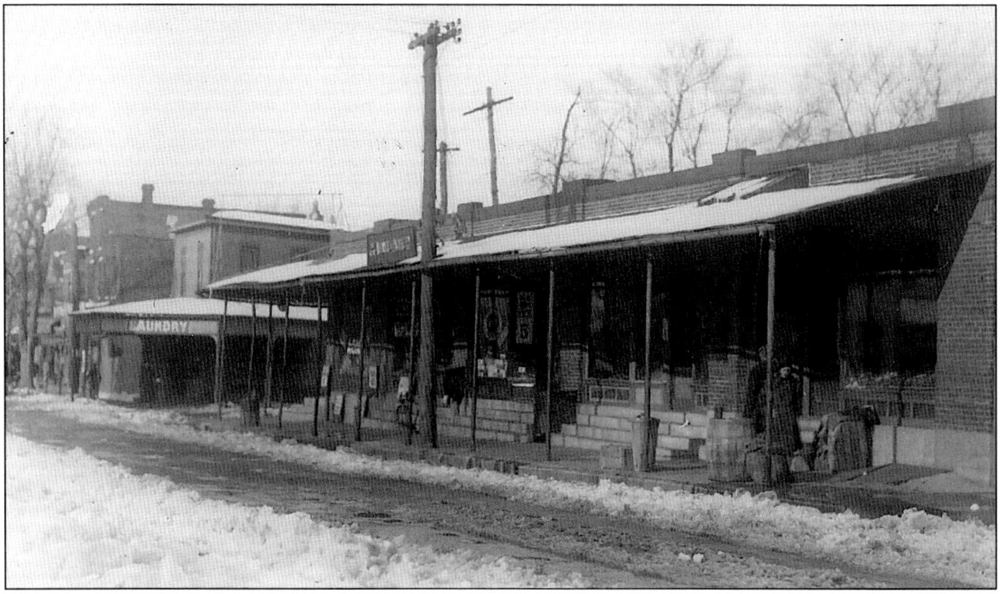

The block on the east side of Centre Street between East Maple and East Park Avenues, c. 1915, housed several stores. At that time, Walter Eastlack's Shoe Store, H.L. Bush's Pool Hall, Dorman's Café, and the first A & P in the borough were located here. (Bob Hanna.)

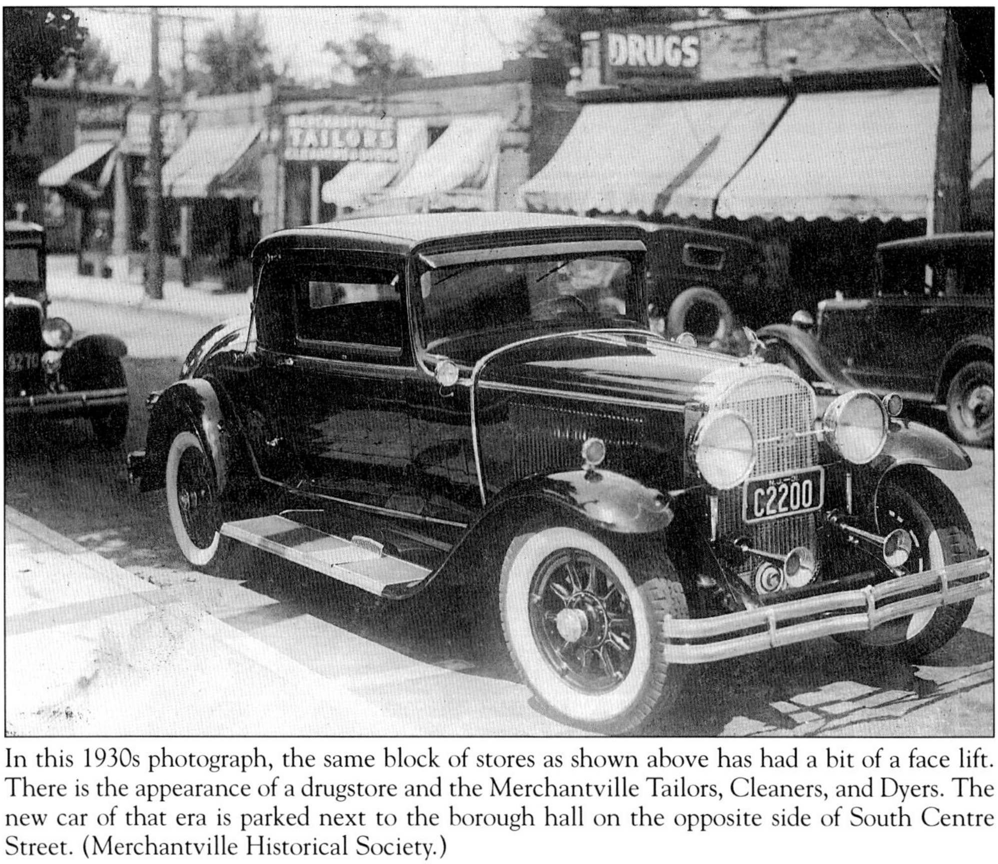

In this 1930s photograph, the same block of stores as shown above has had a bit of a face lift. There is the appearance of a drugstore and the Merchantville Tailors, Cleaners, and Dyers. The new car of that era is parked next to the borough hall on the opposite side of South Centre Street. (Merchantville Historical Society.)

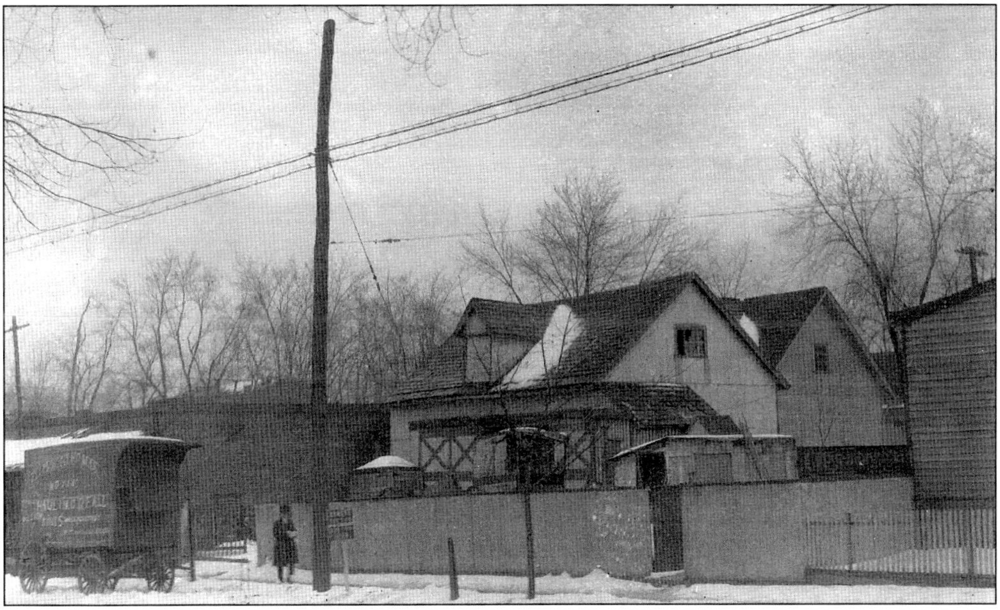

One establishment down from the corner of East Maple Avenue and South Centre Street was Thomas' Hauling of All. Presumably the business began after 1911, since it is not mentioned in the directory that year. (Merchantville Historical Society.)

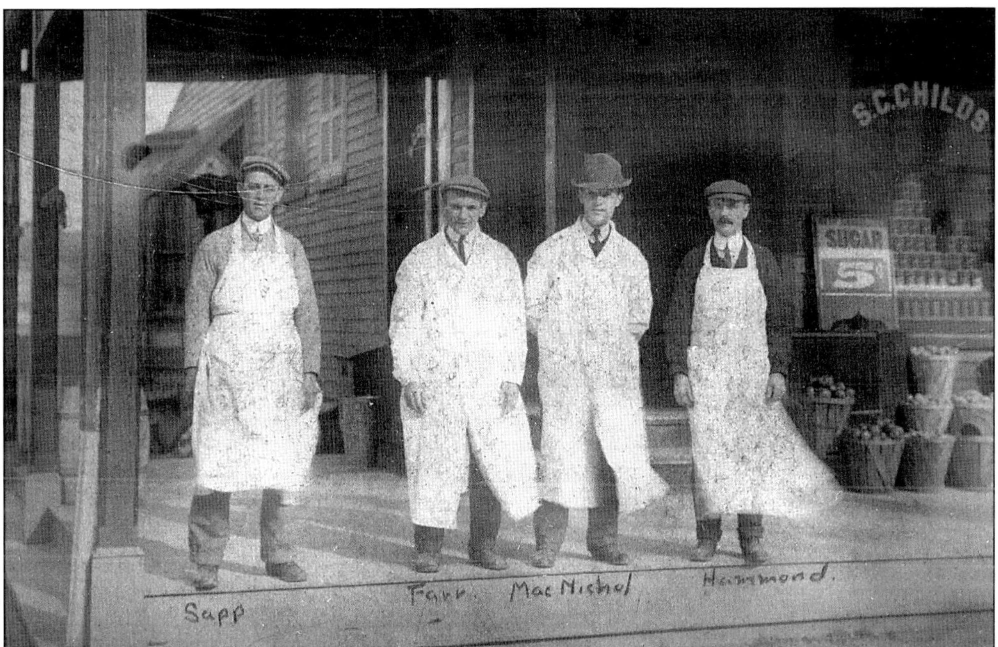

S.C. Childs Grocery Store was located on the northeast corner of South Centre Street and East Maple Avenue. They sold meat as well as groceries. An unusual shopper, a dog belonging to a borough resident, would trot to the store carrying a basket with a note requesting a cut of meat. The meat always arrived home intact. The American Food Store was situated here at a later time. It is now a bank parking lot. (Merchantville Historical Society.)

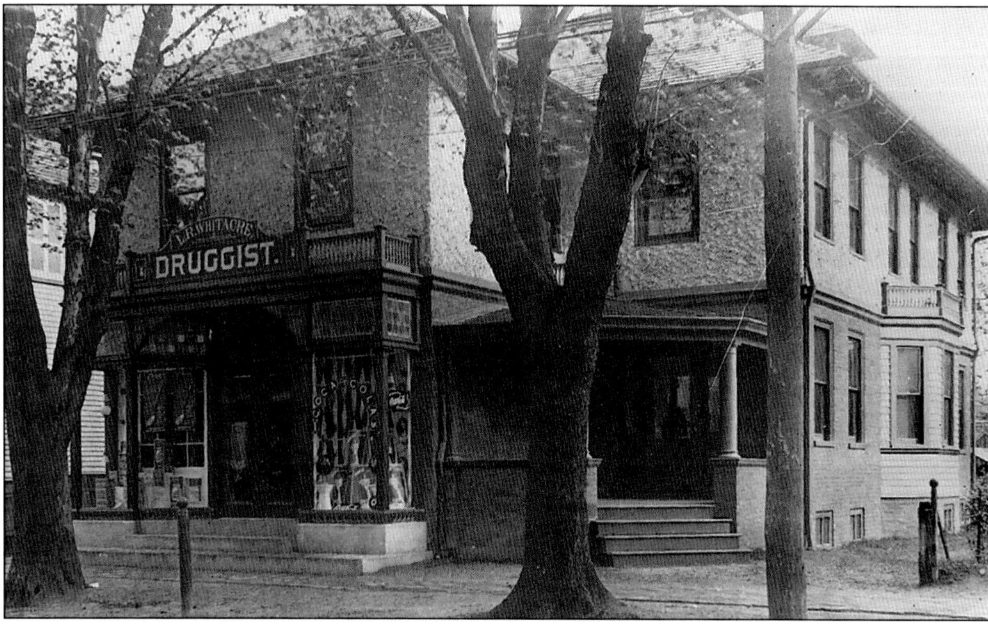

Whitacres Drug Store, at 3 East Maple Avenue, was originally owned and operated by L.R. Whitacre. The store boasted that one could drink the best things at the right place, their new and "down-to-the-minute" soda fountain. The store was sold to a Mr. Gebhardt *c.* 1915. Gebhardt's pro-German sympathies during World War I aroused the ire of the Merchantville citizens, who boycotted the store. This site is now part of Grace Episcopal Church. (Merchantville Historical Society.)

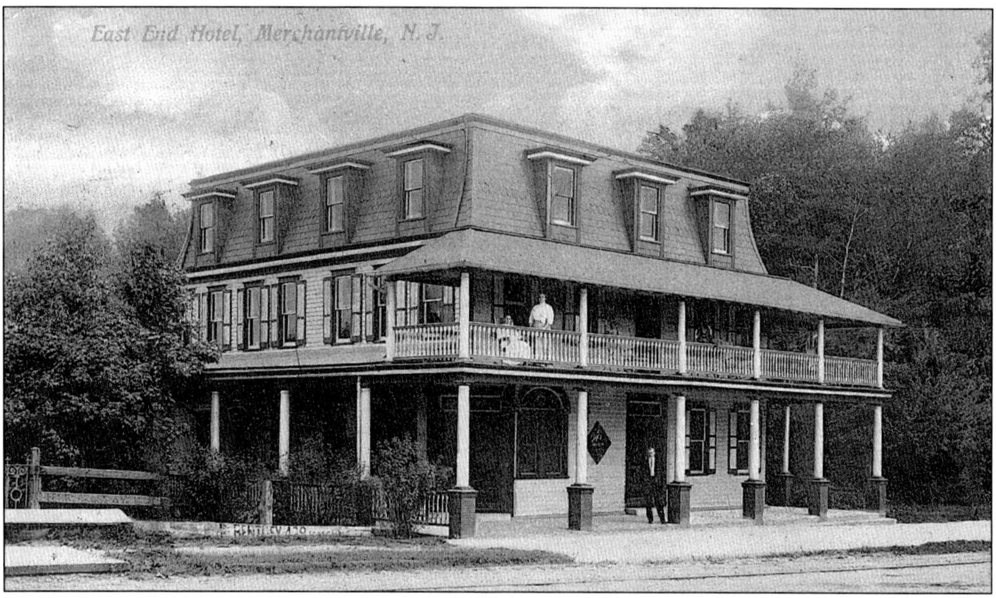

The East End Hotel was located on East Maple Avenue. Originally, it was a popular tavern on the Mount Holly stage road and was known as the Half Moon. The earliest known proprietor was a Mr. Cattell, who operated the hotel until 1825. Then Charles Buzby came into possession of the property and named it the Spread Eagle. This old hotel was razed to make way for the parking lot for the Woodbine Swim Club and Maple Bowling Lanes in 1962. (Bobbi Stagliano.)

Eight

Community Caring

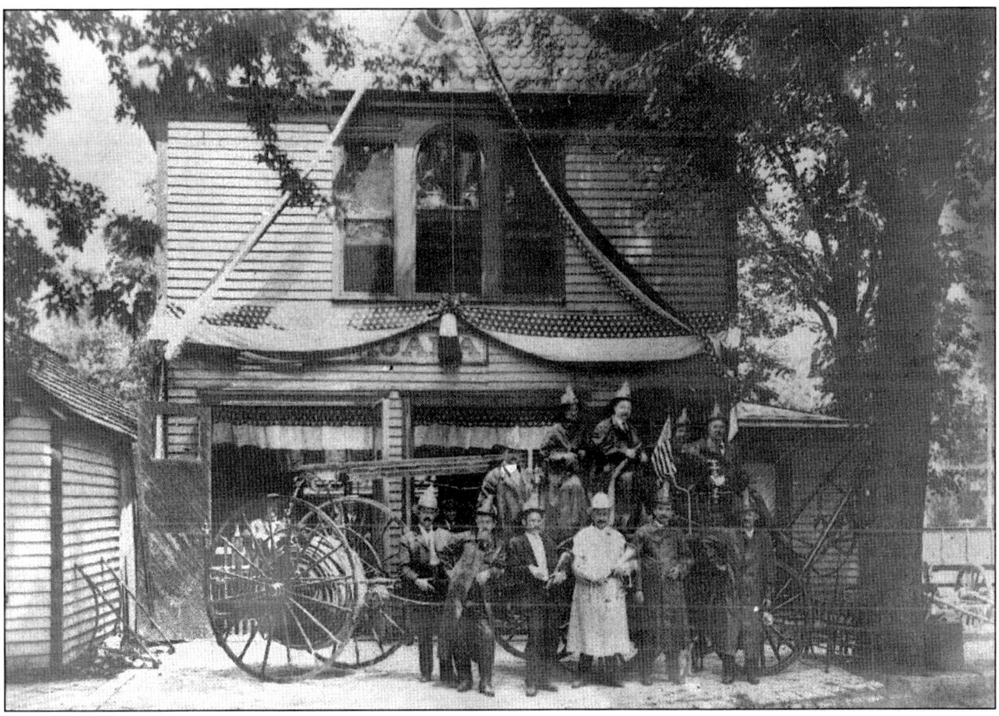

The Niagara Fire Company members are shown *c.* 1900, possibly for a Fourth of July parade. Shown from left to right are the following: (front row) Harry Snyder, George Lewis, Joseph Neumann, Chief Gottlieb Mick, unidentified, and Conrad Kranz; (back row) Walter Eastlack, and Frank Vergason, ? Reid, Roscoe Compton, and William MacFarlan. (Merchantville Historical Society.)

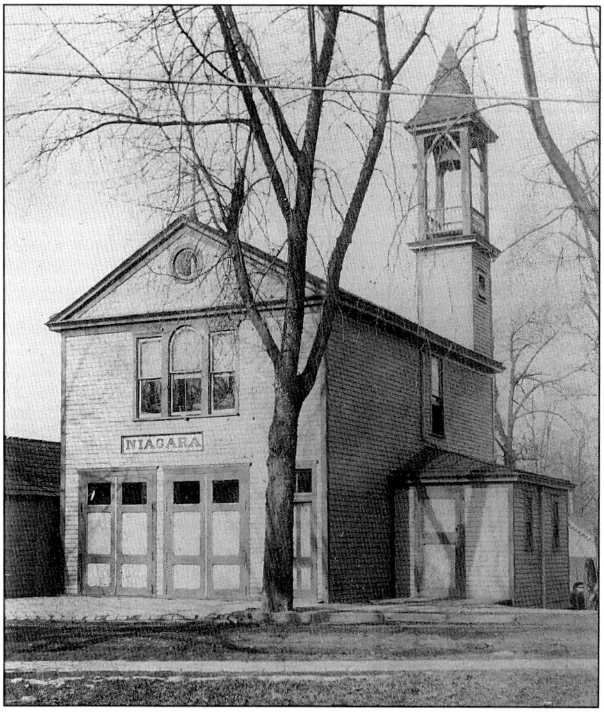

The first Niagara Firehouse was located at 19 East Park Avenue across the street from the present station. It was built in 1888 at a cost of $1,226. In 1889, four electric lights were installed free by the Merchantville Light Company, with the fire company paying $15 for the wiring. On November 20, 1895, a bell tower and hose dryer were added to the building at a cost of $179. In 1896, the bell to hang in the tower was purchased for $50 from the Wecacco Fire Company of Camden. (Merchantville Historical Society.)

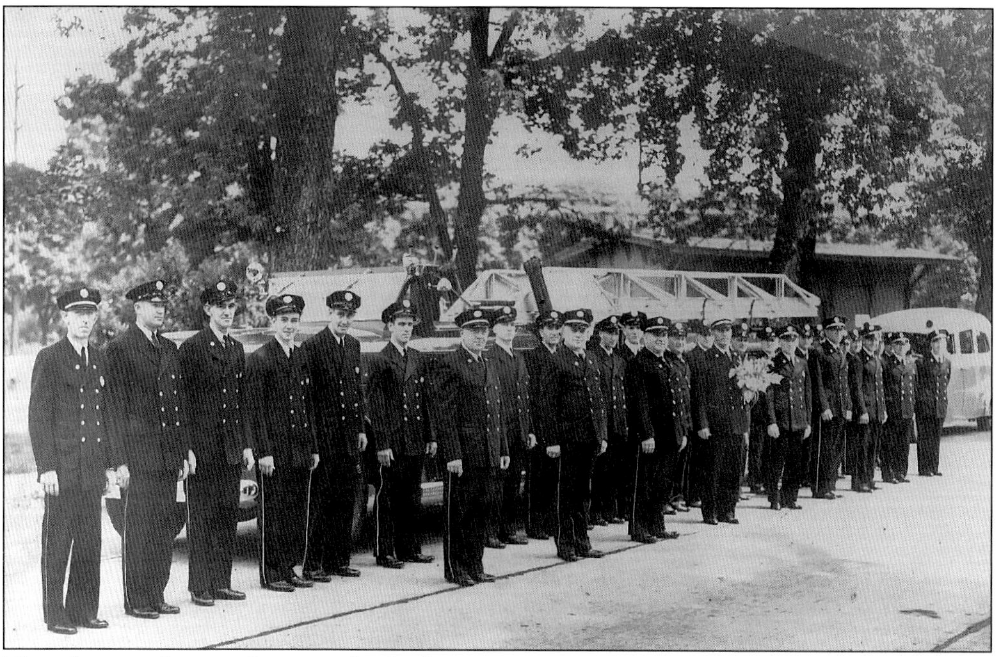

This photograph was taken outside the fire station at 22 East Park Avenue *c.* 1950. From left to right are the following: (front row) unidentified, Bill Wetzel, unidentified, Chief Harold Watson (white hat), Ed R. Plaskett, Burt German, unidentified, Walter Bayne, and Ken Smith; (back row) John Plasket Sr., John Downs, Howard Robinson Sr., unidentified, Otto Robinson, unidentified, Al Klaus, four unidentified, Hap Thomas, Dale Watson (behind the chief), Elwood Thomas, and Roy Hench. (Merchantville Historical Society.)

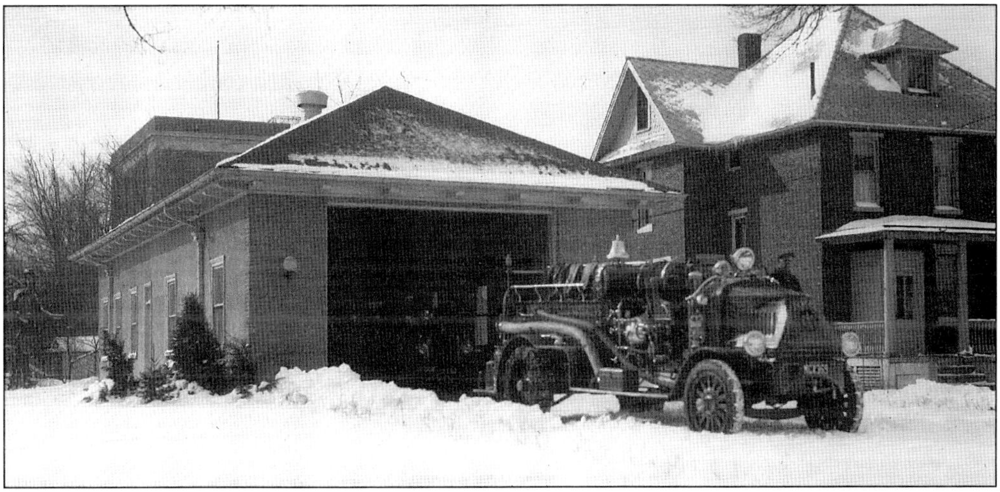

The second firehouse was built in 1926. This one-bay building forms the western quarter of the present station. In 1935, sometime after returning from a fire call, this building burned with a loss of one of the trucks housed in the building. In this photograph is the home of Chief William Lindermann of the police department. He resided at 20 East Park Avenue. (Merchantville Historical Society.)

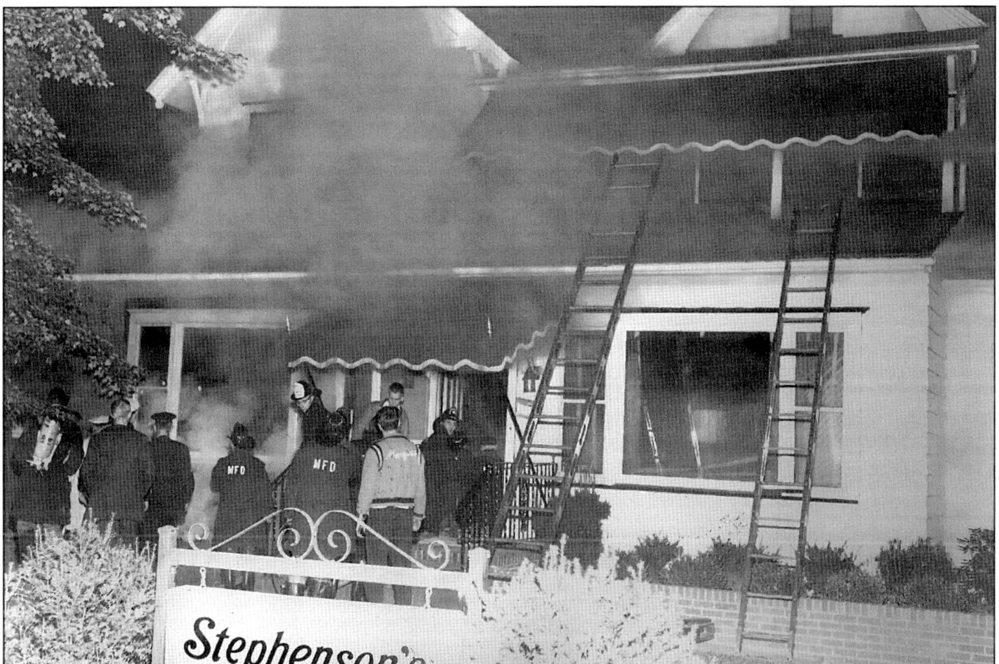

On October 26, 1960, Stephenson's Funeral Home had a fire. The Merchantville Fire Department was on the scene, and the home was saved. The first spectacular fire that the company was called upon to fight was the old Merchantville Inn on September 5, 1892, when the roof and third and fourth floors were destroyed. Other fires were Collins and Pancoast Hall, on January 3, 1893; the loss of the third floor of the Merchantville Hall, on October 23, 1922; and the destruction of all but the foundation of St. Peter's, on January 6, 1924. (Jeff Brown.)

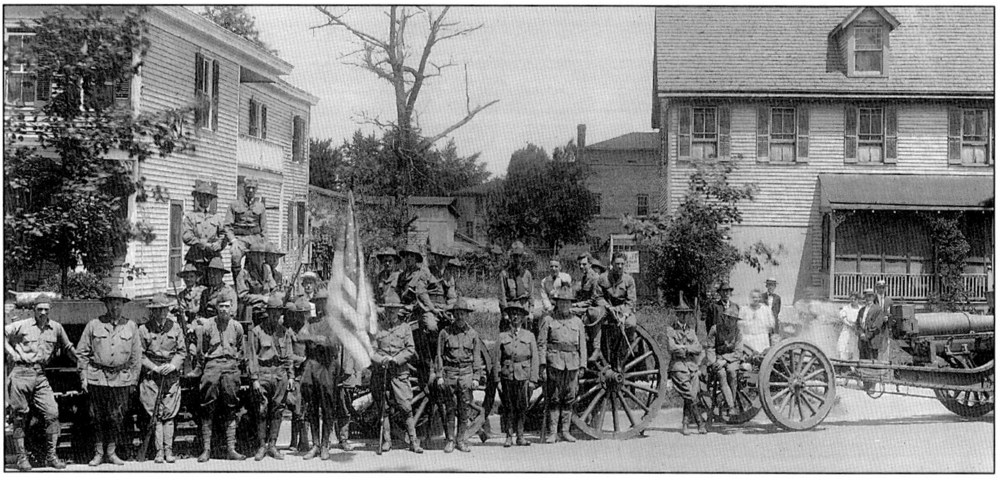

Here, at the corner of West Park Avenue and South Centre Street, World War I soldiers take a moment to pose for the camera. A tablet was erected in recognition of the patriotic spirit and loyal devotion of the men of Merchantville, who served in the military and naval forces of the United States in the Great War. The service monument was dedicated on Armistice Day, November 11, 1921. Four men had given their lives in service to their country. (Merchantville Historical Society.)

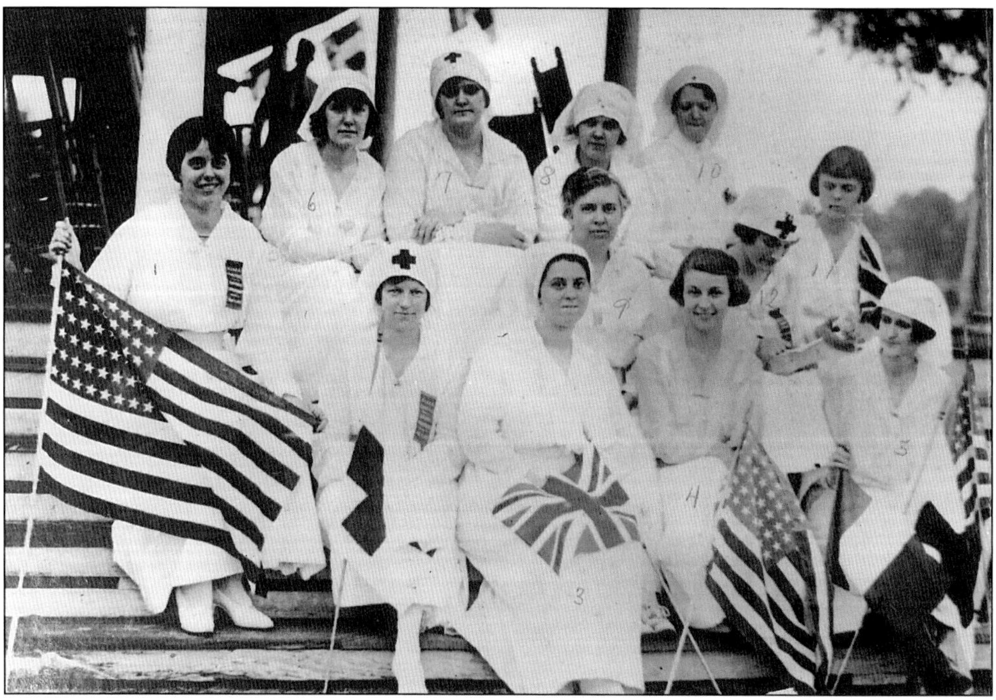

Authority to form a chapter of the American Red Cross for Camden City was established on February 14, 1917. The Merchantville branch was organized on March 3, 1917. Meetings were held in the borough hall. Members shown are, from left to right, the following: (front row) Minnie Wyckoff, Ethel Rudderow, Marion Tichnor, Muff Porter, and Rosiland Mundy; (middle row) Julia Williams and Lavinia Skeggs; (back row) Faith Morse, Deborah Williams, Dorothy Githens, Connie Joline, and Georgie Morgan. (Merchantville Historical Society.)

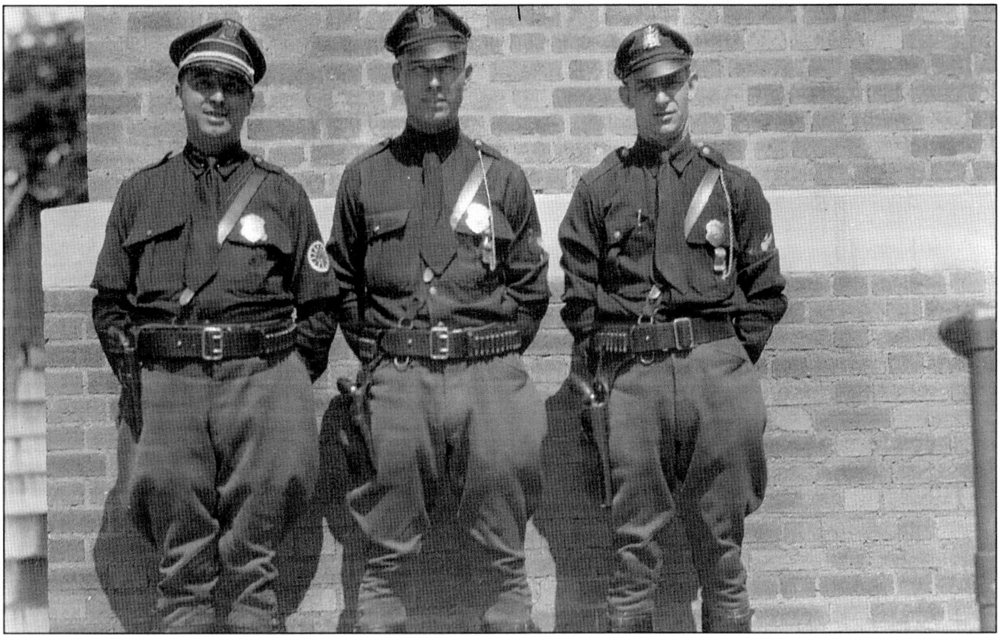

In 1899, Francis F. Eastlack stated in his *History of Merchantville* that Merchantville had a first-class police force and two committing magistrates. The first borough lock-up, in 1874, stood in the rear of Mayor Longstreth's office. Then it was moved to behind the borough building. It was destroyed when the new municipal building was constructed. Standing in the middle of this picture is Rome Tull, who was the chief of police after William Linderman. (Merchantville Historical Society.)

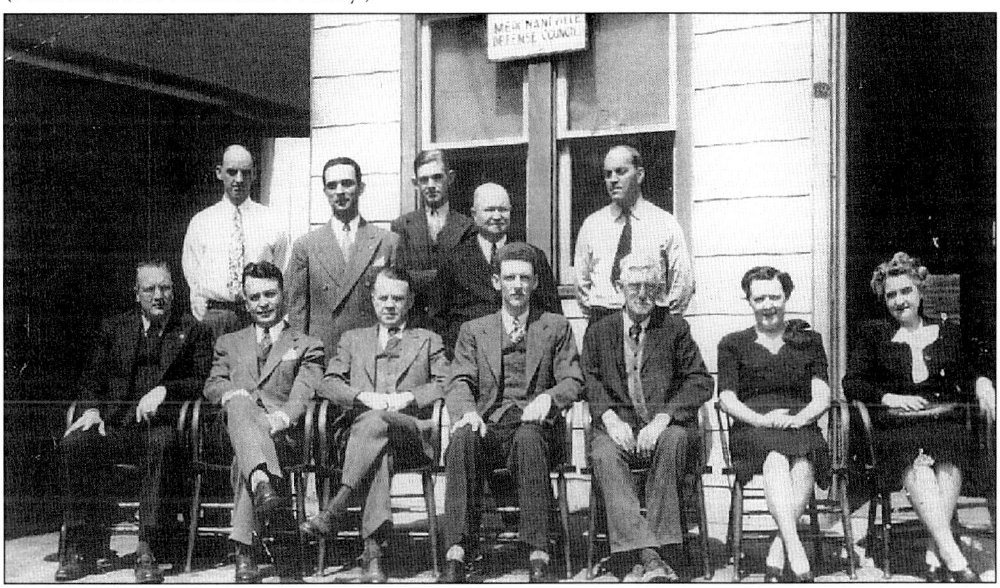

This group of supportive and patriotic Merchantville residents had trucks to be used in case of a need for evacuation during World War II. Shown from left to right are the following: (front row) Clarence Whipple, Harry Kurkian, Bernard Blankenbush, Charles Potter, John Plasket, Ester Evens, and Hazle Hacket; (back row) unidentified, George Partlow, Walter Kurkian, Fritz Plasket, Dory Loffler, and Harold Watson. (Vernon Collins.)

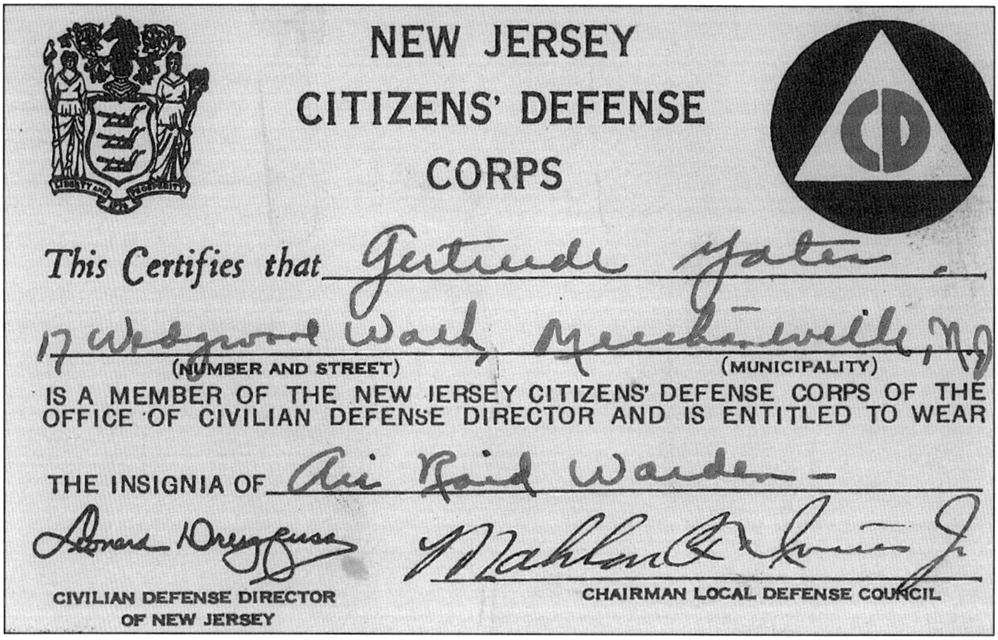

NEW JERSEY
CITIZENS' DEFENSE
CORPS

This Certifies that Gertrude Yates
17 Wedgwood Walk, Merchantville, N.J.
(NUMBER AND STREET) (MUNICIPALITY)
IS A MEMBER OF THE NEW JERSEY CITIZENS' DEFENSE CORPS OF THE OFFICE OF CIVILIAN DEFENSE DIRECTOR AND IS ENTITLED TO WEAR
THE INSIGNIA OF Air Raid Warden

CIVILIAN DEFENSE DIRECTOR OF NEW JERSEY

CHAIRMAN LOCAL DEFENSE COUNCIL

In Wellwood Memorial Park is a tablet dedicated to the patriotic and loyal devotion of the men and women who served the United States in all the wars. On the home front during World War II, townspeople did their part for the cause. Gertrude Yeats was an air-raid warden for the New Jersey Citizen's Defense Corps. She is pictured below in her uniform; on her sleeve is the insignia of the air-raid warden. (Merchantville Historical Society.)

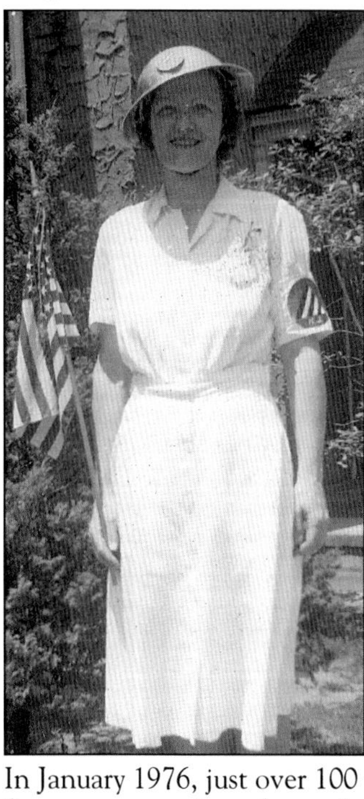

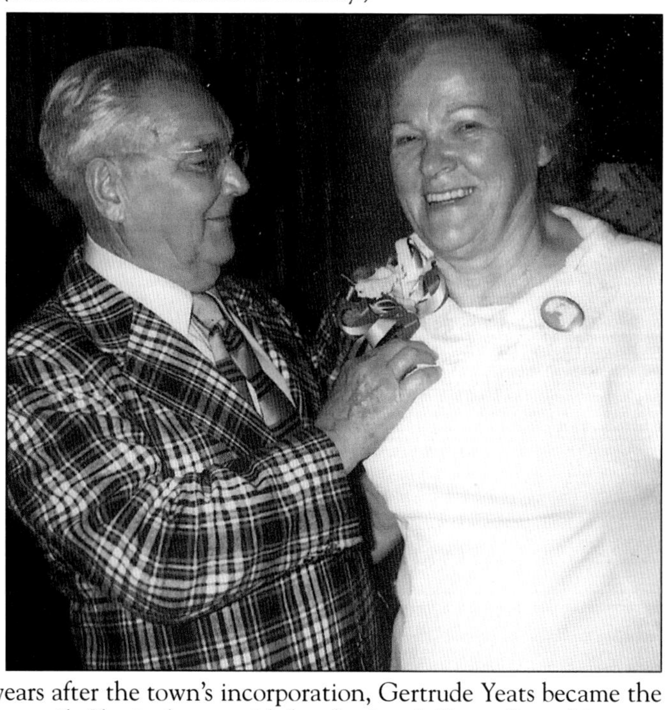

In January 1976, just over 100 years after the town's incorporation, Gertrude Yeats became the first woman to sit on borough council. She is shown with her husband, Harry O., celebrating this momentous event. (Merchantville Historical Society.)

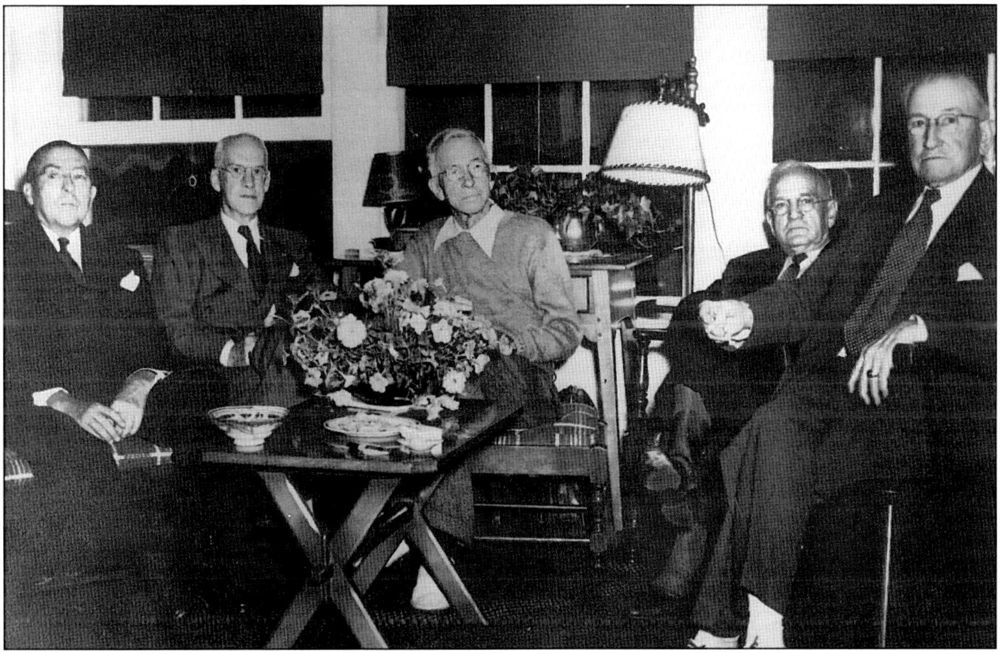

The first Field Club Minstrels show was in 1894. The town could not get along without the minstrels' presentations for 16 years. When the Field Club gave them up, others came along to keep the minstrel habit going. "Doc" Lawrence joined the minstrel troupe *c.* 1900. Pictured *c.* 1950 are, from left to right, the last living minstrels: Albert E. Burling, Jim Cranmer, Will Paul, Frank Homer, and Fred Meade. (Merchantville Historical Society.)

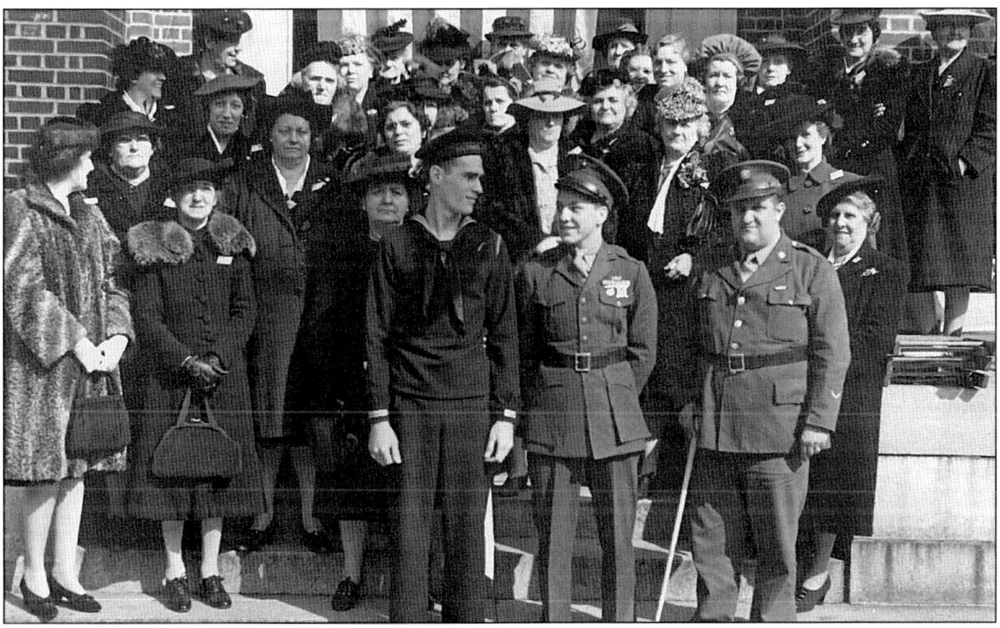

Servicemen and servicewomen received very special attention when they came to Merchantville on leave or for a visit. Here, during World War II, a group of women rallies around a few servicemen on the steps of the bank building at 9 South Centre Street. (Merchantville Historical Society.)

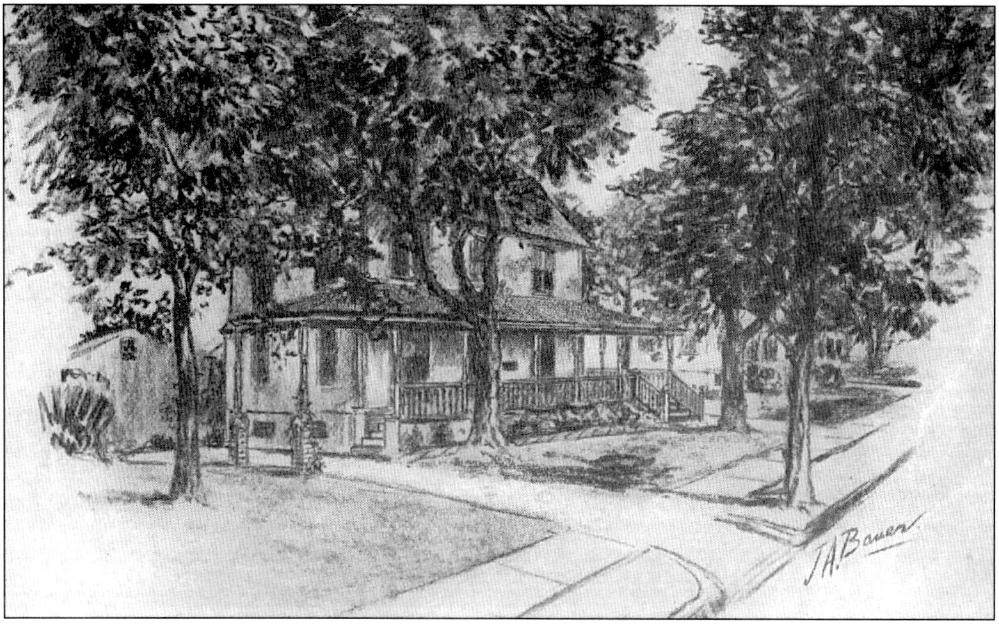

In 1892, a group of women met to promote the habit of reading by giving a half hour each day to the best of literature. They were known as the Half-Hour Club. In October 1919, with a membership of more than 100, the name was changed to the Woman's Club of Merchantville. The members continue to work together to advance social, educational, and charitable interests in the community. The club motto is "Service." Here is a picture of the clubhouse at 9 West Cedar Avenue. The Women's Club moved here in 1927 and sold the clubhouse in 1992, when it relocated to the community center. (Maureen McLoone.)

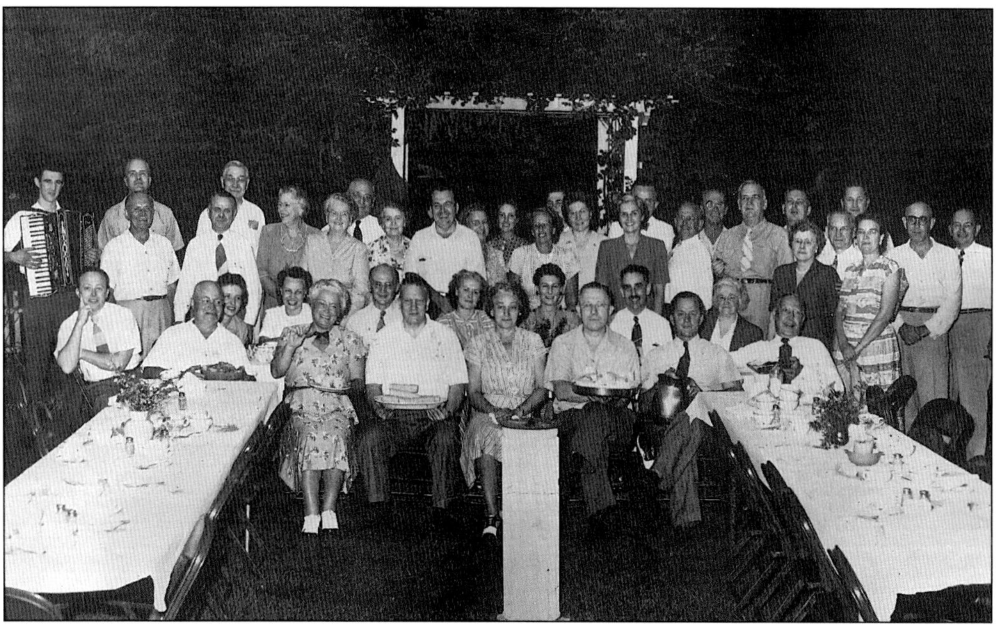

The Lions Club gathers for an outdoor get-together in the backyard of Mayor Chew c. 1950. Among those shown are Harold Stephenson, Jack Ludlum, Bernard Blankenbush, and the mayor's wife. (Merchantville Historical Society.)

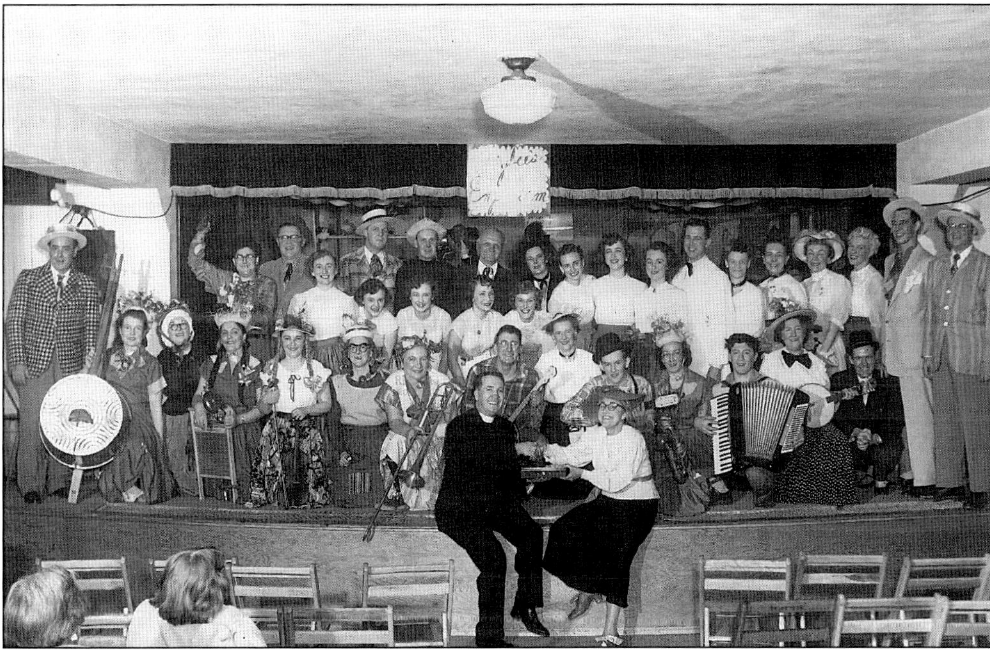

The parish family of St. Peter's Roman Catholic Church prayed and played together. On April 20, 21, and 22, 1950, members of the parish put on a variety show. Msgr. John P. Fallon is center stage among the cast members in the lower church auditorium. (St. Peter's.)

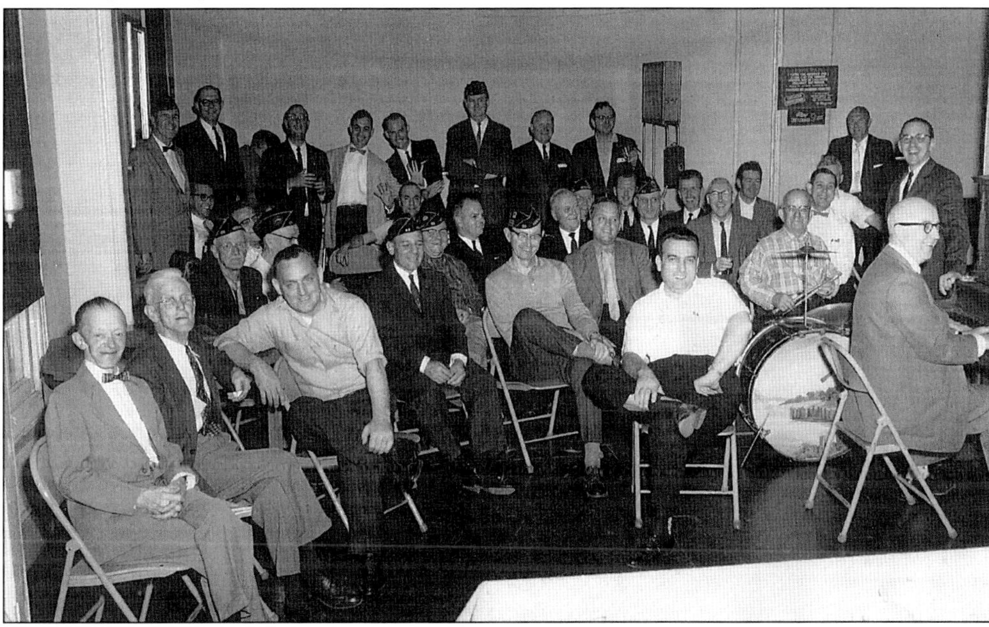

Gathered at the American Legion Frederick W. Grigg Post No. 68 are, from left to right, the following members: (front row) two unidentified, Jim Hogan, Tony Repice, Charles Keeler, John Todd, Bob Hollefup, Bob Heyman, Frank Ferraro, Judge Mitchell (at the piano), and Joseph Zampino (standing); (middle row) Frank Humphries, Joe Matchet, unidentified, Ed Hohen, Bill Fallon, and Charles Snyder; (back row) Don Wolverton, two unidentified, Ted Bittle, unidentified, Frank Whelan, Jerry Belz, and Paul Patri. (Tony Repice.)

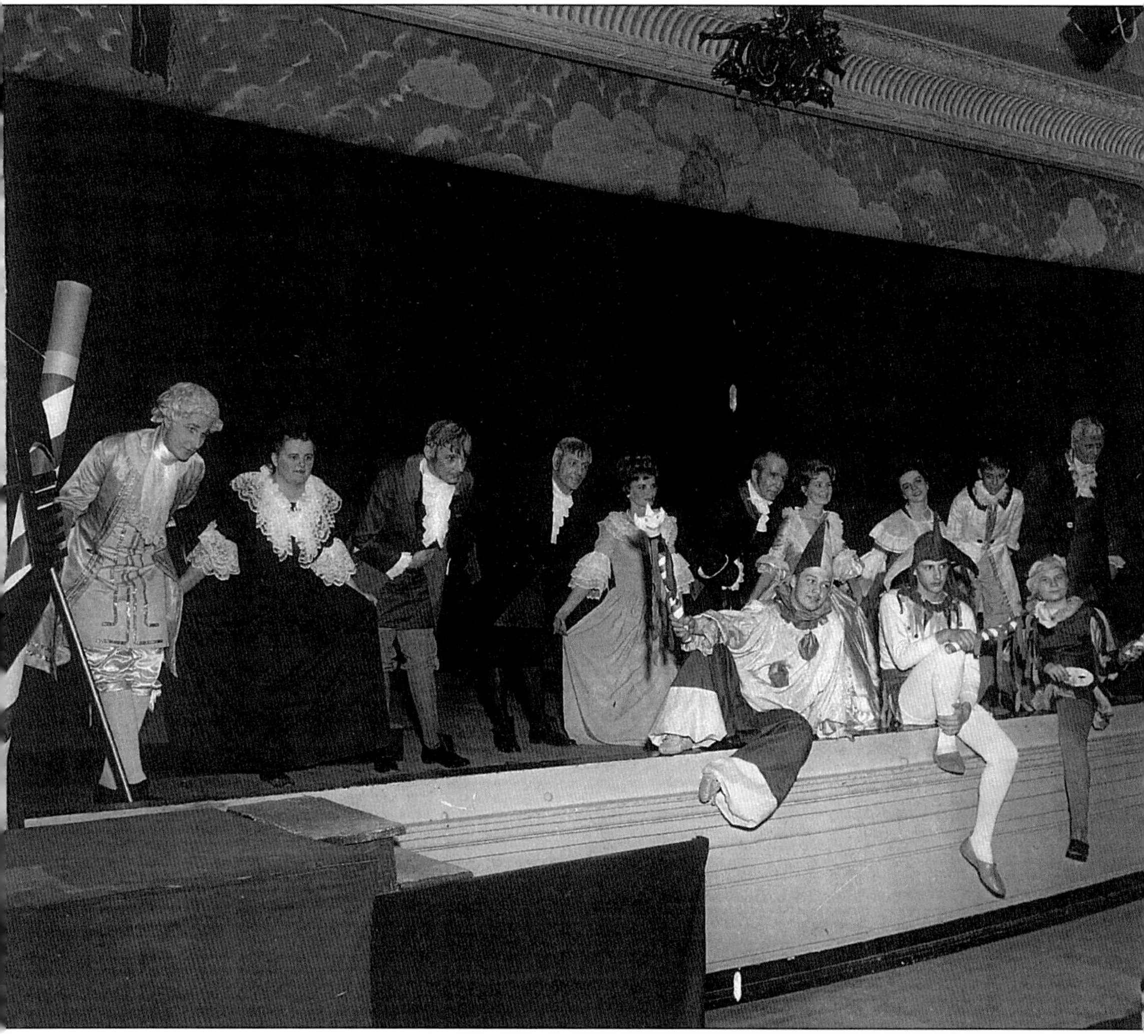

Organized in the spring of 1933, Merchantville Playcrafters ranked among the oldest of theater groups in the area. The founders of the group were Camden High School classmates and former students of Lucy Dean Wilson. Early rehearsals were held in members' homes, and the plays staged at Grace Episcopal Church. In 1937, the membership had grown considerably. The group arranged to lease the auditorium in Collins Hall at the corner of South Centre Street and West Chestnut Avenue. During World War II, the Playcrafters' stage was darkened for several seasons. (Kay Hussong.)

1933-1934 *Thirty-First Season* 1963-1964

MERCHANTVILLE PLAYCRAFTERS

present

"THE VILLAGE GROUCHES"

A Comedy

by

CARLO GOLDONI

directed by

MRS. LEE T. TYBURSKI

Friday and Saturday, February 21 and 22, 1964

8:30 P.M.

PLAYHOUSE, COLLINS HALL MERCHANTVILLE, N. J.

In the 31st season of the Merchantville Playcrafters, a comedy was presented. On Saturday, February 21 and Sunday, February 22, 1964, *The Villages Grouches*, a comedy by Carlo Goldoni and directed by Lee T. Tyburski, was performed. The curtain on the stage portrayed Merchantville people and buildings *c.* 1945. There is hardly a warmer feeling than sitting on your porch and watching the townspeople stroll home from the theater after a lovely evening's entertainment. (Kay Hussong)

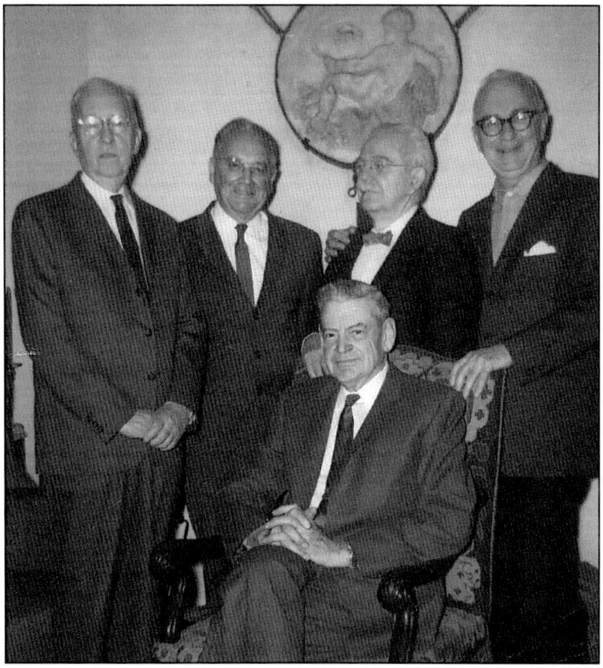

Interest in protecting the shade trees of Merchantville began in 1930. The two citizens appointed to get more trees planted were Carlyle Stephen and Harry Yates. In February 1942, the borough council passed an ordinance establishing a "Shade Tree Commission, for the regulation, planting, care, and control of shade and ornamental trees and shrubbery upon the streets, public places and parks." Here is a 1965 photograph of the first Shade Tree Commission taken in Dr. Henry H. Shirk's home. They are Joseph Truscott Jr., Harry O. Yates Jr., Dr. Henry H. Shirk, Robert Rudolph, and C. Stuart Cooper, chairman. (Merchantville Historical Society.)

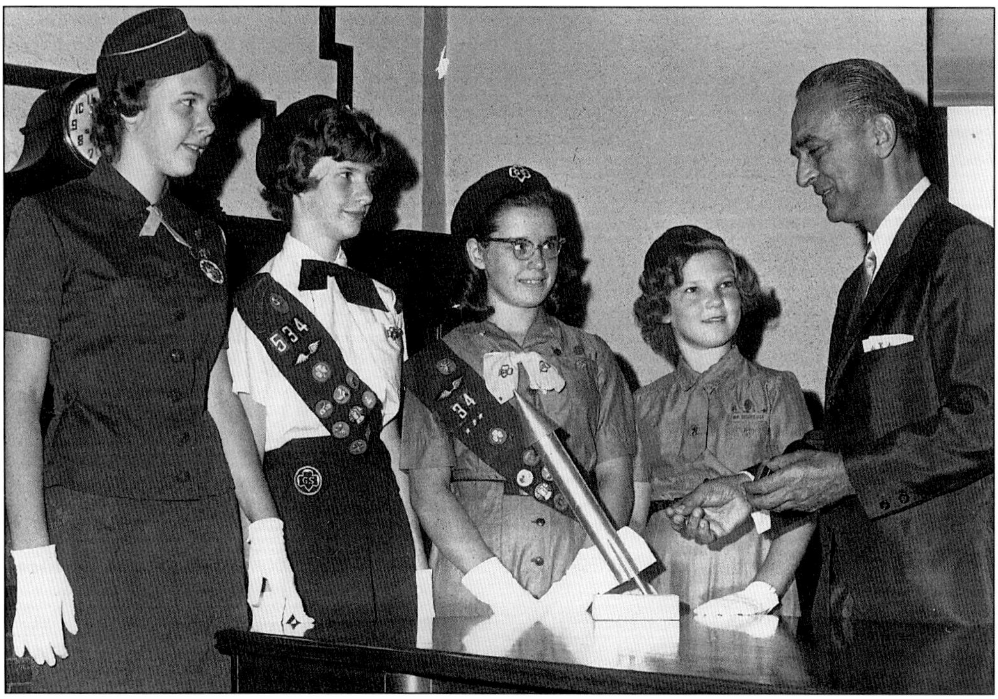

Adults and girls have been interested in scouting since the 1920s. There were two troops then: Troop No. 1 met at the First Presbyterian Church, and Troop No. 2 met at the Hillcrest Community Church in Pennsauken. Loreata Sullender, of 211 West End Avenue, was a captain of Troop No.1 for years and also the director of the Camden Council of Girl Scouts. Shown with the mayor in 1964 are, from left to right, Girl Scouts Peggy Shuler, Eileen Schuler, Carol MacDona, and Dianne Whittaker. (Merchantville Historical Society.)

Nine

Noteworthy Notables

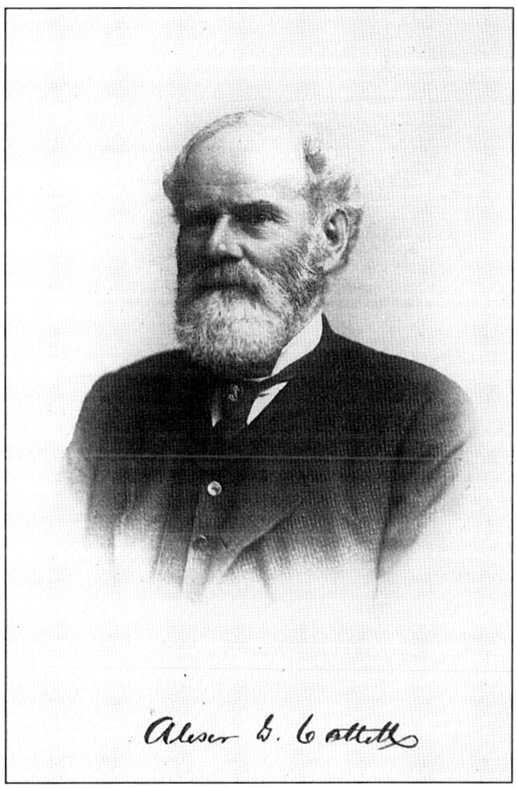

One of our most colorful citizens was Sen. Alexander G. Cattell. He had operated the A.G. Cattell & Company (shipping and commission merchants), organized the Corn Exchange National Bank of Philadelphia, and developed the 79 acres of land in Merchantville known as the Cattell Tract. On June 7, 1862, Cattell bought the estate of Samuel H. McFadden on the north side of Maple Avenue, west of Cove Road. He and his wife, Eliza, moved from Haddonfield. Pres. Ulysses S. Grant said of Senator Cattell, "He is one of my wisest advisors and best friends." Grant made a few visits to Merchantville. (Merchantville Historical Society.)

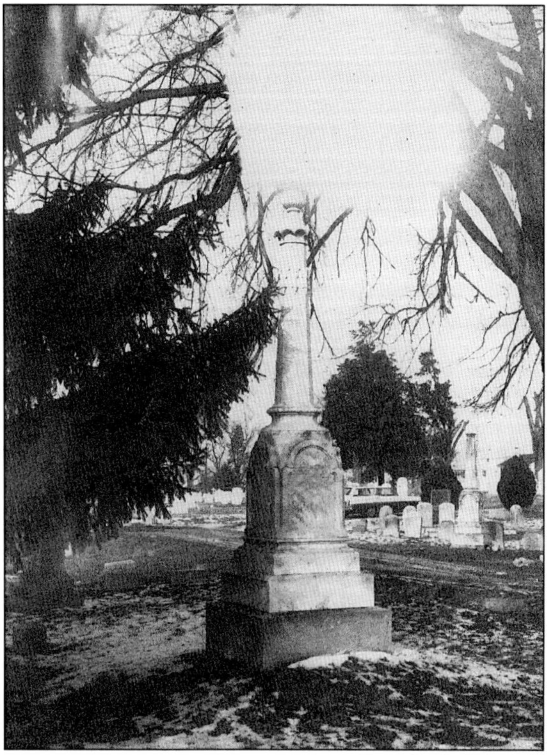

The Cattell burial marker can be found in the Colestown Cemetery on Kings Highway and Church Road in Cherry Hill. Alexander G. and Eliza Gilmore Cattell were laid to rest here. Sen. Alexander G. Cattell died in 1894. (Merchantville Historical Society.)

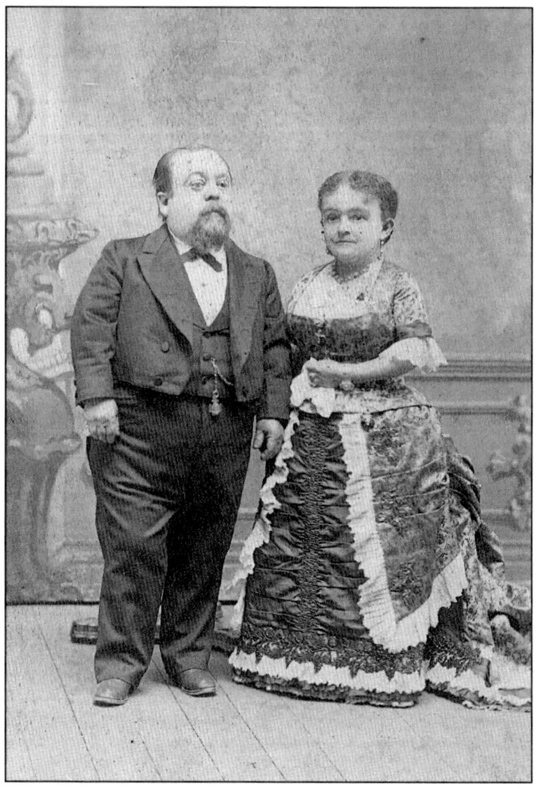

Charles Sherwood Stratton (Tom Thumb) was born in January 1838 in Bridgeport, Connecticut. In 1842, P.T. Barnum discovered him. Stratton married Lavinia Warren on February 10, 1863. He died of a stroke on July 15, 1883. The couple visited Merchantville in 1880. (Merchantville Historical Society.)

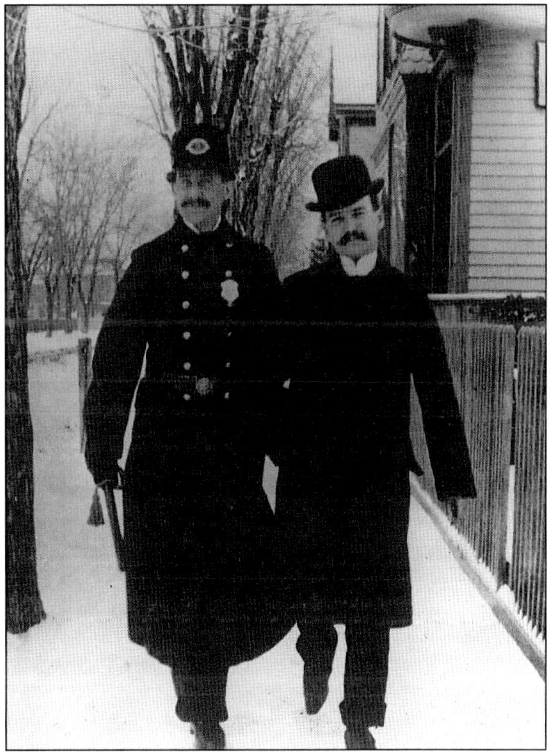

In the winter of 1895, Chief Linderman and Frank P. Homer stroll down North Centre Street outside of the building that became Blankenbush's Pharmacy. The name Linderman has been synonymous with protection of life and property and guidance of our youth. William H. Linderman was a member of the Merchantville police force starting in 1893. At that time, young Billy Linderman was selected to serve the borough for four months over the summer. In 1897, he became our first chief of police. The town never ceased to reap dividends in law and order from the reputation built by Linderman, who died on August 29, 1954, at the age of 80. (Merchantville Historical Society.)

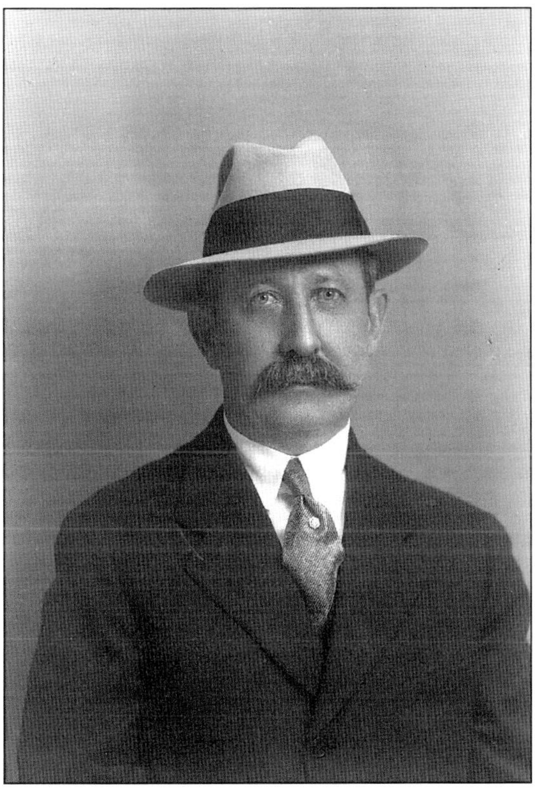

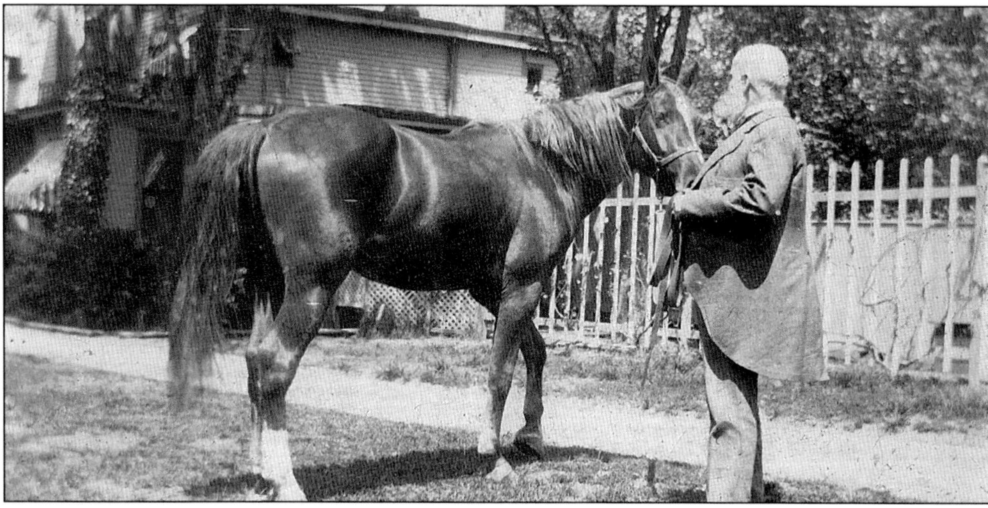

Dr. David Hedding Bartine was born in 1841 in Morrisville. He graduated from the University of Pennsylvania in 1859, where he studied medicine. After service in the Civil War, he returned to civilian life in February 1866. After his marriage to Clementine Hanna, he moved to her father's home, on the north side of Maple Avenue and opened his first office. Later he acquired the double house on the south side of Maple Avenue opposite the Park Avenue intersection. Dr. Bartine was president of the Merchantville Board of Health. He was endeared to the community, and his Merchantville neighbors took great pride in him as might be expected of the physician's family. The village doctor passed away in 1901. The face of Merchantville's first physician, molded in bronze, was placed on the grass plot at Maple and Park Avenues. It was a loving tribute by his fellow townspeople for services faithfully rendered. (Merchantville Historical Society.)

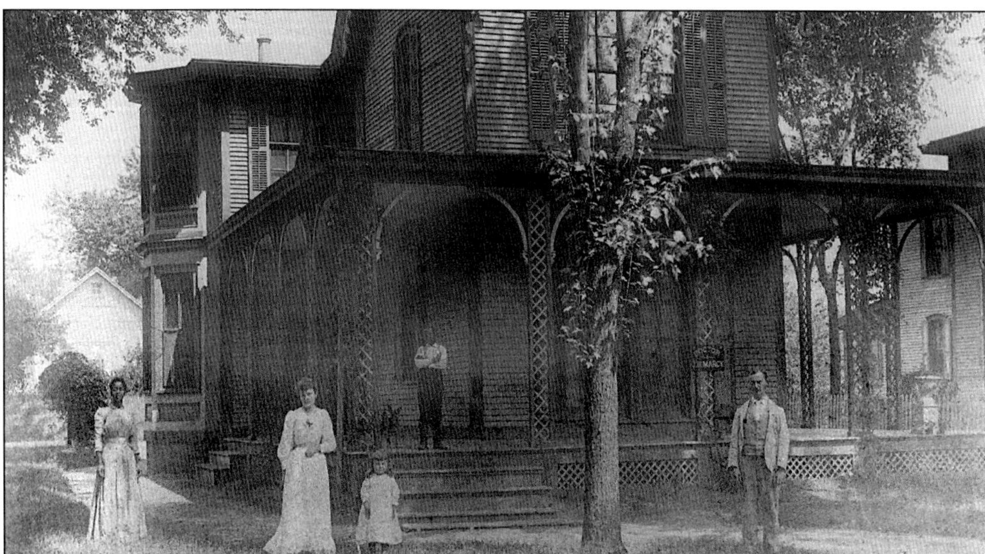

Dr. John W. Marcy practiced medicine at 117 East Park Avenue. He is listed as a physician in Eastlack's *History of Merchantville* in 1899. Around the beginning of the 20th century, his medical records indicate that he had treated Wallace Warfield, during her visit to Merchantville. Wallace Warfield Simpson later became the Duchess of Windsor. (Merchantville Historical Society.)

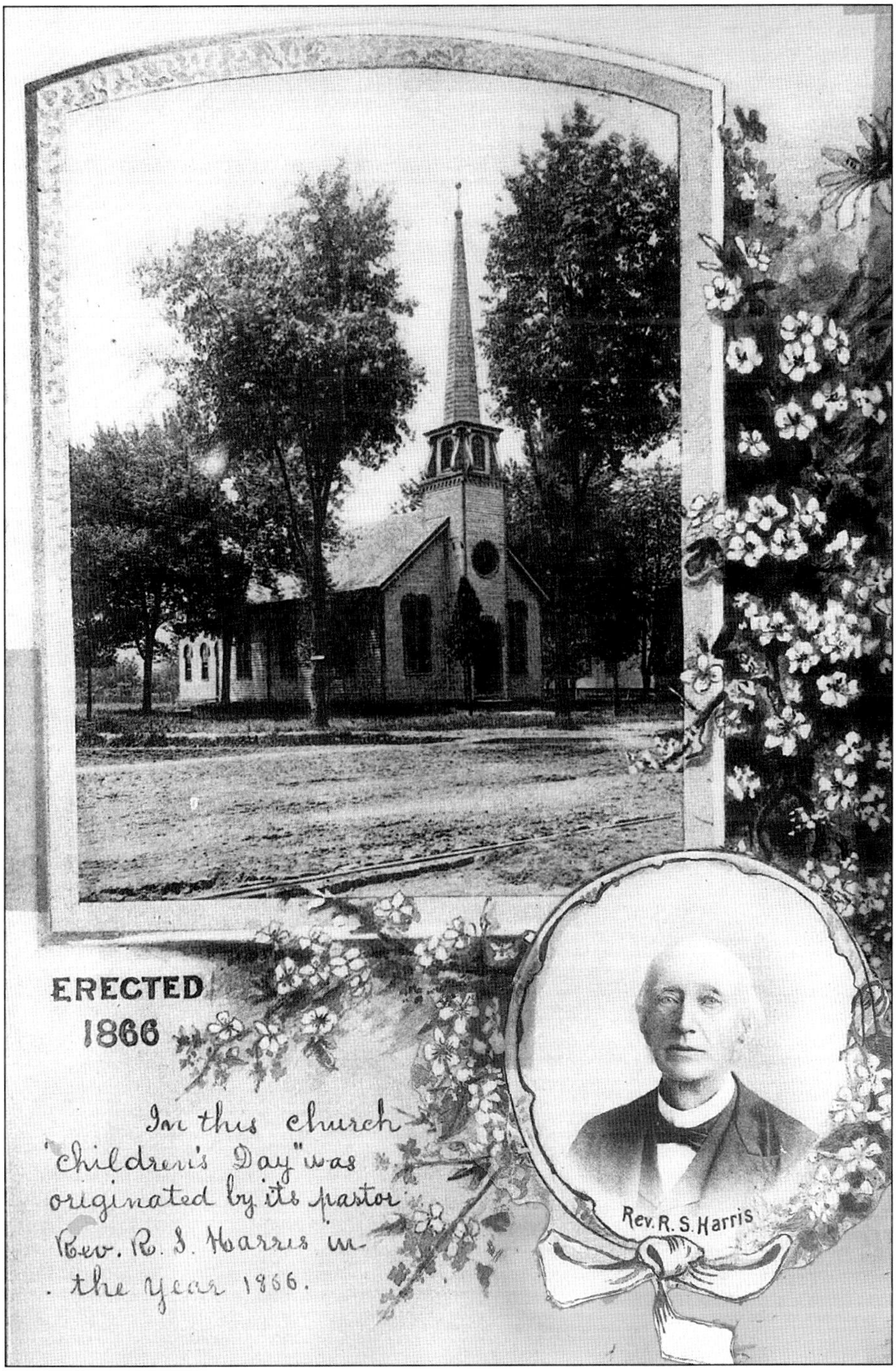

The first church erected in Merchantville was Trinity Methodist Episcopal Church, which was incorporated on May 11, 1865. Rev. Robert S. Harris, who was the first pastor, was the originator of Children's Day, now celebrated in June of each year by churches of all denominations in all parts of the world. It was the enthusiasm of the children of the congregation, coupled with the distress Harris experienced from the loss of his own son, that evoked the urge within him to set aside one Sunday in every year as Children's Day. (Merchantville Historical Society.)

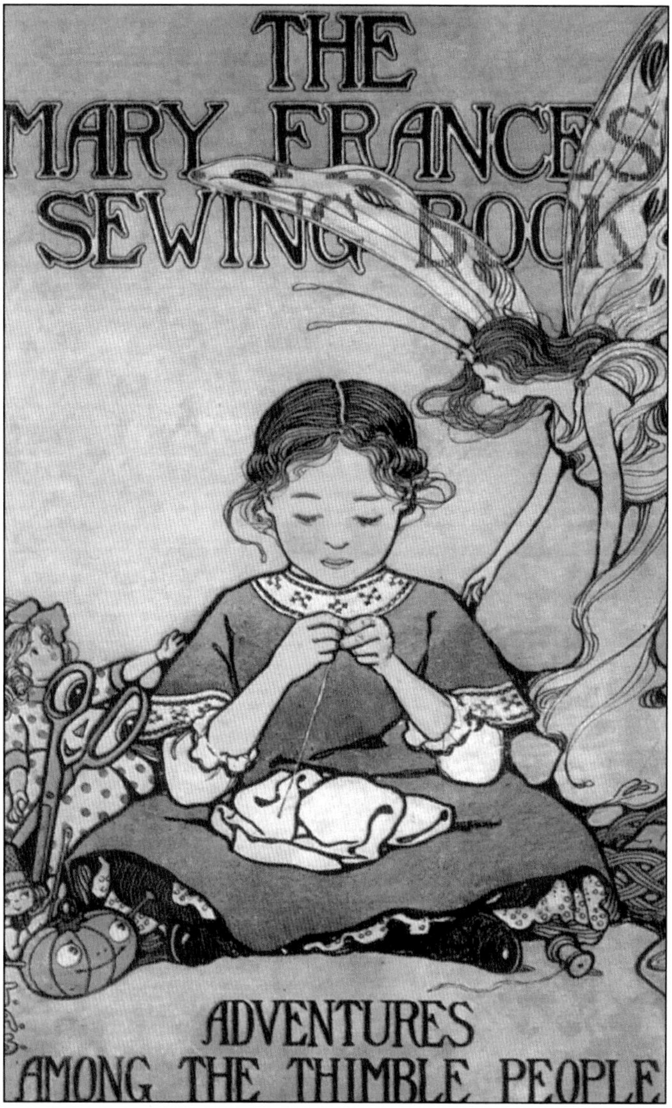

From 1912 to 1918, a series of books was published by Winston Publishers. Written by Merchantville resident Jane Eayre Fryer, they were instruction books in story form for children and were designed to teach "useful things in an entertaining way." Fryer, born in Philadelphia, was a teacher of domestic science and art at the Jacob Tome Institute in Port Deposit, Maryland. In 1902, she married John Gayton Fryer in Providence, Rhode Island. Jane Eayre Fryer lived at 9 Alexander Avenue with her husband and their daughter Stella. John Fryer was a Baptist minister. There were six books written about Mary Francis and her experiences. In 1997, Lacis Publications reprinted several of the series. (Maureen McLoone.)

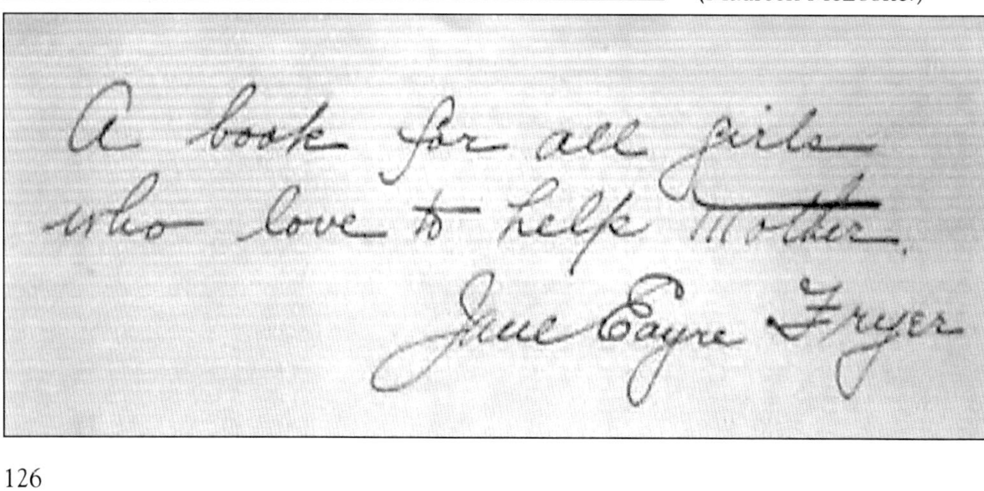

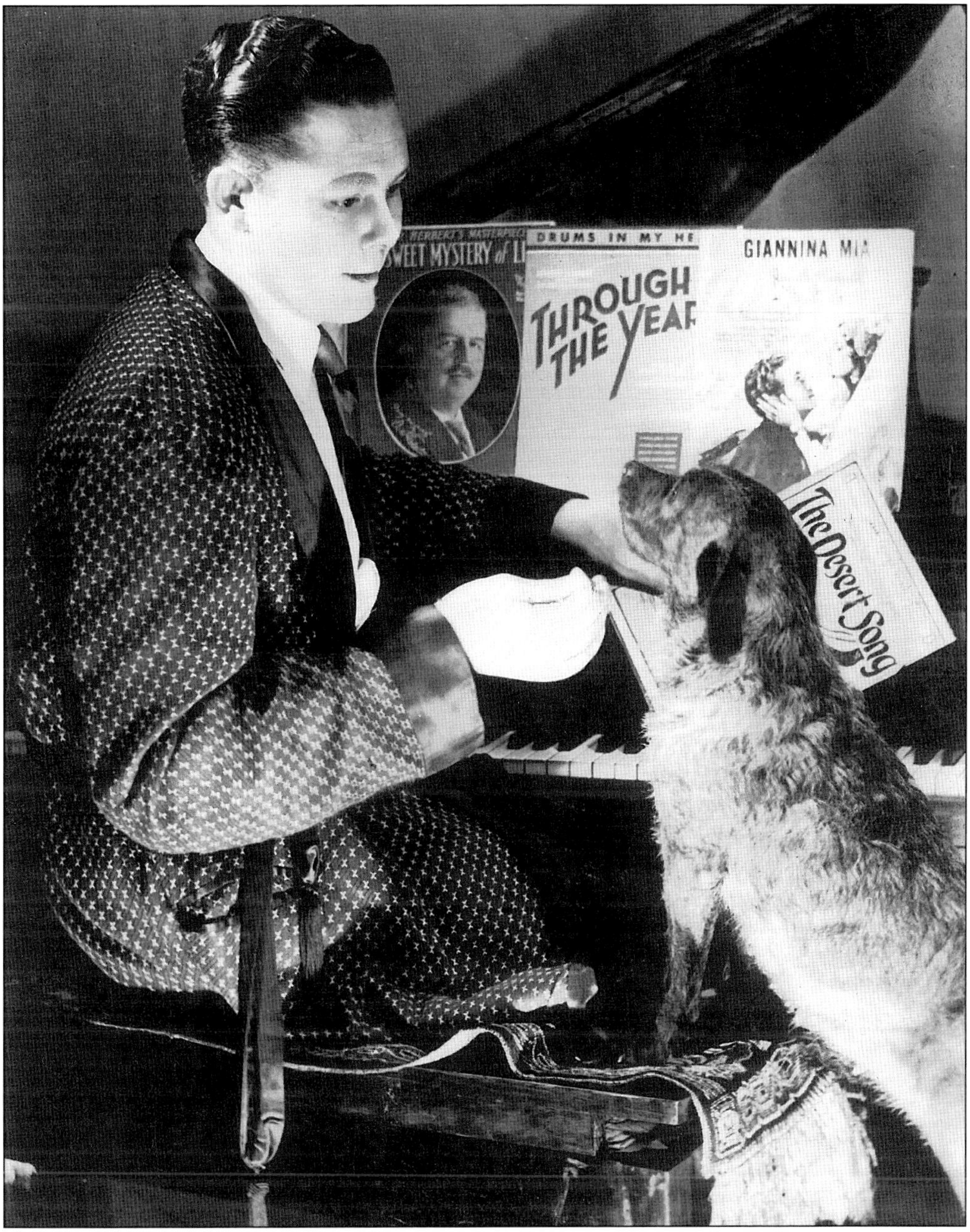

Early on, Eddie Roecker enjoyed a career as a Broadway tenor. The people of Merchantville knew him as a lively person who sang at special events in town. Among his activities in the 1940s and 1950s was his role as holiday singer at the Trinity Church and at many community functions. At the National Little League Championship in 1956, in Williamsport, Pennsylvania, Roecker sang the national anthem. The Merchantville Baseball League named its field at the community center the Ed Roecker Memorial Field. The Roecker family lived at 28 West Cedar Avenue. Roecker passed away in 1975. (Tina Schmidt.)

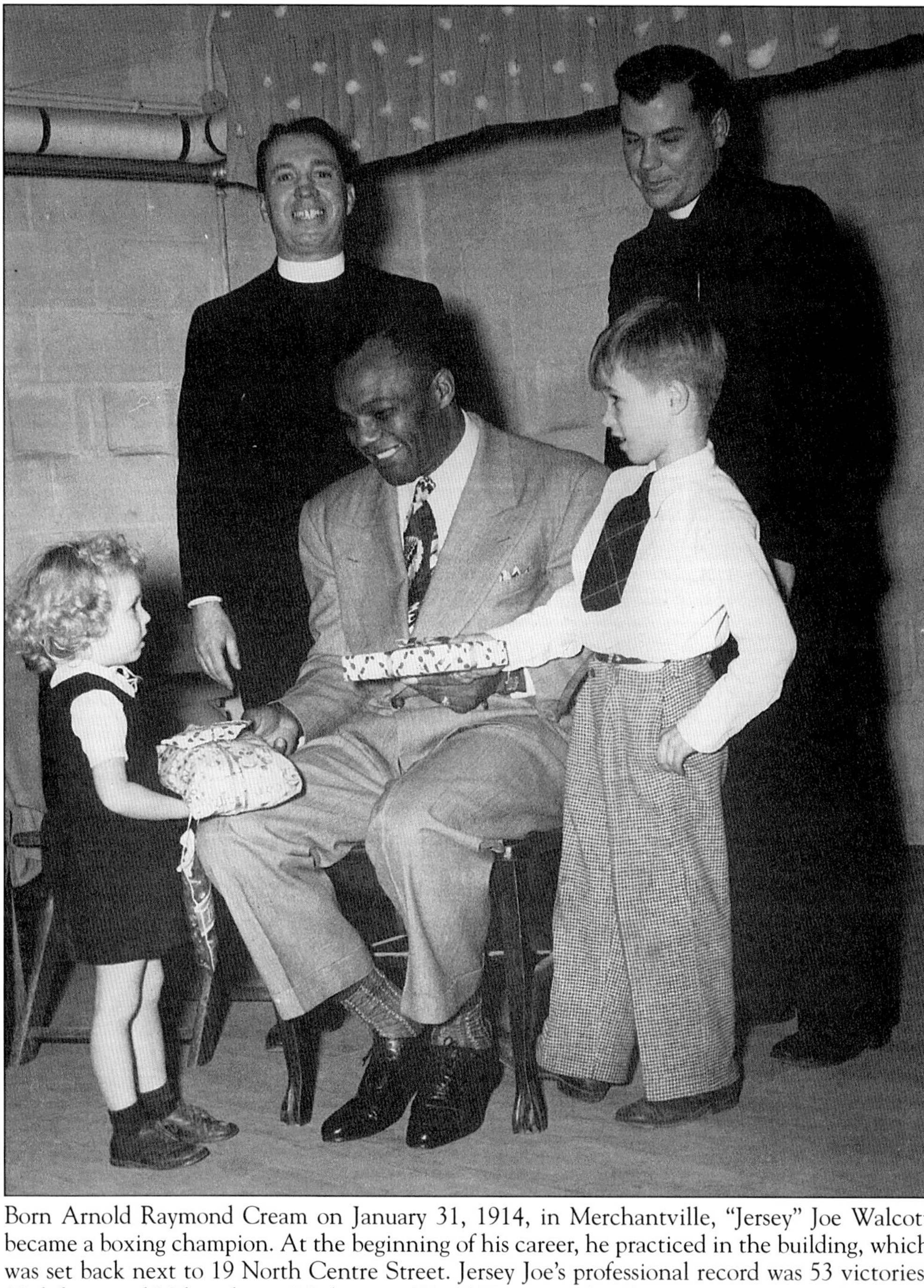

Born Arnold Raymond Cream on January 31, 1914, in Merchantville, "Jersey" Joe Walcott became a boxing champion. At the beginning of his career, he practiced in the building, which was set back next to 19 North Centre Street. Jersey Joe's professional record was 53 victories, 18 defeats, and 33 knockouts. He became World Heavyweight Champion in 1951 and retained the title in 1952 but then lost it to Rocky Marciano. Jersey Joe is pictured here with two schoolchildren and Msgr. John P. Fallon of St. Peter's School. (St. Peter's.)